DATE DUE

COLORADO HOME BUYERS GUIDE

Second Edition

Updated for 2012

Vicki S. Porter
Ideal Properties of Denver
3773 Cherry Creek North Drive #575
Denver, CO 80209

BRADFORD PUBLISHING CO.
Denver, Colorado

DISCLAIMER

This book is intended to provide general information with regard to the subject matter covered. It is not meant to provide legal opinions or to offer advice, or to serve as a substitute for advice by licensed, legal, or other professionals. This book is sold with the understanding that Bradford Publishing Company and the authors, by virtue of its publication, are not engaged in rendering legal or other professional services to the reader.

Bradford Publishing Company and the authors do not warrant that the information contained in this book is complete or accurate, and do not assume and hereby disclaim any liability to any person for any loss or damage caused by errors, inaccuracies or omissions, or usage of this book.

Laws, and interpretations of those laws, change frequently, and the subject matter of this book can have important legal consequences that may vary from one individual to the next. It is therefore the responsibility of the reader to know whether, and to what extent, this information is applicable to his or her situation, and if necessary, to consult legal, tax, or other counsel.

Library of Congress Cataloging-in-Publication Data

Porter, Vicki S.
  Colorado home buyers guide / Vicki S. Porter. -- 2nd ed.
    p. cm.
  Includes bibliographical references and index.
  ISBN 978-1-932779-64-6
  1. House buying--Colorado. I. Title.

  HD266.C6P67 2008
  643'.1209788--dc22

                                                        2008053605

Bradford Publishing Company
1743 Wazee Street, Denver, Colorado 80202
www.bradfordpublishing.com

DEDICATION

To my mom, who would have been so proud.

ABOUT THE AUTHOR

Vicki Porter is an accomplished real estate broker, mortgage broker, lawyer, educator, and business owner who also owns and manages real estate. After practicing law for over 20 years in the Denver area, Vicki established her own real estate company, Porter House Realty, where she has been representing buyers, sellers, and investors in the Denver metro area since 1994. Porter House Realty started doing business as Ideal Properties of Denver in 2010. Vicki also is a licensed mortgage broker in Colorado.

In 2003, Vicki received the e-Pro certification from the National Association of Realtors, which recognizes highly skilled and continuously trained real estate professionals. For the past several years, Vicki has been awarded the Realtor Roundtable Award of Excellence from the Denver Board of Realtors, which recognizes success in real estate. She is a member of the Denver, Colorado, and National Association of Realtors.

Vicki teaches a class through Colorado Free University called "ABC's of Home Buying," and she has taught hundreds of people how to buy a home. She served as an adjunct faculty member at the University of Denver College of Law and taught several real estate and property law classes.

Before starting her real estate business, Vicki practiced law in Denver, specializing in bankruptcy and real estate law. She owned her own law firm for 15 years and was active with the Denver, Colorado, and American Bar Associations, holding various offices in each association. Vicki earned an undergraduate degree in Economics from the University of Colorado and received her J.D. *cum laude* from the University of Miami School of Law.

Vicki lives in Denver with her partner, Mary, and likes to spend her free time playing golf.

ACKNOWLEDGMENTS

In large part, this book is a collection of responses to questions asked by clients, students, and broker associates, so I owe a thank you to each of those people for helping me realize that this book was needed.

Thank you also to Bradford Publishing and a very patient editorial staff.

Vicki

TABLE OF CONTENTS

INTRODUCTION

The process of buying a home seems daunting to most first time buyers, but it is really an uncomplicated process. The purpose of this book is to define the unfamiliar terms and demystify the process.

The entire home buying process can be divided into seven steps:

- Step 1 – Analyze the decision to buy.
- Step 2 – Find a lender and learn about financing.
- Step 3 – Find a real estate agent.
- Step 4 – Find the right home to purchase.
- Step 5 – Enter into a contract to purchase.
- Step 6 – Close on the purchase.
- Step 7 – Move.

This book explains the requirements and the potential pitfalls for each of the above steps. The first chapter will help you analyze your own decision to buy a home. Chapter 2 discusses how to choose a lender and the various kinds of financing available. Chapter 3 will help you find the right real estate agent. Chapter 4 will guide you in finding the right property to buy, and it contains a checklist to help you along. Chapter 5 contains a paragraph-by-paragraph explanation of Colorado's standard contract to buy and sell real estate. Chapter 6 tells you how to prepare for the closing and what to expect there. Chapter 7 discusses a few post-closing matters.

CHAPTER 1
TO BUY OR NOT TO BUY

§ 1.1 Introduction

Since you are reading this book, you have likely been thinking about whether you want to buy a home. Have you considered such factors as your employment, income, lifestyle, and long-term plans and goals? These are the kinds of questions you will want to answer for yourself before you decide to buy a home—your answers will help you decide what to buy when you do get into the real estate market.

How long do you want to live in the property? Do you anticipate changes in your life or your family size, and how will those changes affect your home ownership or needs? Will you have to relocate to care for a needy relative or friend? If you do not expect to live in the property for more than three years, then unless you are confident that the value of the property is going to increase during those three years, you might be better off renting.

How secure is your employment and income? How certain are you of your current income? If you are not confident that your current income will continue, how many months' worth of living expenses do you have saved? Before buying property, it is a good idea to have saved at least six months' of living expenses, which can be used to pay the mortgage if you lose your job. Without that safety net, you might be better off renting. If you have additional savings, on the other hand, it might be safe for you to buy.

It has often been said that owning a home of one's own is the American Dream. According to the last U.S. census report, only about two-thirds (67.84%) of the property in Colorado was owner-occupied. That leaves over one and a half a million properties in Colorado that were occupied by residents who had not achieved the Dream.[1]

What makes home ownership a dream for some and a reality for others? Financial reasons can prevent people from owning a home. Often, however, it is a lack of understanding of what is involved, the lack of desire or will to own, or some other factor. This book provides the roadmap to home ownership, but

---

[1] The following is from the U.S. census report for the year 2010:

Occupied housing units in Colorado	2,167,850	100.0
Owner-occupied housing units	1,478,434	68.2
Renter-occupied housing units	689,376	31.8

one must decide to pursue the goal of owning a home before traveling down the path to buy.

This chapter will help you decide if buying is right for you. It compares the advantages of ownership versus renting, answers your question of when to buy, and helps you decide whether you want to buy in Colorado if you are considering relocating to Colorado. In the next chapter, you will be able to analyze your finances to decide if you can afford to buy.

§ 1.2 Advantages of Home Ownership

Home ownership requires a significant commitment of money and energy—first to acquire the property and then to maintain it. Some very good motivating factors make the effort worthwhile.

§ 1.2.1 Emotional Security

One of the strongest motivators for purchasing a home for most of us is emotional security. Having a place to call home for you and your family provides a sense of stability and emotional comfort that does not exist for tenants. If it is *your* home, then no landlord can announce that your rent will be increased or that your lease will not be extended.

The worst scenario occurs when you are a month-to-month tenant and your property owner informs you that the place you are renting has been sold and that you have to move shortly. I remember receiving a call from such a tenant. She had been renting the same place for more than five years, and the property owner advised her that he had decided to sell the property. The landlord asked her if she wanted to buy the place, and she considered it. She had 30 days' notice that she had to buy or move out. She called me in a panic. I assured her that 30 days was enough time to find a place to buy—and it was. If it had not been for the property owner's decision to sell, this buyer might still be renting.

There is something temporary about living in an apartment or a rental house; people feel more stable in property that they own.

§ 1.2.2 Financial Security

Financial security is another major factor in favor of home ownership. An owner feels secure knowing that the largest portion of his or her monthly housing expense will not change. This is because most homes are purchased with "fixed financing," which means that the interest rate charged for the financing is established at the time of the purchase and the monthly loan payments do not increase during the term of the loan.[2] If, on the other hand, you are renting, it is highly likely that your monthly rent payments will increase over time. In fact, rental increases should be expected. According to data from the Apartment Association of Metro Denver and the Colorado Division of Housing, the average rents in the Denver increased from $842.70 in 2010 to $863.37 in 2011.

§ 1.2.3 Investment

Another advantage of buying over renting is that owning a home is an investment in real estate. There is no way to recover the money that you pay for rent. The money that you pay on a home purchase loan, however, may be recovered in a variety of ways.

Each monthly loan payment you make on a home consists of principal and interest. When you sell the property, even if you sell the property for just what you paid for it, you can recover that portion of your monthly payment that was credited towards paying down the amount you owed on the loan.

Here is an example that will show you why buying can be better than renting from a financial perspective:

Suppose that a buyer is paying $850 per month in rent for a two-bedroom place. Assume the buyer can purchase the same-sized unit for $150,000. The buyer could end up with thousands more dollars in five years if the buyer purchases the place rather than renting. We have to assume that the buyer has sufficient credit to get a loan to purchase the place, as well as money for a down payment.

If the buyer gets a loan and puts 3% ($4,500) down at the time of purchase, the loan amount would be $145,500. Using a 30-year fixed-rate mortgage with an interest rate of 6%, the buyer's monthly payment would be as follows:

Principal and interest	$ 872.35
Taxes	60.00
Insurance	40.00
Total	$ 972.35

(You will learn how to calculate principal and interest payments and how to estimate taxes and insurance amounts in the next chapter.)

---

[2] In addition to principal and interest, a home buyer will have to pay 1/12 of the annual tax bill and insurance premium and both of these amounts will likely increase during the 30-year loan term. These are discussed more fully in Chapter 2.

While taxes and insurance might increase during the next 30 years, the principal and interest figure is fixed. There also may be tax savings to the buyer.[3]

The buyer's rent, however, is not fixed. It is likely that rent will increase over time. Assume that rent will increase $25 a year, so that next year instead of $850 for rent, the buyer has to pay $875, and $900 the year after that, etc.

The total annual rent is easy to figure, as it is the monthly rent times 12. The total cost for buying includes not only the monthly payment for the loan, but also the cost for taxes and insurance. For purposes of this illustration, the taxes and insurance are estimated and no adjustment is made for potential increases in those amounts. Also, no calculation of the buyer's tax savings is included.

It is necessary to use an amortization schedule to see how much of the monthly loan payment is principal and how much represents the interest payment. At the end of five years, the balance due on the amortized loan is $135,394.09. Thus, the buyer has paid off $10,105.91 ($145,500 - $135,394.09) of the principal balance of the loan. On the day that the buyer acquires the home and puts $4,500 towards the purchase, the buyer has $4,500 in equity in the home. Equity is the difference between the current value of the home and the amount of any debts that are owed on the home. If the property value has not changed, the buyer's equity at the end of five years is at least the $4,500 invested plus the $10,105.91 of principal paid.

Here are the financial totals per year for our example:

	2008	2009	2010	2011	2012	Totals
Rent	10,200.00	10,500.00	10,800.00	11,100.00	11,400.00	54,000.00
Home Costs (PITI)[4]	11,668.20	11,668.20	11,668.20	11,668.20	11,668.20	58,341.00
Equity[5]	6,286.76	8,183.72	10,197.68	12,335.86	14,605.91	14,605.91

Over the next five years, the buyer could pay a total of $54,000 in rent—and have nothing to show for it. On the other hand, the buyer could invest $4,500 plus closing costs up front, and pay a little more each month towards his or her own home—and have $14,605.91 in equity at the end of five years.

---

[3] Assuming the buyer is in the 28% tax bracket, when the buyer deducts the total $5,037 of interest paid in the first year, the actual tax savings could be as much as $1,410.

[4] The figure represents principal, interest, taxes, and insurance. There is no increase assumed in these figures in the next five years. It is assumed that any maintenance costs will not exceed tax savings, which have not been included.

[5] "Equity" is the value of property less the balance due on the loan against the property.

§ 1.2.4 Appreciation

Another motivating factor for buying and not renting is that the value of property historically has increased over time, making real estate a good investment. The increase in the value of the property over time is called "appreciation."

If you had purchased an average house in southeast area of Denver in 2004, it would have cost you $385,577. The average-priced home in the same area in 2010 sold for $443,937, so the property appreciated $58,360, or an average of 3.96% per year. Here is how that is calculated:

Value	$443,937
Initial price	− $385,577
Appreciation	$58,360

Appreciation: $58,360 divided by 6 years = $9,726.67 per year

Initial Price: $385,577 divided by $9,726.67 = 3.96% per year

Real estate is an especially attractive investment because the return on investment (ROI) is even greater than the appreciation; this is true because a real estate purchase is a leveraged investment. A "leveraged investment" is one in which the investor uses credit or borrowed funds to increase his or her investment capacity. Most buyers invest only a portion of the purchase price to acquire the property, and borrow the balance. If the value of real estate itself increases over time, the return on the actual investment (i.e., the down payment) can be significant. The initial investment might be only 5% of the current price of the home; but if the property appreciates, the homeowner reaps 100% of that increase.

For example, if property was purchased in 2004 for $385,577, and if the buyer purchased the home with a 5% down payment, then the initial investment would have been $19,278.85 ($385,577 x .05 = $19,278.85). The return on the initial investment, the $58,360, is a nice return on the $19,278.85 actual investment—and that was during some bad economic times.

The true return on investment is more complicated than that. Your actual investment will be greater than the down payment, and your proceeds at the time of sale will be less than the amount of your equity in the property, because there are other costs to pay at the time of purchase and sale, known as closing costs. Closing costs will be discussed in detail in Chapter 6. You also have to maintain the property, and you have to make the monthly loan payments for the five years. A portion of the monthly loan payments will be principal repayment and much of the loan payment will be interest. The principal repayment adds to your equity, and the interest portion of the payment is a tax-deductible item. The monthly loan payments essentially represent the cost of living in the home, which you were able to enjoy for those three years. Otherwise stated, those payments were in lieu of rent that you would have been paying.

In Denver, Colorado, the average home price increased between 7 and 12% a year from 1989 to 1999.[6] Don't you wish that you had purchased a home in 1990 for $80,000 and invested $4,000 (5% down), and then sold the home in 2000 for $225,000? The appreciation and the profit (assuming no other facts) would have been approximately $145,000, and the return on the $4,000 investment would have been more than 362.5%!

Property values in Denver have not done as well since the turn of the century. Home prices went up during the first half of the decade and then went down as the entire country suffered an economic slowdown. In May of 2011, the average priced home in Denver was $230,000.[7]

§ 1.2.5 Tax Savings

Homeowners are able to deduct the interest paid on their residence. The amount of their tax savings depends on such things as the amount of the interest, the homeowners' other deductions, and the owner's income tax level.

In our example above, if the property was purchased in January 2004 for $385,577 with 5% down, the loan balance would have been $366,298.20. The tax savings depend in part on the interest rate that is paid on the loan. Let us assume the interest rate was 6%. The amount of interest paid in 12 payments, the first year, would have been approximately $21,855.55. The amount of the tax savings depends on the individual's tax bracket. If the individual is in the 20% tax bracket, the deduction would have represented approximately $4,371.11 in tax savings.

§ 1.2.6 Pride of Ownership

Another reason many people choose to buy and not rent is that owners do not have to get permission to paint the walls, change the carpeting, or make most other home improvements. Since it is your home, you can do with it as you wish, provided you do not offend your neighbors or neighborhood, or break any laws or rules that govern the property. There is real pride in having

---

[6] Denver Comprehensive Plan 2000, available at
http://www.denvergov.org/Portals/646/documents/CompPlan2000.pdf.

[7] Gilbert Mohtes-Chan, *Denver Home Prices Steady, Some Sellers on Sidelines* (June 27, 2011), available at http://www.inman.com/news/2011/06/27/denver-home-prices-steady-some-sellers-sidelines.

such things as a well-maintained yard or a freshly painted or stained fence when they are yours.

Homeowners have stable housing costs, they benefit from appreciation, and they get a tax deduction. In addition to the investment aspects of home ownership, homeowners enjoy the intangible benefits of owning their own home. If you live in a community with a homeowners' association, being a homeowner allows you to participate in that association and gives you a greater opportunity to get involved with your community.

§ 1.3 Advantages of Renting

We have talked about the advantages of owning a home, but home ownership also comes with liabilities and responsibilities that do not burden renters. There are some real advantages to being a renter, too.

§ 1.3.1 Responsibilities and Liabilities

Renters do not have the same responsibilities as homeowners. For instance, most leases do not require a tenant to make repairs to the property. A tenant will be expected to make repairs if he or she causes the damage, of course; but if there is damage to the roof from a hailstorm, for instance, a residential tenant is not expected to repair the roof. Repairs and maintenance fall squarely on the homeowner's shoulders, and they can be costly.

Major damage, such as a damaged roof, might be covered by homeowners' insurance. If you are borrowing money to purchase your home—and most of us do—then your lender will insist that you acquire insurance to protect the asset (your home) since your home is the security for the loan. The lender needs to know that if the house burns down in a fire, you will have the resources to rebuild or to repay the lender. If the property is adequately insured, the insurance proceeds will be that resource. However, even when the damage to the property *is* covered by insurance, the homeowner will suffer a loss—the expense of paying the insurance deductible and the hassle of getting the repairs done.

There also can be major repairs that are not covered by insurance. A common example of this is a broken sewer line. In many older homes, sewer lines are made of cement. Even a good, functioning sewer can crack and break over time. Age is one factor, but tree roots are also sometimes to blame. Replacement of a sewer line can be quite costly (thousands of dollars). Whether replacement of a sewer line is covered by insurance depends on the insurance policy, of course, but may also depend on the facts. Tree roots may be something that your insurance policy covers you for, but it is unlikely that insurance will cover damage due solely to age. If the repairs required are not covered by insurance, then the homeowner can be faced with a large, unexpected, and unwelcome expense.

As a homeowner, you will have to pay for the many repairs and maintenance issues that are due to wear and tear and are not covered by insurance, or are not expensive enough to report to your insurance company. Many parts of a home have limited lives. For example, many roofs come with a 20-year warranty, a hot water heater may have a 10-year useful life, and many appliances will not even last that long.

§ 1.3.2 House Rich and Cash Poor

Most first-time home buyers face the challenge of calculating just how much house they can afford to buy. It is easy to call a lender or get online and find out how much a lender is willing to loan to a buyer; there are calculators that tell you how much you will qualify for if you enter how much money you have to put down, how much cash you have to apply towards payments, what debts you have already, and whether you have good credit. Go to Ginnie Mae's website for such a calculator:

www.ginniemae.gov/2_prequal/intro_questions.asp?Section=YPTH

Buying a house requires some initial investment (i.e., down payment and closing costs), and often the required monthly payments are higher than rent payments. Many first-time buyers feel a pinch in their budget when they buy, in part because of the initial investment and increased monthly payments, but also because of all the expenditures that are necessary to turn a house into a home. Furniture, window coverings, and the like are items that buyers are anxious to purchase once they have their own new home. In many ways, what you buy is just a house; it needs you to define it as your home.

It is wise, therefore, to do some budgeting before you decide how much house to buy. This will be discussed further in Chapter 2.

§ 1.3.3 Let the Buyer Beware

The concept of *caveat emptor* (which means "let the buyer beware") is alive and well in the real estate business. To avoid surprises after closing, it has become customary for a home buyer to have the property professionally inspected prior to purchase.

A buyer hires an inspector to examine the property and provide the buyer with a report that will more fully disclose the condition of the property. These inspectors are listed in the yellow pages under Home and Building Inspectors. If you hire a real estate agent, he or she will also be able to recommend inspectors to you.

The standard Colorado Real Estate Contract to Buy and Sell Real Property protects the buyer if the buyer is no longer satisfied with the condition of the home or inclusions after the inspection. The buyer can terminate the contract or can ask the seller to remedy the unsatisfactory conditions before the buyer will purchase the home. This will be discussed further in Chapter 5.

§ 1.3.4 Changes in the Market

While real estate has historically appreciated in value, there is no guarantee that property values will continue to increase. If you have to sell your home within a few years after buying it, you might not be able to sell it for as much as you paid for it. In addition, there are costs involved in selling property. The vast majority of people hire a real estate agent to help them sell their home and pay thousands of dollars in real estate commissions at the time of sale. If the property has not appreciated, it is possible that as the seller you will pay money to sell your property *and* get less money for the property than you paid for it.

From 2006 to 2010, the value of properties in many areas of Colorado declined, depreciated. Many buyers who purchased properties without putting much money down could not afford to sell their homes.

§ 1.4 Deciding on the Right Time to Buy

When you buy depends, of course, on when the necessary funds are available to you (either through financing or available cash), and when you have otherwise decided that you are ready to assume the role of homeowner. I am often asked whether there is a good season or time of the year to buy. My answer is a consistent "no." The real estate market follows the rules of supply and demand, and prices reflect the balance of sellers and buyers in the market. In fact, in Colorado more real estate transactions occur in the spring and summer than in the fall or winter. But if you are a buyer, the price for the house is not determined by the number of transactions but by the number of other buyers you are competing with for the same property. In the winter months, there are likely fewer properties on the market *and* fewer buyers in the market.

As this book is being prepared for publication, there is currently a huge inventory of homes on the market; in other words, supply is high. When supply is high, the market favors the buyers; there are more properties to choose from and buyers have more negotiating power because there are too few buyers for all of the properties that sellers are trying to sell. Combine that with the historically low interest rates available in the market today, and you have a very strong buyer's market. It is a great time to buy.

Aside from price considerations, the best time to buy is when it is convenient for you to move. Many people choose to buy in the summer, when their children are out of school and when weather is less likely to be a factor on moving day.

§ 1.5 Relocating to Colorado

As most Colorado residents will happily tell you, it's a privilege to live in Colorado! But before you decide to relocate to Colorado (or anywhere), you should learn all you can about your future home. Colorado ranks eighth among the states in size (104,247 square miles) and, according to the 2000 national census, ranks 24th among the states in total population (4,301,261).

Here is what the Colorado Tourism Office says about our annual climate:

Each year Colorado receives:

- 300 days of sunshine
- more than 300 inches of snow at the mountain resorts
- 16.5 inches of precipitation (8 down low and 23 up high)
- 33 percent humidity
- first snow in September (though it usually snows somewhere in the state every month, except maybe August)[8]

Note that the quantity of snow touted is at the mountain resorts. If you are buying a home in the mountains, you must be willing to live with a lot of snowfall. If you are going to be a "flatlander"—someone who lives anywhere in Colorado that is not the "high country"—then the snowfall you will encounter will not likely be that great. However, if you are moving here from an area where snowfall is a rarity, you may have to do some adjusting. Colorado residents are expected to shovel their sidewalks as soon as the snow stops falling. Snow will accumulate on the north side of your home and could stick around for weeks or months, while snow on the south side is likely to melt away in days.

Most of Colorado is not in the high country. The area west of the Continental Divide is referred to as the "Western Slope," and the area to the east is often called the "Eastern Slope," but only the Continental Divide itself and the area immediately adjacent to it comprises the high county. If you are moving to Colorado to enjoy skiing, hiking, climbing, mountain biking, or other activities in the mountains, you may want to seek a location with easy highway access to the mountains.

---

[8] Colorado Tourism Office, "Weather" page, available at www.colorado.com/static.php?file= weather.

Colorado has a semi-arid climate. Its lack of rain and humidity is a challenge for some. (For most of us, it means we use a lot more lotion than when we are in the Midwest, for example.) But there are health factors to consider if you are relocating to this climate.

Denver is the "Mile High City." Besides being a slogan, it is a fact that Denver sits 5,280 feet above sea level. The state, with an average elevation of 6,800 feet, is the highest of all the states. All of Colorado is more than 3,300 feet above sea level, and altitude can be a real challenge for some people—especially those with heart, lung, or circulatory disease.

If you are a sports fan, you will be glad to know that all four major-league professional sports have teams in Denver: the Denver Broncos football team, the Denver Nuggets basketball team, the Colorado Avalanche hockey team, and the Colorado Rockies baseball team.

§ 1.6 Conclusion

If you have decided that you want to call Colorado home and you are convinced that buying rather than renting is right for you, then you are ready to start the home buying process. The next step is determining how much house you can afford. In Chapter 2, you will learn about lenders, loans types, loan terms, and how to figure out the amount of loan you can qualify for.

CHAPTER 2
FINANCING THE PURCHASE OF YOUR HOME

§ 2.1 Introduction

According to the 2000 U.S. Census report, the average purchase price of a home in Colorado was more than $166,000, and the average annual income was just over $24,000. Since most of us buy a home that costs two or more times our annual income, it is a rare individual who can purchase a home with cash. Most of us have to borrow money to purchase a home. The interest that we pay on a loan to purchase our home is a tax-deductible item, so there is actually an incentive to borrow money to buy your home.

There are different types of lenders, different types of loans, and different loan terms. The right loan for the empty nester might not be the right loan for a recent college graduate, even if their income and credit scores are the same. This chapter covers how to find a lender, how to decide which loan is right for you, and how to qualify for a loan.

§ 2.2 Lenders

Until 2007, mortgage lenders in Colorado were not required to be licensed or registered. Beginning in 2007, most mortgage brokers doing business in Colorado were required to register with the Colorado Division of Real Estate, and in 2008, mortgage brokers must be licensed. In 2008, the Secure and Fair Enforcement for Mortgage Licensing Act (S.A.F.E. Act) was passed. It is a federal mandate for all states to license and regulate mortgage loan originators (MLOs), and it requires the registration of all MLOs on the Nationwide Mortgage Licensing System and Registry (NMLS).

Licensing requirements for a mortgage loan originator (MLO) now includes fingerprints for a criminal history check to the Colorado Bureau of Investigations and the FBI, pre-licensing education and exams, a surety bond, and errors and omissions insurance.

There are exceptions on who has to be licensed, so you should choose a lender who is recommended to you or who you know to be reputable. Below are some questions that will help you evaluate whether a potential lender is right for you.

§ 2.2.1 How to Choose a Lender

A good lender acts like your partner, helping you get the loan type and terms that best fit your needs. The lender will need to know your financial situation—your income, assets, current debts, and credit history—to be able to tell you what kind of loan he or she can offer you. A good lender will explain all of your options, show you how the payments would differ under various scenarios, and help you decide which loan makes the most sense for you. Deciding on the loan type will depend on factors such as your budget, how long you expect to stay in the property, and what you anticipate your future income to be.

§ 2.2.2 Is the Lender a Mortgage Broker or a Mortgage Banker?

Both mortgage brokers and mortgage bankers originate, sell, or service loans that are secured by mortgages on real property. Both provide a variety of loan packages or products to different quality levels of borrowers. The main difference is in the source of their loans; the mortgage broker is a middleman between a lender and the borrower, whereas the mortgage banker *is* the lender. Even though the source of the loan differs depending on whether the lender is a mortgage broker or a mortgage banker, all lenders try to have competitive rates and services—and they want your business.

Which is better for you? The benefits of working with each are discussed below to help you decide which better meets your needs.

Mortgage Brokers

Mortgage brokers do not hold or service any loans, and they typically work with a variety of companies or investors. If you do not have good credit or if you cannot fully document your income, you may have better luck with a mortgage broker. Because a mortgage broker has several lending sources to choose from, the mortgage broker may be able to offer loans to more types of borrowers. A mortgage broker works directly with borrowers, taking the loan application and collecting and verifying all required information and documentation. Once the mortgage broker has a complete loan package, he or she submits it to an appropriate lender.

Because the mortgage broker is independent, he or she has the luxury of searching for a loan based on the borrower's needs rather than the needs of any particular lender. After the mortgage broker matches the client with a lender, the broker submits the paperwork for final approval and loan funding. The fee for the mortgage broker is paid by the lending institution and therefore does not directly affect the buyer.

Loan approvals always require a review by an underwriter who is employed or authorized by the lender that is funding the loan. A disadvantage of working with a mortgage broker is that he or she is not working with an in-house underwriter. The mortgage broker is not in the same office—and may not even be in the same state—as the actual lender, and even if the mortgage broker has provided all that the lender has published as requirements for the loan, the underwriter may come up with additional requirements after the specific loan is reviewed. Because the mortgage broker may not do a lot of business with any particular lender, the mortgage broker may not be able to anticipate all the hurdles that a lender will require. Thus, the mortgage broker will not have much control over the loan after it is submitted to the lender, and may not know how long approval will take.

Mortgage Bankers

A mortgage banker actually funds the loan and can approve or reject loans directly. Some mortgage bankers, such as savings and loans and mortgage banks, have lenders who work in-house to place loans with customers. Other mortgage bankers work with a pool of investors as sources for loans, but the mortgage banker still controls the loan.

Since mortgage bankers are direct lenders, working with them eliminates the middleman. A mortgage banker can also work with many outside lenders, but the mortgage banker has delegated underwriting authority, i.e., has the ability to approve the loan for other lenders. Mortgage bankers generally work with institutions with significant net worth, since the institution makes the loans. Mortgage brokers, on the other hand, can be small operations. Because mortgage bankers and mortgage brokers compete for business, they each have no choice but to maintain competitive rates.

§ 2.2.3 Does the Lender Have Experience Placing Loans in Colorado?

It is wise to choose a lender who has placed loans locally. Many sad stories are told about individuals who applied for a loan online and sent in an application fee, but never received the loan funds. Colorado has some unique real estate practices, and if the lender has not made loans in Colorado, then you are taking a risk by using that lender.

A good example of a problem with out-of-state lenders is that in Colorado, all payments and title transfers are made at a designated time and place: the closing. At the closing, either (1) the funds must be wired to the title company that is handling the closing, with instructions directing when and if to disburse the funds, or (2) a cashier's check must be brought or sent to the closing by the lender. In other states, the funds are not expected or due until some time after the closing, sometimes days or even weeks later. If the lender does not understand that the funds have to be at the closing and does not have them there, the buyer in Colorado cannot purchase the property and will be in default under the contract.

§ 2.2.4 Comparing Rates

You will want to choose a lender who offers the right type of loan for you, at the lowest rate you can find. It is wise to contact a few lenders when you are shopping rates, and include at least one mortgage banker and one mortgage broker. On any given day, you may find a better loan package for yourself with one or the other. When comparing rates, it is imperative to get quotes on the same day. Interest rates vary daily and often fluctuate during the day. To truly find out which lender can offer you the best rate, you must compare their quotes from the same market conditions, i.e., the same date and time.

I am always suspicious of lenders who advertise their rates in the newspaper or on the radio. First of all, rates change frequently (again, not just daily, but also throughout the day), so rates that have been published may no longer exist by the time you call about them. Since lenders know that rates change, you may not be able to trust lenders who advertise rates. In some advertisements, lenders offer an unbelievably low rate, but the rate is actually a teaser rate—and is much higher when you apply for the loan. The advertisements can be deceptive, for example, when the consumer thinks the rate offered is a fixed-rate loan, but it is actually a rate that will increase early and often. Also, advertisements may not explain that there are points involved, i.e., extra fees that will be charged in order to get the lower rate. Generally, if the rate being advertised seems too good to be true, it probably is!

§ 2.2.5 Comparing Fees

The interest rate for a loan is a major factor in choosing a lender, but it is not the only consideration. Lenders will all try to sell you on the service they provide. It is important to have confidence that the loan will be properly handled, even after closing, but much of the service you will receive from a lender is in placing the loan in the first place.

In addition to different interest rates and terms, and being confident in the service that you will receive, you need to compare the fees that the lender will charge you for the loan. Real estate agents often refer to most of these lender charges as "junk" fees. Some examples of these fees are:

- Document preparation – You are charged for this even though lenders almost always use standard forms and merely fill in the blanks.

- Underwriting fee – A fee for deciding it is okay to grant you the loan.

- Escrow fee – A fee for holding and accounting for your money (they hold your funds, do not pay you interest, and charge you to do so).

- Origination fee – Typically, this fee is 1% of the loan amount; it is somewhat negotiable, though most often the lender will charge more interest if it does not receive an origination fee.

There are also third-party fees that the lender pays to others for your loan. Third-party fees, which differ among lenders, include:

- Credit report – The fee for pulling and reviewing your credit report.

- Appraisal fee – The fee for getting an appraisal of the value of the property you plan to purchase.

You will have to pay additional fees that might not vary much among lenders, such as the fees for title work, for recording the documents, for the closing company to handle the closing, for ordering a tax certificate, and for a flood certificate.

The best way to compare lender fees is to obtain from each lender a Good Faith Estimate of your costs. You want to be sure that when a lender claims that they will charge you a flat fee (for example, "$500 total closing fees") the lender is not excluding third-party charges. Lenders, like all business people, can be very creative in the ways they advertise their fees. The Truth-in-Lending Act [9] is a federal law that requires a lender to disclose the terms and costs of the loan to you, including all of the lender's fees. Fortunately, the Good Faith Estimate does not allow a lender to hide fees, so you can actually compare total fees among lenders. It is great to be aware of all of these costs in advance so that you do not suffer sticker shock at closing. For a copy of a Good Faith Estimate form, see *Appendix 1, Form 1: Good Faith Estimate*.

The Real Estate Settlement Procedures Act (RESPA) requires the mortgage banker or mortgage broker to deliver or mail the GFE to the applicant within three business days after the application is received.

§ 2.3 Pre-Qualification

You can get a letter from a lender stating that you are pre-qualified for a loan, usually after a phone call with the lender, if you provide satisfactory financial information. The lender will need to know your income, current assets, current debts, and will have to run your credit report.

It is wise to get a pre-qualification letter when you start looking for properties. Most sellers will require that a lender letter be submitted with any offers on their property. So it is good to have a lender letter in hand when you start house hunting, just in case you find the right property.

The fact that a lender gives you a letter saying that you are pre-qualified for a loan does not mean that the lender is prepared to make a loan to you; it just means that if the facts are as you stated to the lender, and if you decide to purchase a property for fair market value, then the lender may make you a loan.

---

[9] 15 U.S.C. §§ 1601 *et seq.*

Certain circumstances may make the loan unavailable to you, such as when your financial picture changes, the property you choose is not worth what you have agreed to pay (in the bank's opinion), or market interest rates have changed.

§ 2.4 Pre-Approval

If you submit a full loan application, a lender can process the application and you can get credit-approved for a loan. The lender will not commit to make a loan until it knows which property you are going to buy and it hires a professional to appraise the property. However, getting credit-approved means that the lender has reviewed your credit, has verified your employment, and has determined that your credit and income satisfy the lender's requirements for a loan.

Pre-approval, as opposed to pre-qualification, may give you an advantage in your home-buying venture. Advantages of pre-approval over pre-qualification include:

- Pre-approval can save you from wasting time looking at houses you cannot afford.

- If you make an offer on a home and then apply for a loan, you may not have sufficient time to shop around for the best lender and loan.

- A pre-approval letter from a lender gives you an edge when multiple offers have been made on a house. A seller will take an offer from the stronger buyer, if all else is equal. Being pre-approved, rather than just pre-qualified, gives the impression that you are a stronger buyer.

- Pre-approved buyers can generally close escrow more quickly because most of the work has already been done. Having an earlier closing date may give you more negotiating power on other terms or may make your offer more attractive to a seller.

Depending on the lender you choose and the type of loan you apply for, you may be able to get pre-approved quickly because many lenders use automated underwriting.[10]

§ 2.4.1 The Loan Application

The application requires information about your employment and income, your assets (property, cars, bank accounts, and investments), and your liabilities

---

[10] Automated underwriting systems include Desktop Underwriter (DU) and Loan Prospector (LP). Desktop Underwriter is Fannie Mae's program, and Loan Prospector is Freddie Mac's program. Each program is comprised of complicated formulas that take into account your income, assets, debts, and credit scores to decide if you will qualify for any particular loan.

(auto loans, installment loans, mortgages, credit card debt, household expenses, and others).

To complete an application, you will need to provide documentation, including:

- Paycheck stubs.
- Bank account statements.
- Tax returns.
- Investment earnings reports.
- Rental agreements.
- Divorce decrees.

For a copy of a standard loan application, see *Appendix 1, Form 2: Uniform Residential Loan Application.*

§ 2.4.2 Locking in a Loan

A lock-in holds an interest rate and points for a specified period of time, usually 30 to 60 days. Depending on the lender, you may be able to lock in a rate either when you submit your application, during loan processing, at the time of loan approval, or later. Some lenders require buyers to be under contract to purchase a home before they will lock in a rate. Lenders who work with builders sometimes allow a buyer to lock in the rate once the buyer is under contract to buy a newly constructed home, even though the closing may be several months away. A lock-in is useful when interest rates are on the rise because a lock-in protects against rate increases. If interest rates are falling, it may be best to wait until after application approval to lock in. Unfortunately, you might not know whether interest rates are rising or falling.

Locking in a loan rate is not always free. Some lenders charge up-front fees, which may or may not be refunded upon withdrawal or denial of your application. Other lenders charge the fee at closing. The fee may be a flat fee, a percentage of the mortgage amount, or a fraction of a point added to the lock-in rate. If you believe that interest rates are going up, it may be worth it to pay the lock-in fee.

§ 2.4.3 Credit Impact of Shopping for a Loan

You should avoid asking several lenders over a long period of time for credit, because each time a creditor runs a credit check, it is reflected on your credit report. Credit inquiries are a negative factor because statistical studies show that multiple inquiries are associated with a higher risk of default. Distressed borrowers often contact many lenders hoping to find one who will approve them.

Shopping for the best mortgage will not negatively impact your credit rating if you do all your shopping within a short period. Since the market can change from day to day, this is the only effective way to shop anyway. Credit scorers ignore inquiries that occur within 30 days of a score date. To avoid biasing the credit score from earlier shopping episodes, the scorers treat all of the same types of inquiries that occur within a 14-day period as a single inquiry.

For example, if you shop for a lender on September 30, that lender pulls your credit score that day. Even if you had shopped 50 other mortgage lenders in September and they had all checked your credit, none of those inquiries would affect your credit score on September 30. Inquiries from August and the previous 11 months, however, would be counted on September 30. If you shopped 50 lenders during August 1-14, they would count as one inquiry. If you spread them over August 1-28, they would count as two inquiries. Thus, you will damage your credit if you spread your shopping over many months.

Because the market can change from day to day, it makes little sense to do this in any case. When you are ready to start the process of buying a home—and not until then—you should contact lenders and allow them to pull your credit scores.

§ 2.5 Loan Types

Loans are either conventional or fall into a special category of loan. If you are a first-time home buyer, you should check with lenders that offer special loans for first-time buyers. The Federal Housing Administration (FHA) and Veterans Administration (VA) both have loan programs. FHA and VA loans are guaranteed to be paid back by the government. These loans can only be obtained from designated FHA or VA lenders.

§ 2.5.1 Federal Housing Administration

With FHA insurance, you can purchase a home with a very low down payment (3.5% of the FHA appraisal value or the purchase price, whichever is lower). FHA mortgages have a maximum loan limit that varies depending on the average cost of housing in a given region. The maximum loan limit has increased over time and is posted on the FHA website at www.hud.gov. In 2011, the maximum FHA loan in the Denver-Aurora Colorado area was $406,250 for a single-family residence.[11]

§ 2.5.2 Veterans Administration

The VA guarantee allows qualified veterans to buy a house with no down payment; that is, a qualified borrower can get 100% financing for the purchase of a home. There is a cap on the purchase price of a home, which was increased

---

[11] FHA, *FHA Limits: Lending Limits for FHA Loans Insured for Colorado Counties*, http://www.fha.com/lending_limits_state.cfm?state=COLORADO.

to $417,000 in 2008. The qualification guidelines for VA loans can be less flexible than those for either FHA or conventional loans. If you are a qualified veteran, this can be an attractive mortgage program. However, if you have good credit, better loan options may be available to you. This is because the interest rate on the VA loans is not always competitive with current market rates. To check out the current VA interest rates, go to www.homeloans.va.gov.

§ 2.5.3 Conventional

"Conventional loans" include any loans that are not FHA or VA loans, and that meet certain requirements. Freddie Mac[12] (FMC) and Fannie Mae[13] (FNMA) set the standards that determine which loans are conventional, and most lenders seek to make loans to borrowers who meet these standards. In 2011, the single-family residence conventional loan limit is $417,000. If the amount that you will borrow is larger than that, then you will be looking for what is referred to as a "Jumbo loan," and you will have to find a lender willing to make Jumbo loans.

In addition to the size of the loan itself, there are other requirements for a loan to be a conforming loan. Typically, a 5% down payment is required. For a loan to be a conforming, conventional loan, the borrower must have a credit score of at least 640. Also, the property being purchased must contain only one to four dwellings (as distinguished from a larger apartment building).

If the property or the borrower do not fit into the conforming requirements, the borrower will need to find a lender that does non-conforming loans. These lenders exist, but the loans will likely carry higher interest rates.

§ 2.5.4 Secondary Market

Many lenders sell loans on what is called the "secondary market." The lender makes money by charging fees to establish the loan, and by selling the established loan to other financial institutions after closing the loan with the borrower. If the lender intends to sell the loan on the secondary market, the loan must meet certain criteria. Lenders seek to make loans that are

---

[12] The Federal Home Loan Mortgage Corporation (FHLMC), commonly referred to as Freddie Mac, was created by Congress in Title III of the Emergency Home Finance Act of 1970 (12 U.S.C. §§ 1451 *et seq.*). FHLMC is a stockholder-owned corporation, a portion of whose board of directors is appointed by the President of the United States.

[13] The Federal National Mortgage Association (FNMA) is referred to as "Fannie Mae" and is the largest mortgage investor in the nation. FNMA was created in 1968 by an amendment to Title III of the National Housing Act (12 U.S.C. §§ 1716 *et seq.*). FNMA is a stockholder-owned corporation, a portion of whose board of directors is appointed by the President of the United States.

"conforming" (i.e., loans that fall within certain guidelines), so they can sell the loans easily.

Fannie Mae and Freddie Mac are two private, secondary mortgage market companies that buy mortgage loans from lenders, thereby ensuring that mortgage funds are available at all times in all locations around the country. The most important difference between a loan that conforms to Fannie Mae and Freddie Mac guidelines and one that does not is its loan limit. Fannie Mae and Freddie Mac will purchase loans only up to a certain loan limit ($417,000 for 2011). The mortgage loan may also follow slightly different underwriting requirements, particularly in regard to your required down payment amount.

§ 2.5.5 Portfolio Loans

Some lenders make loans that they have no intention of selling on the secondary market. These are referred to as "portfolio loans" because the lender keeps the loan in the lender's own portfolio. A lender may seek to have a portfolio of loans in a certain area or of a certain amount as part of the lender's business plan. A portfolio loan, by its nature, does not have to conform to any resale guidelines.

§ 2.6 Loan Terms and Rates

How do you decide which loan is right for you? If you anticipate living in your home for many years, then the interest rate may be the main factor for you. But if you expect to keep the house for only a short period of time, then the closing costs may be more important to you. If you want to have any mortgage debt paid off by the time you are facing your children's college bills or your own retirement, you may wish to consider a shorter-term loan, such as a 15-year fixed-rate mortgage. If your own retirement is years away, you may be less inclined toward a shorter-term loan, preferring to extend payments over a longer period of time by taking on a 30-year mortgage loan.

Following is a chart showing a comparison of five different scenarios for a $200,000 loan. Some of these loans are amortized, so that the principal balance of the loan is paid over time. Others are interest-only, meaning interest is paid monthly, but the entire balance remains due. The payments reflect only principal and interest, and do not include other payments that you will have to make to a lender, such as taxes and insurance. This is all explained further in this chapter.

	30-year fixed		15-year ARM		Monthly ARM
	amortized	interest only	amortized	interest only	interest only
Interest Rate	5.750%	6.000%	4.750%	5.000%	3.875%
Monthly Payment	$1,168.00	$1,000.00	$1,044.00	$833.33	$645.83

§ 2.6.1 Fixed

The most common loan is a 30-year fixed-rate loan. There are also 15-year fixed-rate loans. A "fixed rate" is one where the interest rate is established at the outset for the entire term. During the term of your loan, you will pay back your mortgage by making regular monthly payments of principal and interest. In the early years of your loan, most of the money you pay will be for the interest you owe. Toward the end of your loan term, you will be paying primarily principal. A fixed-rate mortgage ensures that your interest rate (and your payments) will stay the same over the life of your loan—which may be an important consideration if you plan to stay in your home for several years. When you choose the length of your repayment (usually 15, 20, or 30 years), keep in mind that while shorter-term loans may have higher monthly payments, they also let you build equity faster. In the long run, you also pay less total interest on a shorter-term loan.

If you borrow $225,000 on a 30-year fixed-rate loan with an interest rate of 5.75%, the total interest that will be paid on the home (if the loan gets paid off according to its terms) will be $247,694.01. The monthly principal and interest payment is $1,313.04.

However, the same loan amount for a 15-year fixed-rate loan might carry an interest rate of 5.25%, and your total financing charge could be $100,570.47. The 15-year loan requires $147,123.54 less in interest to be paid than does the 30-year loan ($247,694.01 – $100,570.47). In this scenario, the monthly principal and interest payment is $1,808.72.

If you borrow $225,000 on a 30-year fixed-rate loan with an interest rate of 5.75%, but make one extra mortgage payment a year, say with a year-end bonus, then your loan will be paid off in just under 25 years and the total interest you will pay is $198,993.30. So by paying an additional $1,313.04 per year, you reduce your total interest paid by $48,700.71 ($247,694.01 – 198,993.30).

As a practical matter, most homeowners do not stay in their home for 30 years, so the total interest amounts above may never be paid. However, you can see the savings potential from getting a shorter-term loan or making prepayments.

§ 2.6.2 Adjustable-Rate Mortgages

An "adjustable-rate mortgage" (ARM) is one where the interest rate may change during the term of the loan, based on an index and margin and an established time of adjustments. There are loans that are amortized over 30 years that will adjust every year. The amount of each adjustment and the total of all adjustments are limited at the start of the loan. For instance, you may have a loan that starts with an interest rate of 4% that will adjust every year by no more than 1% and will adjust during the life of the loan no more than 6%. An ARM has an interest rate that varies during the life of the loan; it may increase or decrease, based on market interest rates. Consequently, your mortgage payments may go up or down.

This means that when market interest rates go up, your monthly mortgage payments may go up as well. On the other hand, when interest rates go down, your monthly mortgage payments may also go down. ARMs are attractive because they may initially offer a lower interest rate than fixed-rate mortgages. Because the monthly payments on an ARM start out lower than those of a fixed-rate mortgage of the same amount, you might be more comfortable with a larger loan that would make it easier to buy a more expensive home. You will likely benefit from an ARM if you are planning to move or refinance in the near future, if there is a high likelihood that your income is going to increase in later years, or if you need lower initial interest rates on the mortgage to be able to buy the home you want.

Before applying for an ARM, be sure you know the worst-case scenario: how high your monthly payments could potentially be. An ARM has two "caps," or limits, on how much the interest rate can increase: there is a cap on how much your interest rate can go up during each adjustment period and another cap on the maximum total amount of all interest adjustments over the life of the loan. The rates on an ARM usually change once a year, but could change more often—even monthly. For example, if your loan starts at 5%, has a 2% per-adjustment cap, and has a lifetime adjustment cap of 6%, then you know that your loan might go up to 7% the first time the rate changes. You also know that the rate can never go higher than 11% over the life of the loan (5% start plus 6% lifetime cap). Only you can determine whether you would feel comfortable paying this interest rate sometime in the future.

Here is the best way to analyze whether an ARM makes sense: Assume that the options are: (1) a 30-year fixed loan with an interest rate of 6%, or (2) an ARM that has an initial rate of 4.75% that will adjust annually no more than 1% and will adjust during the life of the loan no more than 6%. If the loan amount is $200,000, then the monthly principal and interest payment for the first year will be $1,200 for the fixed-rate loan and $1,050 for the ARM. So during the first year, the ARM saves the buyer $150 per month.

Assume the worst-case scenario, that the ARM rate increases to 5.75% for the second year. In that year, the monthly principal and interest payment for the ARM loan will be $1,168. The fixed-rate loan payments, of course, remain at $1,200 per month. The ARM saves the buyer $32 per month.

Assume that in the third year, the ARM rate again increases by the maximum amount, so the rate is 6.75%. The monthly principal and interest payment on the ARM in the third year will be $1,298. The ARM loan costs the buyer $98 per month more in the third year. However, at the end of the third year, the buyer has paid more over the three years with the fixed-rate loan than with the ARM. In fact, after three full years of payments, the ARM loan has saved the buyer $1,008.

If the buyer does not expect to be in the property for longer than three years, or if the buyer can refinance the loan before the buyer loses all of the benefits of the ARM, the buyer may be better off using the ARM option—even under the worst-case scenario of adjustments.

Whether an adjustable-rate mortgage makes sense depends on its initial interest rate, the potential for increases in the rate, and the length of time the buyer expects to own the home.

Some ARM loans allow you to convert from an adjustable-rate to a fixed-rate loan at a designated time. Ask your lender about this feature when researching ARMs.

One important thing to know when comparing ARMs is that the interest rate changes on an ARM are always tied to a specific financial index. A "financial index" is a published number or percentage, such as the average interest rate or yield on Treasury bills. Some common indices are:

- CD-indexed (certificate of deposit) – adjusted to a certificate of deposit index.

- Treasury-indexed – indexed to the weekly average yield of U.S. Treasury securities.

- Cost of funds-indexed (COFI) – indexed to the actual costs that a particular group of institutions pays to borrow money (for instance, the monthly weighted average cost of savings, borrowings, and advances of members of the Federal Home Loan Bank of San Francisco).

- The London Interbank Offered Rate (LIBOR) – the average interest rate at which international banks lend and borrow funds in the London market, as published in *The Wall Street Journal.*

- MTA – the "Twelve-Month Average" of the annual yields on actively traded United States Treasury securities, adjusted to a constant maturity of one year as published by the Federal Reserve Board. The Twelve-

Month Average is determined by adding together the Monthly Yields for the most recently available 12 months and then dividing that number by 12.

If you are considering getting an ARM, you should make sure you know which index it is tied to. It would be wise to find out the history of that index (i.e., how much it has varied in the past), so that you may have some idea how much it might vary in the future. You also should compare your interest rate to the current amount of the index plus the factor that will be used to determine your loan interest rate. Often, the stated initial interest rate on an ARM is below what the index and factor actually equal. If this is the case, your loan interest rate will increase at the time of the first adjustment even if the index does not change.

§ 2.6.3 Blended and Hybrid Loans

These loans offer you several years of fixed payments before there is an interest rate change. You might get a three-year, five-year, or seven-year fixed-period loan that will adjust after the agreed fixed term. Your interest rate would be set for the first three, five, or seven years at an agreed rate, and then, at the end of the fixed-rate period, your interest rate would adjust every year. These loans might be referred to as 3/1, 5/1, or 7/1 ARMs; the first number identifies the fixed-rate period and the second number identifies how frequently the loan will adjust after that.

This type of ARM protects you against rapid interest rate increases in the early years of your loan. It may be the best loan, rate-wise, for you if you only plan on owning the property for the fixed-rate term. These loans will also specify the maximum amount for each annual adjustment after the fixed term and the maximum of all adjustments during the life of the loan. These loans are typically amortized over a 30-year period.

§ 2.6.4 Balloon Payments

There are short-term loans (usually five, seven, or ten years) that offer lower interest rates, but only a portion of the amount you borrow is paid off during the term of the loan. The payment is calculated as if it were a 30-year loan; however, at the end of the five, seven, or ten years you have to pay off the remaining balance in a lump sum or else refinance it. That balance due is referred to as a "balloon payment." (It is an inflated payment compared to the principal and interest payments due during the term of the loan itself.)

If you think you will be selling or refinancing your home in five to seven years, then you may benefit from obtaining a loan that includes a balloon payment. The interest rate on a balloon mortgage is lower than that of a 30-year, fully amortized, fixed-rate mortgage.

Some lenders will permit you to extend your loan beyond the agreed term if you pay a fee and refinance your loan. The loan would be at the current interest rate. This type of loan should not be pursued if you have concerns about the conditions at the time you will have to refinance or if you think the agreed term will expire before you are ready to sell or refinance.

§ 2.6.5 Points

Some loans include an option to make a payment (called "points" or "discount points") up front to lower your interest rate. Points are a fee that you pay to your lender. Simply put, one point is equal to one percent of the loan amount. So one point on a $150,000 loan would be $1,500.

These discount points represent extra money you pay to the lender at closing to buy down the interest rate on your loan. For each point you pay for a 30-year loan, your interest rate is generally reduced by about 1/4 (or .25) of a percentage point. So, if the current interest rate on a 30-year mortgage is 6.5%, paying one point means you could get that mortgage for an interest rate of 6.25%.

If you are interested in paying less interest, you can ask the lender to quote you interest rates where you pay one, two, or three discount points. Usually, the longer you plan to stay in your home, the more sense it makes to pay discount points. It is easy to analyze whether paying any points makes sense if you know how long you will be making the loan payments.

If you are given the option of a 30-year fixed-rate loan with an interest rate of 6.5% with no points, and a rate of 6.25% if you pay a point, it is easy to calculate the value of the point. If your loan amount is $180,000, the price of the point is $1,800 (1% of the loan amount). The principal and interest payment at 6.5% would be $1,137.60 and the principal and interest payment at 6.25% would be $1,108.80—a savings of $28.80 per month. It would take you 62.5 months to recover the price of the point ($1,800/28.80). If you are confident that you will be in the property for more than 62.5 months, then the point would pay off in the long run.

Whether paying a point makes sense depends on the cost of the point, the monthly savings that the borrower will obtain, and the length of time that the borrower will reap the benefit (i.e., how long the borrower will be paying on the loan).

§ 2.6.6 Mortgage Insurance

On most conventional loans, if your down payment is less than 20% of the purchase price, the lender will require that you purchase private mortgage insurance (PMI). This mortgage insurance is an additional charge that you pay to the lender monthly along with your principal and interest payment on the loan itself.

Paying mortgage insurance can be avoided by putting 20% down on the purchase or by obtaining two loans rather than one. If a buyer obtains a first loan for 80% of the value of the property, no mortgage insurance is due on that loan because it meets the 20% down requirement. Mortgage insurance is never required on a second mortgage, so a buyer can take a second mortgage for the portion of the 20% that the buyer is not putting down for the purchase. For instance, if the buyer has the ability to put 5% down on the purchase, the buyer can take out one loan for 80% of the purchase price and a second loan for the remaining 15%. Interest rates on a second loan tend to be higher than rates on a first, and the buyer needs to compare the cost for the extra insurance to the cost for mortgage insurance to decide which option makes more sense.

On FHA loans, mortgage insurance is always required for single-family residences. An amount of mortgage insurance is added to the loan balance from the start, and your monthly payment of principal and interest then includes repayment of debt with interest and an amount for the mortgage insurance premium.

§ 2.7 How Much House Can You Afford?

Your buying power depends on how much you have available for the down payment and how much a financial institution will agree to lend you. How much you can borrow depends on your income, the amount you put down on the house, your other assets and debts, and your credit history. How much you can borrow also depends largely on current interest rates.

If you are buying a house with someone else, such as a relative, friend, or business associate, your co-purchaser's earnings and existing debts will be considered as well as your own. Remember, if you apply for a loan with somebody else, you and your co-borrower are both legally responsible for repayment of the mortgage. Sometimes a couple will have more buying power if only one of the individuals—the one with better credit—applies for the loan, especially when the other partner has poor credit or a lot of existing debt.

§ 2.7.1 Down Payment

In the typical transaction, the buyer pays a down payment and pays closing costs at the time of the purchase. The down payment is the amount of the purchase price that the buyer pays directly, and the balance of the purchase price is the amount of the loan that the buyer borrows. It is possible for a buyer to purchase a home without investing *any* money up front. This will be discussed below under special financing.

§ 2.7.2 Loan-to-Value Ratio

The amount of the down payment will influence the rate and terms of the loan that the buyer can obtain. The larger the down payment, the more secure the lender is that the loan will be repaid.

Assuming that you do not overpay for your property (i.e., you do not agree to pay more for the house than it is worth), the loan-to-value ratio is determined by the amount of money that you pay as a down payment.

For example, if you purchase a home for $130,000, and you pay $13,000 and hope to borrow the balance, your loan amount, $117,000 (130,000 – 13,000), is 90% of the value of the house. The loan-to-value ratio is 90%. If you paid $6,500 down and borrowed the rest, $123,500, the loan-to-value ratio would be 95%.

Your down payment can come from your checking and savings accounts, mutual funds, stocks and bonds, the cash value of your life insurance policy, and gifts from parents or others. Discussed below are options for purchasing property with no money down.

Remember, putting less than 20% down often means you will be required to purchase private mortgage insurance to protect the lending institution in case you fail to make payments on your mortgage.

To decide how much money you feel comfortable paying as a down payment, you should think about the many other expenses that go along with buying a home. There will be moving expenses and possibly home decorating costs. Some lenders like to see that you will have sufficient funds after closing to make a few mortgage payments.

§ 2.7.3 Down-Payment Assistance Programs

Most loans require a minimum of 3% down payment, meaning on a $100,000 house you must pay $3,000 of the purchase price at the time of purchase. If you do not have money for a down payment, there are still ways that you can purchase and finance a home.

There are a number of ways to get assistance with the down payment if you do not have the ability to pay it or if you want to save your cash for other purposes. Some of the programs are statewide, like the Colorado Housing and Finance Authority program. There are programs specific to counties or cities. These organizations are all listed on the HUD website at www.hud.gov/local/co/homeownership/buyingprgms.cfm.

CHFA and Local Loan Programs - Bond Financing

The Colorado Housing and Finance Authority (CHFA) sponsors programs to help first-time home buyers or low-income buyers qualify for mortgages.

Local housing agencies also offer attractive loan terms to eligible home buyers. These programs typically offer competitive loan terms (low down payment or low interest rate) to first-time home buyers who meet specified income guidelines. CHFA also offers assistance with the down payment and closing costs. For information about this program, visit the Colorado Housing and Finance Authority website at www.colohfa.org/.

Seller Financing (Owner Carry Backs)

Sometimes a seller will offer to finance the purchase for the buyer. This is most likely to occur either when the seller is an investor or when the seller is looking for a way to sell property that is not otherwise selling. Basically, rather than going to a lender to finance the purchase, you will give the seller a down payment and execute a note and a deed of trust on the property in favor of the seller for the balance. The terms of the seller financing can be whatever you and the seller negotiate.

Seller carry back financing is not common, and I highly recommend that you hire a lawyer to represent you if you are going this route.

1sts and 2nds – No Money Down

Though not readily available these days, there are financing options that will allow a buyer with good credit to buy a home with no money down. Usually, this is accomplished through the use of two loans. The first loan is in the principal amount of 80% of the purchase price of the home. The second loan is for the balance of the purchase price, less the down payment.

A common loan of this type is referred to as an "80/20." If the purchase price of the home is $200,000, then the buyer seeks one loan for $160,000 (80%) and another loan for $40,000 (20%). Since the first loan is for 80% of the value of the home, the buyer can avoid mortgage insurance and can get an attractive interest rate because of the loan-to-value ratio. To complete the purchase, the buyer takes a second loan for the remaining 20%. The second loan has a higher interest rate because it is in a second position, but it does not require mortgage insurance.

Lease Option and Lease Purchase (Rent to Own)

Another creative financing option available on some properties is a lease option or a lease purchase. A seller who is an investor or who is looking for a way to sell property that is not otherwise selling might offer the lease purchase as an option. In this kind of transaction (often called "rent to own"), the buyer signs a lease and becomes a tenant in the property, paying rent for an agreed term. Under the terms of the lease, the tenant either (1) has the option to buy the property at the end of the lease term (called a "lease option"), or (2) commits to buy the property at the end of the lease term (called a "lease purchase"). The terms of the lease, including both the rent and the length of the lease period, are items for the parties to negotiate. Also, the parties will have to agree to the purchase price and terms at the time the lease option or lease purchase agreement is executed.

A lease option or lease purchase allows a buyer to move into the home that he or she wants right away, but to buy it later. Such an arrangement can be a useful way for an individual with poor credit, greater future earnings, or other special circumstances to buy a home.

§ 2.7.4 Calculation of Loan Payments

The bulk of your monthly loan payment will be principal and interest if you get an amortized loan. Below is a chart that will help you calculate the principal and interest portion of your loan payment. The factors in this table can be used to calculate the principal and interest due per $1,000 of loan. For example, if you borrow $75,000 at 8% for 30 years, you take 75 (which is 75,000/1000) x 7.34 (which is the factor for 8% for 30 years) to calculate the principal and interest due (75 x 7.34 = $550.50).

AMORTIZATION TABLE

Interest Rate	YEARS				
	10	15	20	25	30
4	10.12	7.40	6.06	5.28	4.77
4.25	10.24	7.52	6.19	5.42	4.92
4.5	10.36	7.65	6.33	5.56	5.07
4.75	10.48	7.78	6.46	5.70	5.22
5	10.61	7.91	6.60	5.85	5.37
5.25	10.73	8.04	6.74	5.99	5.52
5.5	10.85	8.17	6.88	6.14	5.68
5.75	10.98	8.30	7.02	6.29	5.84
6	11.10	8.44	7.16	6.44	6.00
6.25	11.23	8.57	7.31	6.60	6.16
6.5	11.35	8.71	7.46	6.75	6.32
6.75	11.48	8.85	7.60	6.91	6.49
7	11.61	8.99	7.75	7.07	6.65
7.25	11.74	9.13	7.90	7.23	6.82
7.5	11.87	9.27	8.06	7.39	6.99
7.75	12.00	9.41	8.21	7.55	7.16
8	12.13	9.56	8.36	7.72	7.34
8.25	12.27	9.70	8.53	7.88	7.51
8.5	12.27	9.70	8.53	7.88	7.51
8.75	12.53	9.99	8.84	8.22	7.87

9	12.67	10.14	9.00	8.39	8.05
9.25	12.80	10.29	9.16	8.56	8.23
9.5	12.94	70.44	9.33	8.74	8.41
9.75	13.08	10.59	9.49	8.91	8.59
10	13.22	10.75	9.65	9.09	8.78
10.25	13.35	70.90	9.82	9.26	8.96
10.5	13.49	11.05	9.98	9.44	9.15
10.75	13.63	11.21	10.15	9.62	9.33

Insurance and Taxes

In addition to requiring a monthly payment of principal and interest, the lender needs to know that the property is insured, so that if the property is damaged by fire or other casualty, there is insurance to replace it (and the lender is assured of being repaid). The lender also needs to know that real property taxes are being paid because unpaid property taxes are a lien against the property—to which the lender's lien will be junior. Lenders do not take any chances on these matters, so they require borrowers to deposit with the lender amounts to pay the insurance and the taxes. The lender establishes escrow accounts to which the borrower contributes 1/12 of the annual insurance premium and 1/12 of the annual tax bill each month. When the annual insurance premium and annual taxes are due, the lender pays those bills with the funds it has been holding in escrow.

Thus, with each monthly principal and interest payment that a borrower pays to the lender, the borrower also deposits a payment towards taxes and insurance. The full monthly payment is sometimes referred to as a "PITI payment" (Principal, Interest, Taxes, and Insurance).

Homeowners' Dues

If you are going to buy a townhome, condominium, or any property in a common-interest community, then in addition to your loan payments, you will have to pay homeowners' dues. These are dues paid to the homeowners' association (HOA) for services it provides, which could include the purchase of insurance, maintenance of the common elements of the community, trash removal, and snow removal. When analyzing how much home you can afford, you need to include the amount of your HOA dues.

§ 2.7.5 Closing Costs and Fees

It is customary in Colorado for the title company to prepare closing statements for the parties, which itemize all of the credits (deposits) and all of the debits (charges) due to and from each of the parties. A buyer's closing statement is typically prepared after the buyer's lender notifies the title company of the amount of the loan and the "lender fees" (the amounts that the lender is charging the buyer for the loan). Lender fees include such things as interest until the end of the current month, a document preparation fee, an underwriting fee, a credit report fee, and an appraisal fee. For the form closing statement, see *Appendix 1, Form 3: Closing Statement.*

It is customary for the lender to contact the buyer and advise the buyer of the closing costs and fees, i.e., the total amount that the buyer needs to bring to the closing table. This amount includes the buyer's down payment and all of the closing costs and fees, less the amount of the earnest money deposited, which is a credit to the buyer. The amount that the buyer must bring to the closing should be in the form of a cashier's check. It is safest for the buyer to have the check made out in the name of the buyer and then endorse the check over to the title company at the end of the closing—once the buyer knows that all has gone well.

Sometimes you can negotiate with the seller of a property to pay some of your closing costs, which will reduce the amount of money you will need to bring to closing. Common items to be paid at the closing are:

- Transfer taxes and recording fees.
- Title insurance premium and endorsements.
- Survey or improvement location certificate.
- Loan discount points.
- Attorney fees.
- Various lender fees for underwriting the loan and preparing the legal documents.

When you apply for a loan, the lender must give you a Good Faith Estimate (GFE) of the costs that you will have to pay. The Real Estate Settlement Procedures Act (RESPA) requires the mortgage banker or mortgage broker to deliver or mail the GFE to the applicant within three business days after the application is received.

§ 2.7.6 Credit Scores – FICO

FICO is a measure of creditworthiness. It is an objective, mathematical way to determine whether you meet a lender's criteria. The formula was created by Fair, Isaac & Co. Factors that affect your score include the following:

- Delinquencies will lower scores, and scores drop when several credit accounts are opened in a short period.

- A long credit history is better than a new one, and too few revolving accounts make it harder to evaluate the ability to manage credit.

- Consumers with "maxed out" credit cards may have trouble making payments. Too many revolving accounts indicate overextension.

- Tax liens, bankruptcies, and use of consumer credit agencies can all lower a FICO score.

- Small credit card balances and no late payments show responsibility.

- As discussed above, credit inquiries can negatively impact credit scores.

You can obtain your score, for a fee, at www.myfico.com. At a minimum, a score should be over 640 to easily qualify for a loan. If your score is above 700, that is a good score and it will open up more lending options for you.

In Colorado, you are entitled to a free report from the credit bureaus every year. The report, however, does not include your FICO score. There are three major credit bureaus, and you might want to request copies of your credit reports and make sure they are accurate. Contact information for each credit bureau is below.

Equifax Consumer Relations
P.O. Box 740241
Atlanta, GA 30374
(800) 685-1111
www.equifax.com

Experian
National Consumers Assistance Center
P.O. Box 2002
Allen, TX 75013
(888) 397-3742
www.experian.com

TransUnion
Consumer Disclosure Center
P.O. Box 1000
Chester, PA 19022
(800) 888-4213
www.transunion.com

§ 2.7.7 Loan Qualification Information

Lenders are comfortable making a loan to a buyer only if the amount of the loan is reasonable considering the property value and the buyer's income, assets, other debts, and credit score. Because the first source for repayment of the mortgage loan is the borrower, the lender needs to be convinced that the borrower has the ability to repay the loan.

When you apply for a mortgage, the lender will consider both your earnings and your existing debts in determining the size of your loan. To determine what size mortgage you are eligible for, lenders generally use the following two qualifying guidelines:

1. Housing expense ratio – the amount of money you owe for mortgage payments, property taxes, insurance, and HOA fees, if applicable, should total no more than 28% of your monthly gross (before-tax) income.

2. Debt-to-income ratio – the amount of money you owe for the above items plus other long-term debts should total no more than 36 percent of your monthly gross income.

Basically, lenders are saying that a household should spend not much more than one-fourth of its income (28%) on housing and not much more than one-third of its income (36%) on total indebtedness (housing plus other debts). Lenders believe that homeowners who follow these guidelines will be able to pay off their mortgages fairly comfortably.

These lender ratios are flexible guidelines. If you have a consistent record of paying rent that is very close in amount to your proposed monthly mortgage payments or if you make a large down payment, you may be able to use somewhat higher ratios. Some lenders offer special loans for low- and moderate-income home buyers that allow them to use as much as 35% of their gross monthly income for housing expenses and 45% for total debt.

When you apply for a mortgage, the lender will use all of the relevant data—your income, your existing debts, the purchase price of the house, your down payment, the interest rate on the loan, and the cost of property taxes and insurance—and calculate whether you qualify to borrow the amount of money you need to buy the house.

Following is a sample worksheet for calculating a loan qualification.

LOAN QUALIFICATION WORKSHEET

Income

Your monthly gross income[14]	$1750	
Overtime/bonus[15]		
Co-borrower gross income	1750	
Overtime/bonus		
Net rents		
Total monthly income:	3500	**A**

---

[14] If you are self-employed, take the past two years' average gross income plus your year-to-date net income and divide by total months to determine average income.

[15] Use a 24-month average for overtime and bonuses.

Expenses

Auto	250
Alimony/childcare	
Student loans	75
Minimum payments on credit card debt(s)	0
Other mortgage	
Other debt obligations	0

Total monthly expenses:	325	**B**

Housing Expenses

Principal and interest	647.90[*]
Taxes[16]	104.00
Homeowners insurance[17]	22.50
Homeowners' dues	
Mortgage insurance[18]	61.20

Total housing expenses	835.60	**C**

[*] $95,000 ($100,000 house with $5,000 down) at 7.25% interest for 30 years.

Qualification ratio:

Total housing expenses **C** ÷ total gross income **A** should not exceed 28% for a conventional loan[19] or 29% for a government-guaranteed loan (FHA or VA).[20]

Total monthly expenses **B** + total housing expenses **C** ÷ total gross income **A** should not exceed 36% for a conventional loan or 41% for a government-guaranteed loan (FHA or VA).

C ÷ A < 28%

835.60 ÷ 3500.00 = .24

(B + C) ÷ A < 41%

(325.00 + 835.60) ÷ 3500.00 = .33

---

[16] Sales price x .00104 is a good estimate of the monthly tax burden.

[17] Loan amount x .00025 is a good estimate of the monthly cost of homeowners insurance.

[18] Loan amount x .00068 is a good estimate of the monthly cost of mortgage insurance.

[19] As a rule of thumb, a buyer can qualify for a conventional loan where the housing expense ratio does not exceed 28%.

[20] As a rule of thumb, one can qualify for an FHA loan where the housing expense ratio does not exceed 29%.

CHAPTER 3
FINDING THE RIGHT REAL ESTATE AGENT

§ 3.1 Introduction

Most home buyers choose to hire a real estate broker to help them find and buy their homes. The terms "broker" and "agent" are used interchangeably in Colorado. It makes sense to take advantage of the expertise, experience, and efforts of an agent when making a home purchase. The buyer rarely has to pay the agent's commission, at least not directly. Buyers have to choose the type of relationship they wish to have with the agent, and which agent to hire. There are many real estate agents, and choosing the right agent—like choosing any professional—should be done carefully.

§ 3.2 The Pros and Cons of Using a Real Estate Agent

§ 3.2.1 Researching Properties

Not that long ago, only real estate agents knew what properties were on the market. Sure, there were signs on the front lawns of homes that advised the public that a home was for sale, but organized information about properties currently on the market, and information about properties that had sold (and at what price), was not as readily available as it is today. More and more, the information that once was known only by real estate agents is available in one form or another to the general public.

For instance, buyers can obtain information about properties through county websites. Currently, the information provided by counties does not identify which properties are on the market, and the information available varies by county, but there is a lot of information about sold properties. Generally, information provided by counties includes legal descriptions of properties, assessed values, names and addresses of property owners, and historic sold information. Appendix 2 includes a list of Colorado county websites that provide real property records for their counties.

Any buyer with a computer can also research and find many properties that are currently on the market. The Multiple Listing Service (MLS) is available throughout the state and can be accessed at various websites. Unfortunately for the consumer, the information available on public website is not as complete as the information available by subscription to real estate agents. This is discussed more in Chapter 4.

Researching available properties and comparative properties that have sold is only one of the services that a real estate agent provides. A competent real estate agent also has knowledge about the areas and neighborhoods, property values, financing, contracts, negotiations, real estate law, and every other aspect of a real estate transaction.

§ 3.2.2 Showing Properties

One great reason for using a real estate agent is the fact that an agent can schedule you to see many properties in one day. There is a system in place that allows a licensed agent to schedule a showing of a property without the seller or seller's agent being present, if the property is listed for sale by another licensed real estate agent. Your agent can make a telephone call and schedule a time to show a property to you. The agent must provide to the seller's agent (or his or her office) information about the agent who seeks to show the property, and can then obtain the combination to a lockbox that is placed at the property (usually on the front door). Generally, properties that are on the market are available for viewing during daylight hours by your broker.

If you are trying to view properties without your own agent, you must contact each of the listing agents or sellers to schedule a showing. Since the seller or the seller's agent must be there for you to view the property, scheduling is a little more challenging. Trying to schedule viewings of several properties in one day can be very difficult logistically.

§ 3.2.3 Preparing the Legal Documents

Real estate brokers have a limited license to practice law. This means that they can prepare contracts for their clients, provided that they use the standard forms created by the Colorado Real Estate Commission (or forms created by an attorney for the real estate company).[21]

A successful agent has written many contracts and can fully explain the terms of the contract to the buyer. The real estate agent completes the contract with input from the buyer. For instance, your real estate agent will be able to help you decide how much to offer as the purchase price for the property. The contract itself is discussed in detail in Chapter 5. If it is necessary to change the contract at any point, your agent will prepare the document needed to amend the contract.

§ 3.2.4 Selecting Financing

Your real estate agent is a great source for a recommendation for a lender. A good real estate agent will help you find the right loan from the right lender. Because real estate agents have worked with lenders on other transactions, your

---

[21] Conway-Bogue Realty Inv. Co. v. Denver Bar Ass'n, 135 Colo. 398, 312 P.2d 998 (1957).

agent will have lenders to recommend to you—ideally lenders who have provided impressive service to the agent's other clients.

Some real estate companies are now offering what they call "one-stop shopping," which means their company or a related company provides loans as well as real estate services. This may be an acceptable option, depending on the financing terms offered. On the other hand, if you could get better financing elsewhere, you may be obtaining a loan that is convenient but unnecessarily expensive or inappropriate.

§ 3.2.5 Educating and Advising You

An agent will help you understand every step of the real estate transaction, including both the legal process and also the required documentation. There are many deadlines in the contract, and you should expect your agent to watch the dates and make sure all required actions are timely completed.

You should have an attorney review information that you receive about the title to the property. Your agent will also review the title commitment and tell you if there are any potential issues that require legal assistance, but a real estate agent is not legally trained or licensed and cannot give you legal advice. Most buyers in Colorado do not hire an attorney for a residential real estate purchase, and title problems are not common, but the contract form and your agent will recommend that you seek legal counsel. In this author's opinion, hiring an attorney is a pretty inexpensive way to assure yourself that you are getting the title to the property that you expect.

The agent will do all that he or she can to make sure all legal and contractual requirements are satisfied for the property to close. The agent will review the closing statement and other closing documents to make sure they are accurate and will attend the closing to make sure all goes well. Keep in mind that the buyer's agent has a vested interest in making sure that the transaction closes because he or she earns a commission only if and when the transaction closes.

§ 3.2.6 Negotiations

You have probably heard the expression that "a lawyer who represents himself has a fool for a client."[22] The reasons that even a capable attorney should not represent himself or herself are the same reasons that a home buyer should not go it alone. A real estate agent or attorney who is involved in all of the negotiations will provide dispassionate, objective advice to you when you are emotionally involved in the matter. The judgment of an independent third

---

[22] *See* Kay v. Ehrler, 499 U.S. 432, 438 (1991).

party can be quite useful. Sometimes buyers and sellers get so emotionally involved in the negotiations that they forget their own self-interest.

In addition to negotiating the purchase price and additional terms of the contract, the agent will assist you with negotiations that will be necessary after contracting and before closing. For instance, if you find any unsatisfactory conditions after you inspect the property, your agent will prepare a notice to correct (demanding that the seller make the required repairs) and will negotiate a resolution of those objections on your behalf.

§ 3.3 Real Estate Broker's Commissions

In most circumstances, the seller pays the real estate commission for the buyer's real estate agent. This is how a typical real estate deal works from the agent's perspective: The seller contracts with an agent to sell the property. The seller and that agent, called the "listing broker," negotiate an agreement (called a "listing agreement" because the agent lists the property for sale). The listing agreement states how much of a commission the seller will pay. In the listing agreement, the seller and the listing broker also agree on how much of the commission the listing broker will offer to the agent who brings the buyer to the transaction (called the "selling broker"). The share of the commission paid by the listing broker to the selling broker is known as the "co-op."

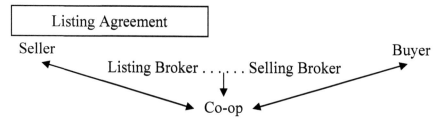

The seller knows that he or she will be paying commission, and because most properties are listed and sold by real estate agents, the market price of homes already reflects the commission as a cost of sale. Thus, in effect, every buyer pays the commission indirectly as part of the purchase price.

If the property has been listed with a real estate broker, and you do not work with an agent representing you as the buyer, the listing broker may retain the entire commission or, if previously agreed between the seller and listing broker, the listing broker will charge the seller less commission because there is no co-op. Many buyers incorrectly believe that they can get property at a lower price if there is no buyer agent involved. But the buyer cannot obtain the co-op—the co-op can only be paid to a licensed real estate broker. The contract between the seller and the listing broker pre-exists the buyer's involvement, and the buyer does not have any ability to force those parties to renegotiate the terms of the listing agreement.

Because the co-op is there for the taking and will not affect the price the buyer pays for the property, every buyer would be wise to use a real estate agent. It costs the buyer nothing extra to hire a broker if the buyer is purchasing listed property. Moreover, because the typical agent earns a fee or commission only if a customer buys a property as a result of the agent's efforts,[23] there is no obligation to pay your agent anything if you do not end up buying a property.

Buyers sometimes agree to pay other fees to their agents. Agency agreements and the various compensation options are discussed in detail below.

§ 3.4 Relationships with Real Estate Brokers

In Colorado, you must decide whether the real estate agent you hire will act as a transaction-broker or as a buyer's agent. A Colorado statute, C.R.S. § 12-61-803(2), makes a broker a transaction-broker unless there is an express written agreement to the contrary. For the contract for hiring a broker, which is discussed in Section 3.6 below, see *Appendix 1, Form 4: Exclusive Right-to-Buy Contract (All Types of Properties)*. Following are the definitions of each relationship.

§ 3.4.1 Transaction-Broker

A transaction-broker is defined in the Colorado statutes as "a broker who assists one or more parties throughout a contemplated real estate transaction with communication, interposition, advisement, negotiation, contract terms, and the closing of such real estate transaction without being an agent or advocate for the interests of any party to such transaction."[24] The transaction-broker must use reasonable skill and care in the performance of any oral or written agreement. The transaction-broker must disclose to potential sellers (1) all material facts concerning the buyer's financial ability to perform the terms of the transaction, and (2) whether the buyer intends to occupy the property. No written agreement is required to engage or employ a broker as a transaction-broker.

§ 3.4.2 Buyer Agency

Many home buyers do not know what a buyer agent is or why it is to their benefit to hire one. All agents in Colorado are presumed to be working with the buyer as a transaction-broker unless the parties agree otherwise in writing. However, only the buyer agent works solely on behalf of the buyer and owes

---

[23] The agent must be the *procuring cause*. "Whether the broker is the procuring cause rests on whether the broker set in motion a chain of events which, without break in continuity, resulted in a sale . . . ." Winston Fin. Group, Inc. v. Fults Mgmt., Inc., 872 P.2d 1356 (Colo. App. 1994).

[24] C.R.S. § 12-61-802(6).

duties to the buyer, including the duties of good faith, loyalty, and fidelity. The buyer agent will negotiate on behalf of, and act as an advocate for, the buyer. However, the buyer agent must make the same disclosures as the transaction-broker about adverse material facts concerning a buyer's financial ability to perform the terms of a transaction and whether the buyer intends to occupy the property.

All real estate agents have duties to their customers, including the duty to perform any oral or written agreement made with the customer and the duty to exercise reasonable skill and care.

The major difference between a buyer agent and a transaction-broker is that the buyer agent is an advocate for the client, and the transaction-broker is a neutral party. In today's market, most buyers choose to work with a buyer agent.

§ 3.4.3 Choosing an Agent

Because you are hiring someone to help you with an expensive and very personal purchase, it is important that you find someone you trust and with whom you feel comfortable. It is not unusual for buyers to spend several hours in a day with their agents, so it is reasonable to look for an agent who is not only competent, but also whose company you will enjoy.

Here are some interview questions to help you compare possible agents:

1. What is your *experience* in the real estate business?

    You should learn how many years of experience the agent has in Colorado; how long the agent has been with his or her current company; how many properties the agent sells in a year; the average price of the property the agent sells; which neighborhoods the agent works in; and the type of property the agent works with most often, e.g., condos, single-family, or multi-family.

2. What kind of *clients* do you have?

    Knowing that the agent has experience working with others who are like you may be helpful in finding the right agent for you. You should ask what percent of the agent's business consists of first-time home buyers, move-up buyers, or sellers. You also might ask demographic questions (e.g., the age, sex, and marital status of most of the agent's clients) to find out whether you are a typical client for the agent.

3. What kind of *agency* relationship do you offer?

    Will the agent act as a transaction-broker or a buyer's agent for you? If the agent represents the seller on a property that you are interested in, how will the agent deal with that conflict? Will he or she require you to sign an exclusive agreement, i.e., that you will not work with another agent during the term of the agreement? Ask how the agent is paid and whether he or she charges any up-front fees.

4. How does the *agent* prefer to communicate—by e-mail or telephone?

   Will the agent be working directly with you or will the agent assign a broker associate or an assistant to work with you? What days and hours does the agent work?

These questions will help you determine what kind of service you will get from this agent. Is the agent working with too many other clients to give you the time and attention that you need? How easy will it be for you to reach the agent?

§ 3.5 Real Estate Agent Designations

There are many designations available to agents. These designations generally represent the education and qualifications an agent has beyond those required to obtain a license. Here are some of the designations that may help you decide on the appropriate agent for your needs.

§ 3.5.1 Realtor® Designation

Realtor® is probably the most familiar title, and is the designation of a real estate agent who is a member of the National Association of Realtors (NAR) as well as the state and local association of realtors. NAR claims to be the largest professional association in the country, and provides its members with access to education and information resources. All NAR members must subscribe to professional ethics and standards.

§ 3.5.2 Accredited Buyer Representative (ABR®)

ABR® designees have completed the Real Estate Buyer's Agent Council (REBAC) course, passed the test, and provided documentation of buyer agency experience.

§ 3.5.3 Accredited Seller Representative (ASR®)

ASR® designees have completed the Seller Agency Council course, passed the test, and provided documentation of seller agency experience.

§ 3.5.4 Council of Residential Specialists (CRS)

This association was created to attract and retain those Realtors® seeking the knowledge, tools, and relationship-building opportunities needed to maximize their income and professionalism in residential real estate.

§ 3.5.5 Seniors Real Estate Specialist (SRES®)

SRES® designees demonstrate the knowledge and experience to counsel senior clients through the major financial and lifestyle transitions involved in relocating, refinancing, or selling a home.

§ 3.6 Negotiating the Agency Contract

When you hire a real estate agent, you will be asked to sign a contract with that agent. The Colorado Real Estate Commission creates standard forms for these agency agreements, which establish the terms of the relationship between the buyer and the real estate agent. They also designate whether the agent is being hired as a transaction-broker or a buyer agent. There is a different form for non-residential properties.

For the standard residential form, see *Appendix 1, Form 4: Exclusive Right-to-Buy Contract (All Types of Properties)*. You should review this form before you meet with a real estate agent so that you are well aware of its terms and your options. Some significant terms of the contract are described below.

The agent must indicate whether he or she is with a multiple-person firm or is a one-person firm. If the agent is with a multiple-person firm, you will want to know each broker who may be designated to work with you. The agency relationship created by the agency contract exists only with the designated broker or brokers (i.e., those listed on the agreement) and does not extend to the employing broker, brokerage firm, or to any other brokers employed or engaged by the brokerage firm who are not so designated.

The contract includes a description of the property that you are seeking to buy. The agent will earn a commission if you purchase property that substantially meets the requirements described in the agreement or similar real estate acceptable to you. Since the buyer does not know which property he or she is going to buy when hiring the agent, this section will describe generally what kind of property the buyer is looking for, and the description tends to be fairly generic, like "residence."

The term of the contract is often six months, and it is designated in the agreement. The expiration of the agreement is either a specific date, or will continue through the completion of the purchase of the property, whichever occurs first.

The agreement describes the obligations of the broker and the buyer. For instance, the broker must disclose to any prospective seller all adverse material facts actually known by the broker, such as the buyer's financial ability to perform the terms of the transaction or whether the buyer intends to occupy the property as a principal residence. However, the broker is prohibited from disclosing the following information about the buyer without the buyer's informed consent:

- That the buyer is willing to pay more than the purchase price offered for the property.

- What the buyer's motivating factors are.

- That the buyer will agree to finance terms other than those offered.

The broker has no duty to conduct an independent inspection of the property for the buyer's benefit, nor any duty to verify the accuracy or completeness of statements made by a seller or independent inspectors. Moreover, the broker has no duty to conduct an independent investigation of the buyer's financial condition or to verify the accuracy or completeness of any statement made by the buyer.

You may want to purchase property that your broker has listed for the seller—meaning that the seller and you, as the buyer, could be working with the same broker. Therefore, the contract requires you to indicate whether the broker will represent you as (1) Buyer's Agent only, (2) Buyer Agency Unless Brokerage Relationship with Both, or (3) Transaction-Broker.

You, as the buyer, have obligations under the agreement as well. You agree to conduct any negotiations for the property only through the broker, and to refer to the broker all communications you receive from real estate brokers, prospective sellers, or any other source during the term of the contract. You also must represent that you are not currently a party to any agreement with any other broker to represent or assist you in the location or purchase of property.

You also may have to pay the broker a "success fee" under certain circumstances. This fee is earned when the property is purchased and is payable at the closing of the transaction. If any transaction fails to close as a result of the seller's default (with no fault on the part of buyer), then the success fee is waived. If any transaction fails to close because of the buyer's default, then the success fee will not be waived, and it will be payable at the time of the buyer's default or, at the latest, on the date that was scheduled for closing. A success fee applies to property contracted for during the term of the contract or during a holdover period. The holdover period is generally 90 days. You are still responsible to pay the success fee if the agent introduced you to property during the term of the agreement and you buy it after the term of the contract but before the expiration of the holdover period.

Even though you agree to pay the broker's fee, the contract allows you to instruct the broker to request payment from the listing brokerage firm or from the seller. In cases where the property is listed, the buyer's broker will get at least some of the broker's fee paid by the seller or the listing broker.

In addition to, or instead of, the success fee, you may be asked to pay the broker an hourly fee, a retainer, or other compensation. These are negotiable items, and you should be sure that you are comfortable with the compensation that you agree to pay. The most common practice is to agree to pay the broker a commission at closing, and most buyers never have to pay that success fee directly.

The buyer agency agreement recommends consultation with legal and tax counsel. Any time you sign a legal document, you should be confident that it reflects your agreement—and that you understand what it says—before you sign it. If not, you should always consult with an attorney.

The agreement provides that if a dispute arises between the buyer and the broker, either prior to or after closing, and is not resolved, then you must first proceed in good faith to submit the matter to mediation before bringing any court action.

The agreement also provides that if the buyer is concerned about the presence of a registered sex offender in the neighborhood where he or she is looking to purchase a home, then the buyer must contact local law enforcement officials to obtain such information. (This paragraph refers to Megan's Law, which requires convicted sex offenders to register with the police.) Your real estate broker has no duty to research this issue for you.

§ 3.7 Fair Housing Laws

The Fair Housing Act[25] and other federal and state laws were enacted to guarantee a right to a national housing market that is free from discrimination. The conduct of real estate agents is covered by the fair housing laws. Real estate agents are prohibited by federal law from discriminating based on race, color, religion, sex, handicap, familial status, and national origin, and are prohibited by state law from discriminating based on race, creed, color, sex, marital status, national origin, familial status, physical or mental handicap, religion, or ancestry of any person.

The National Association of Realtors® prints a brochure called "What Everyone Should Know About Equal Opportunity in Housing," which is available on their website at http://www.realtor.org/.

§ 3.8 Conclusion

Once you have decided whether to hire a real estate agent, and you have selected the agent you want to work with (if you want one), then you are ready to start looking for the right home.

---

[25] 42 U.S.C. §§ 3601 *et seq.*

CHAPTER 4
FINDING THE RIGHT PROPERTY TO BUY

§ 4.1 Introduction

The most time-consuming portion of the home-buying process is the search for a home, but it can also be the most fun. The right property is the one that fits your budget, your needs, *and* your taste. Finding a property that does all that in a location that you like—and that is exciting enough that you are willing to invest much of your savings and income into it—takes some time and strategy. The search is especially challenging because the inventory (homes for sale) is constantly changing. Thus, it is imperative that you have a plan for how and where you will search for your home.

§ 4.2 What Are You Looking For?

There are many ways to look for properties, but the first step is to define what you are looking for. Many first-time home buyers are not conscious of the fact that they have preferences for a home, since they have never bought one before. But we have all lived somewhere, we all have visited family and friends in other homes, and as a result we all have some definite ideas of what makes a "home." These ideas will surface as you start looking for a place to buy, but to the extent you can describe them or define them at the start of the process, you can be a more productive home shopper. There may be hundreds (possibly even thousands) of properties for sale in your area; even if you try to look at them all, some will be sold before you get to see them. However, if you know some of the objective criteria that you are looking for in your home, you can eliminate all of the properties that lack those criteria. You will have to decide what you *want* in your next home, as well as what you *need*. Following are some items for you to consider that might generate the objective criteria for your search. Keep in mind that part of creating the best search criteria for your next home also includes deciding what you do *not* want.

§ 4.2.1 Price

Before looking at any properties, you should consult with a lender to check on current interest rates and to calculate your financial buying power. Do not spend any time looking at properties that you cannot afford; not only is it a waste of valuable time, but it also may depress you when you look at properties that actually are within your price range.

We all have a limit as to how much we can spend—or are willing to spend—on a home. Once you know your price limit, that will also reduce the number of properties that you will have to consider. Decide on a price range that works with your budget and is comfortable for you. Because many people view their home as an investment and not just a residence, buyers often look for the highest-priced properties they can afford. (See Chapter 2 for information on financing and determining how much house you can afford.)

§ 4.2.2 Location

There are many aspects of a home that you can change after you own it, but location is not on that list. Where do you want to live? What areas appeal to you and are convenient for you? Do you want to be in a certain school district? What is most important to you: proximity to where you work, proximity to where you spend your free time, or proximity to family or friends? Do you need or want to be close to public transportation? Do you want an older community with established trees, or do you prefer a newer area with greater conveniences? Consider where you are living currently; why did you choose that location?

Decide on the areas where you would most like to find your new home, and start searching those areas first. You may not be able to find what you are looking for in your price range in your first choice of location. You will then have to decide what is most important to you and what you can be flexible on. Do you want to change what you are looking for or where you are looking, or can you adjust your price to find what you want where you want it?

§ 4.2.3 Size

Start by defining the minimum number of bedrooms and baths you need in your home. Also decide on the minimum square footage for the place that you will buy. This may sound challenging at first, but after you look at a few properties you will know what feels too small to you. Decide on the amount of square footage without including any below-grade or basement area, garage, or enclosed porches or patios. If you want a basement or a garage, add those as additional requirements; that will make your search more accurate and complete.

§ 4.2.4 Attached or Detached Housing

Do you want a detached single family residence, i.e., a house? Or do you want to buy attached housing, which would include any property called a condominium, townhome or row home, cluster or patio home, or half a duplex? Are you interested in a common interest community (CIC), a development with common areas maintained through an association of owners?

Attached housing can be mislabeled and misunderstood, but there are some significant differences in the kinds of attached housing. There is a legal difference in the ownership of a condominium and other forms of attached housing. When you purchase a condominium, you own the airspace of the unit you purchased and you own an undivided interest in the common elements of the condominium complex. Common elements generally include the condominium buildings themselves, as well as any clubhouses, parking areas, or other structures. Developers of a condominium project record covenants, conditions, and restrictions (CCRs) that apply to each condominium unit and owner. The CCRs provide for the creation of a condominium owners' association that is responsible for the management of the common elements. Each condominium owner contributes dues to that association and has voting power on how the association maintains and oversees the complex.

Townhomes and other forms of attached housing do not have to be owned like condominiums (although they can be formed that way). Non-condominium attached housing may or may not have an owners' association. Generally, when you buy attached housing that is not called a condominium, you get ownership of the real estate itself, but there is a common wall or some common facilities. There may be a formal agreement, that has been recorded, specifying how the owners will maintain the common wall, common roof, water bill, or any other shared feature or utility. Or there may not be a formal agreement regarding the shared elements, leaving the current owners to deal with issues as they arise.

Buying your home in a common interest community has advantages and disadvantages. Often CICs have common grounds that are maintained by the association, which add to the beauty of the neighborhood. The association may provide services such as exterior maintenance, grounds maintenance, water and sewer, and trash and snow removal as part of the homeowners' dues. For those who travel often or who do not want the burden of maintaining the outside of their home, these types of properties may be perfect.

Attached housing is often smaller and less expensive than the detached housing in the same area. When there is damage to the property, owners of attached housing have the benefit of others to share the costs. On the other hand, the owners of attached housing have added risk, since damage to any of the common elements affects each owner.

Detached housing generally affords more privacy. Also, there generally are not as many restrictions on the use of the property as there are with attached housing.

Before buying any attached housing, you should review all of the documents that govern the use of the property and the owners' association, including CCRs, bylaws, minutes of previous meetings, financial information, and any rules and regulations. This is discussed further in Chapter 5.

§ 4.2.5 Style and Age

Do you want a one-story or a multi-story property? Do you like a split-level home? Is there a particular architectural style that you are looking for? Do you prefer an older home or a newer one? Does it matter to you?

It is important that you identify the factors that will make a property appeal to you , as well as those factors that will help you eliminate properties as possibilities right off the bat. If you do not have a preference about a particular criteria, or if you know you can be flexible on that criteria, you should not include it as a requirement. You should be as specific as you can without eliminating any properties that might be acceptable to you. Think about what are non-negotiable requirements for you.

§ 4.2.6 Other Considerations

Do you have any special needs? For example, do you want a home that is handicapped accessible? Do you have pets? Household pets are generally not an issue when you buy a detached single-family residence, but if you are looking to buy in an attached-housing community, there may be restrictions on pets that apply to all owners.

Think also in terms of things that you can and cannot change. You can change or add many features to a home, but some changes or additions may be very expensive or impractical. Location is not something you can change, size is not something you can change easily, and adding a fireplace could be a challenge. On the other hand, adding a fence could be accomplished easily.

At the end of this chapter is a questionnaire that summarizes options for you to consider and will help you focus your search.

§ 4.3 How Can You Find It?

§ 4.3.1 Internet Searches

Most properties are advertised for sale, in one fashion or another, on the Internet. If you do not have the ability to search for properties online, then you miss the opportunity to consider all possibilities in a timely manner. Find a real estate broker who will take the time to create a search for you, show you the properties currently on the market that satisfy your criteria, and keep you updated on new listings.

§ 4.3.2 Multiple Listing Service—Online

The Multiple Listing Service (MLS) is a local or regional database of all homes listed by local real estate agents. The vast majority of all homes that are for sale are listed with a real estate agent and are on the MLS.

Metrolist, Inc provides the MLS that serves the greater Denver metro area, now known as Prime Access. It serves seven Realtor® associations: Aurora Association of Realtors®, Denver Board of Realtors®, Douglas/Elbert Realtor® Association, Jefferson County Association of Realtors®, Mountain Metro Association of Realtors® North Metro Denver Realtor® Association, and South Metro Denver Realtor® Association. Metrolist's Property Data Center (PDC) offers Assessor/Treasurer and Deed information for the following counties: Adams, Arapahoe, Broomfield, Boulder, Denver, Douglas, Eagle, El Paso, Jefferson, Larimer, Mesa and Weld. There is also a Multiple Listing Service in the Colorado Springs area, created by the Pikes Peak Association of Realtors, and there is one in Northern Colorado (with real estate and homes in Boulder, Fort Collins, Greeley, Loveland, Longmont, Denver, Fort Morgan, Larimer County, and surrounding areas) called Information and Real Estate Services. Real estate agents can search any of these databases through the Colorado Cooperative MLS.

The Multiple Listings Service has public websites where you can search listings and view most of the listings on these services. The Denver MLS can be viewed at *www.recolorado.com*, the Colorado Springs area MLS can be viewed at *www.ppar.com*, and the Northern Colorado Information and Real Estate Services can be viewed at *www.ires-net.com*.

Not all of the listings in MLS are on the public sites because real estate agents and sellers have the choice of whether to make their listings available to the general public.

The benefit of Internet searching is that the information can be more current; unfortunately, this is not always the case. Each individual realtor has the ability to add a listing and to make any updates or changes to it. Since there are thousands of individuals contributing to the database, it is easy to understand why it is not always accurate, complete, or current. Also, some of the public databases are not updated as often as the database used by real estate agents.

§ 4.3.3 IDX

Many realtors subscribe to IDX, which allows individual brokers or companies to have a search engine on their website that is a portal to their MLS. In this way, clients can search for properties while being told of the advantages of using a particular real estate agent or company. These portals to the MLS are useful, and although they do not contain all of the listings that a real estate broker can search (again, agents and sellers can elect not to have their listings published on other agents' sites), the database is at least as complete and current than the general public access to the MLS.

§ 4.4 For Sale By Owner

Searching for property that is for sale by owner (FSBO) is not as easy. Generally, the best way to find a home that is a FSBO is to see a sign in the front yard to that effect. FSBO listings can also be found in newspaper ads. Recently, websites have been created to advertise FSBO properties, such as *www.forsalebyowner.com*. There are many others and, no doubt, new ones every day. The most significant weakness of many of these sites is the lack of objectivity of the listings. There is rarely consistent information about the various properties to allow a consumer to adequately compare the properties. Another weakness is the fact that the number of listings is often insignificant. This is due to two factors: (1) the small number of properties for sale by owner, generally; and (2) the lack of a centralized marketplace for those that do exist.

§ 4.5 New Construction

If your goal is to purchase a newly constructed home, the Internet is also a great resource. Many builders have their own websites with pictures, floor plans, prices, and other information. Many builders in Colorado list their new construction at *www.homebuilder.com*.

If you want a real estate agent to represent you in the purchase of a newly constructed home, most builders require that the agent register you as a buyer. It is, of course, to your advantage to have a real estate agent and/or a lawyer represent you in the purchase of a new home. The contract used by a builder is not the standard commission-approved form, so there may be even more of a reason for you to have representation.

§ 4.6 Real Estate Agent Searches

If you have chosen to work with a real estate agent, that agent will do property searches for you and will work with you on your search criteria. Many agents have software programs that make searching easier, and the database available to real estate agents allows for more detailed searches. A real estate agent can search for listings based on any of the criteria that are entered into a listing.

§ 4.7 Mountain Property

It never ceases to amaze me how many people think they want to live in the mountains, but ultimately do not buy there. There are some great communities in the mountains, but if you are dreaming of buying a mountain retreat, you will want to consider the possible inconveniences and added expenses discussed below.

§ 4.7.1 Water and Sewer

In many mountain areas in Colorado, the property does not have public water or sewer service. As a result, occupants must have a well and septic tank or find other creative ways to make their property inhabitable. A well has a limited life, and creating a new well is difficult and expensive. Sewer service also adds an expense to the property.

§ 4.7.2 Snow

Snow removal and inaccessibility due to snowfall are other concerns you must consider before choosing a mountain property.

§ 4.7.3 Schools

School proximity is a potential concern, depending on where you are looking.

§ 4.7.4 Water Rights

Another issue with some property in Colorado is water. Because we are in a dry climate and often in drought conditions, our water is a treasured resource. If you are looking at a property that is unimproved, it may not have any water available to it. In some counties, the charges for a water tap can be outrageous, if a water tap is even available.

§ 4.8 Second/Vacation Home

If you are looking to purchase a second home, the process is the same. You may have additional requirements for financing the property if you still have a balance owing on your existing home. If the second home will not be owner-occupied, lenders typically charge a higher interest rate than they do for your primary residence.

§ 4.9 Fix-Up Properties

If you are handy, you may be able to earn some "sweat equity" by buying a home that needs some repairs and investing your own efforts to make the necessary repairs or improvements. Properties in Colorado can be listed as fix-up properties, so it is easy to find these diamonds in the rough. Just how rough the property is may require a professional analysis. Before jumping into a fixer-upper, make sure you know what the repairs will cost; consider the cost of both the materials and the labor, even if the labor is your own. You do not want to end up a slave to your own project and find out down the road when you sell the property that your efforts generated little or no profit for all of your hard work.

It is good to fully analyze the potential value of the fixed property. If you are working with a real estate agent on the purchase of the property, ask him or her for a market analysis of the property as if it were not a fixer-upper. Then, if you can estimate the cost of the repairs and the financing and selling costs you will incur, you can fully evaluate the asking price and potential value of the property.

§ 4.10 Foreclosure Properties

Foreclosure is the process a lender undertakes to enforce its rights in the collateral (i.e., the property) that was given to obtain a home purchase loan. A borrower signs a deed of trust when the loan is created, and the deed of trust gives the lender a security interest in the property being purchased with the loan funds. If the borrower fails to make payments, or otherwise fails to perform the obligations under the promissory note, the deed of trust spells out how the lender may proceed with foreclosure. The Colorado statutes also define the foreclosure process.[26]

The foreclosure process requires the Public Trustee of the county in which the property is located to advertise the property for sale and to conduct a public auction for the sale of the property. There are essentially three distinct time frames within which you might be able to buy property that is involved in a foreclosure, and the requirements and processes differ at each stage. Each of these is discussed below.

§ 4.10.1 Before the Foreclosure Sale

Before the Public Trustee has conducted the sale of the property, it is possible to purchase the property from the owner. It is not uncommon for a property that is headed for foreclosure to be placed on the market. A purchase of property pre-foreclosure is like any other real estate purchase. Any lender who has a lien on the property must be paid from the proceeds at sale for the lien to be released from the property.

If there are insufficient funds to pay off the lender, the lender may nonetheless agree to release its claim on the property. This situation is known as a "short sale."

§ 4.10.2 At the Foreclosure Sale

At the foreclosure sale, the highest bidder gets a Certificate of Purchase to show that he or she purchased the property at the sale. It is difficult to participate in the foreclosure sale, and the purchaser must immediately pay the purchase price to the Public Trustee (which is generally done by a certified

---

[26] *See* C.R.S. §§ 38-38-101 *et seq.*

check). It is very difficult to find a lender who is willing to make a loan to someone to purchase property at a foreclosure sale.

Moreover, buyers at foreclosure sales are bidding against the lender that started the foreclosure. The lender can bid in the total amount of its debt and interest and late fees, plus the costs incurred to conduct the foreclosure (such as attorney fees, title work, postage, etc.) The lender does not have to pay the Public Trustee, but merely has to tender a written bid. It is the exception, not the rule, that the lender's bid is significantly below the market value of the property.

§ 4.10.3 After the Foreclosure Deed is Issued

After the redemption period for the owner of the property expires, there may be rights to redeem by other lienholders. Once all of the rights to redeem expire, the holder of the Certificate of Purchase can request a deed from the Public Trustee. Once the public trustee's deed is issued, the grantee on the deed is the title owner to the property and may sell it just like any other owner may sell property.

§ 4.11 Checklist of Options

If you know what you're looking for, it's easier to find it. A checklist is provided here to help you identify what features you are looking for in a home. Keep in mind that you should only include criteria that are important to you. It is also helpful for you to define what you do *not* want.

HOW MUCH
   Price range: _____

WHERE
   Location of Property: _____

SIZE
   Minimum Square Footage: _____

   Minimum Number of Bedrooms: _____

   Minimum Number of Bathrooms: _____

TYPE
   ☐ Single-Family Detached Home

   ☐ Townhome/Duplex Attached Home

☐ Condominium

    ☐ High-rise

    ☐ Low-rise

If attached housing, list any specific features that you want in the complex, such as

☐ Clubhouse

☐ Pool

☐ Tennis Courts

☐ Fitness Center

☐ Other: _____

STYLE

☐ Ranch/One Story

☐ Bi-level

☐ Tri-level

☐ Two-Story

☐ Three-Story

☐ Other: _____

ARCHITECTURE

☐ Contemporary

☐ Traditional

☐ Tudor

☐ Victorian

☐ Other: _____

CONSTRUCTION

☐ Brick

☐ Frame

☐ Stucco

☐ Other: _____

PARKING

☐ Garage

☐ Attached

☐ Detached

☐ Carport

☐ Reserved

Minimum number of spaces required: _____

OTHER SPECIFICS

Home Features	Required	On Wish List	Not a Factor
Fireplace			
Yard			
Fence			
Patio, Deck, or Balcony			
Mountain View			
Air Conditioning			
Wood Floors			
Carpeting			
Eat-in Kitchen			
Separate Dining Room			
Basement			
Sunroom			
In-law Apartment			
Pool			
Master Bath			

§ 4.12 Quality Checklist—Questions to Ask Before You Decide to Buy

Here are some suggestions of things to help you make sure you are getting a home that will *not* be a money pit.

When you look at properties, you will look for the things that you need and want in a home. If you find one that you are interested in, you also have to look at what issues or problems the property may have. This is a checklist of items to look for and questions to ask to make sure you know what you are getting.[27] This is not intended to be a substitute for having a professional inspection of any home that you buy; this is just the first step.

You do not want to do this with every home you view, but most buyers will take a second look at properties they like before making an offer. At that time, you want to take a thorough look. You will want to do things like:

- Lift rugs to see condition of the floor underneath.

- Run the water to see the water pressure and how quickly it drains.

- Open and close doors and windows to see that they operate properly.

Structural problems can be very expensive. So you should watch for:

- Cracks in the foundation.

- Water damage or cracks on ceiling, floors, or walls.

- Standing water in basement or crawl space.

- Doors and windows that do not open and close properly.

- Added support posts in the basement.

- Old ceiling tiles or flooring that might contain asbestos.

Questions you should consider asking (some of this will be on the Seller's Disclosure Statement that you will receive):

- How old is the roof? Does it have a warranty?

- How old is the furnace, and when it was last serviced?

- How old is the hot water heater?

It is useful to bring a tape measure with you to make sure that any special furniture you have will fit into this prospective new home. Of course, you will be looking for all the things that matter most to you, as well.

- Is there adequate space for your needs?

- Is there adequate lighting?

- Are the appliances newer, or will you have to replace them soon?

- Is there adequate storage for your purposes?

- Is there air conditioning or another type of cooling system, such as an evaporative cooler, whole house fan, or ceiling fans?

---

[27] I created this checklist from one a client gave to me (which her mother had created after buying and selling many properties).

- Is the heat the type (e.g., gas, forced air, hot water) that you want?

- Are there washer/dryer hook-ups?

Discovering some issues or failings of the property should not be a deal killer. It is rare that a buyer will find the perfect home. But this information should help you decide what to offer if you do proceed to buy the property. You need to factor in the property condition and specific features to determine how much a property is worth to you.

CHAPTER 5
CONTRACTING

§ 5.1 Introduction

Once you find the property that you want to buy and call home, you must enter into a contract to purchase it. The purposes of the contract are: (2) to evidence that both parties are committed to the transaction; and (2) to define all of the terms, such as the agreed-upon price and the closing date. In Colorado, contracts concerning real property must be in writing to be enforceable.

It is important that a home buyer have some understanding about contracts generally, and specifically about the real estate purchase contract. Fortunately, in Colorado, the Real Estate Commission creates standard forms that may be used for the purchase and sale of residential real estate, and they are fairly straightforward. All of the real estate contract forms are available online at *www.dora.state.co.us/real-estate* in the "Consumer Corner."

This chapter includes a complete discussion of the Colorado Real Estate Commission's standard form entitled "Contract to Buy and Sell Real Estate (All Types of Properties)." (In this book, this form will be referred to simply as the "Contract"). For a copy of the Contract, see *Appendix 1, Form 6*. This Contract is revised periodically, and the most recent revision before the publication of this book was in September 2008.

§ 5.2 The Value of Using a Lawyer

The first line of text in Colorado's Contract to Buy and Sell Real Estate (Residential) says: "This form has important legal consequences and the parties should consult legal and tax or other counsel before signing."

Paragraph 20 of the Contract also includes a statement that your real estate broker has advised you that the document has important legal consequences and has recommended that you examine the title and consult with legal and tax or other counsel before signing the Contract.

As a rule, lawyers are not involved in most residential real estate transactions in Colorado. I always recommend seeking legal counsel if you have any doubt about what you are being asked to sign, if you have any questions about the title you will be receiving, and if you are not going to carefully read every document you receive. *If you are not going to read it all, hire someone who will.* When you think about how much money you are about to invest in the real estate, paying for a lawyer is a relatively small cost for the assurance that you understand the title that you will receive and that all of the documents and the transaction comply with current laws.

§ 5.3 Offer and Acceptance

Typically, the buyer prepares an offer by filling out the entire Contract with the terms and conditions that are acceptable to the buyer. If the buyer has a real estate agent, the buyer's agent will draft the offer for the buyer, explaining the terms and filling in the blanks with the price and terms that the buyer wants to offer. Real estate agents in Colorado have a limited license to practice law,[28] in that all licensed real estate brokers can complete the standard forms for their clients.

Once the offer is completed and signed by the buyer, the offer must be given to the seller (or to the seller's agent, who will then present it to the seller). If the seller signs and returns the offer to the buyer, then the offer becomes a contract that legally binds both parties.

If there is no timely response to an offer, then the seller has rejected the offer. In that case, the buyer may submit a new offer. Sometimes the seller will not sign the Contract, but will present a counteroffer containing those changes to the terms of the offer that will make the offer acceptable to the seller. Counteroffers are discussed in § 5.10 below.

§ 5.4 Types of Ownership

One of the first items that must be inserted into the Contract is the identity of the buyer. Paragraph 2.1 of the Contract requires you to list the name or names of the buyer or buyers. Because the seller will issue a deed to the buyer or buyers identified in the Contract, be careful to include the full legal name of each buyer.

Paragraph 2.1 also requires you to check a box specifying whether the buyer or buyers will take title to the real property as joint tenants, tenants in common, or "other." Information you will need to make this decision is included in the following sections.

§ 5.4.1 Joint Tenancy

"Joint tenancy" means that the persons purchasing the property will each have equal rights to the use, possession, and enjoyment of the property. Most significantly, joint tenancy includes the right of survivorship, which vests title in the surviving owners if another owner dies. This is because when the joint

---

[28] Conway-Bogue Realty Inv. Co. v. Denver Bar Ass'n, 135 Colo. 398, 312 P.2d 998 (1957).

tenants take title to the property, they each already—and jointly—own all of the property.

If you designate in the Contract that the buyers wish to take title in joint tenancy, then the deed that will transfer title from the seller will transfer title to all of the buyers and will state that title is being taken as joint tenants. The requirements for joint tenancy are that: (1) the interests of all joint tenants are created at the same time by the same document; (2) all of the joint tenants are equally vested in the same property; (3) all of the joint tenants have equal interests in the property; and (4) all of the joint tenants have an equal right of possession of the property. It is common for spouses or significant others who purchase properties together to take title as joint tenants.

§ 5.4.2 Tenants in Common

The other option for multiple buyers is to take title to the property as "tenants in common." (Note that if joint tenancy is not specified, a tenancy in common will be created.) As tenants in common, the owners may take unequal interests in the property, and each owner has an undivided interest in the property without a right of survivorship. Thus, each owner can transfer his or her respective interest in the property independently of the other owner or owners, and may even transfer the property by will or through a trust.

Upon the death of one of the tenants in common, that tenant's interest will pass to his or her heirs, not to the other tenant or tenants in common.

§ 5.4.3 Sole Ownership

If you will be the sole owner, you will want to check the box on the Contract form for "Other" and fill in the blank that follows with the term "solely" or "individually."

§ 5.5 Dates and Deadlines

On the front of the Contract form is a chart where all of the deadlines for the Contract are to be listed. These deadlines are binding, and once the Contract has been executed by both parties, any change to any of these dates has to be negotiated and agreed upon by both parties. Neither party has the power to unilaterally change a date on the Contract.

"Time is of the essence" is a legal phrase meaning essentially that the dates and deadlines are important. This phrase is contained in Paragraph 21 of the standard form Contract. If either party fails to perform any requirements of the Contract by the specified deadline for performance, there is a default on the Contract. It is very important, therefore, that you are aware of all the deadlines established in the Contract. A good real estate agent will keep you advised and will help you meet all of the required deadlines.

§ 5.6 Inclusions and Exclusions

While the entire Contract must be filled out completely and accurately, this is perhaps most obvious in Paragraphs 2.5 and 2.6, "Inclusions" and "Exclusions." A buyer should be careful to identify all of the fixtures ("fixtures" are items attached to the property, such as carpeting) and all of the personal property ("personal property" refers to items included in the sale that could easily be removed, such as a washer and dryer) that the buyer wishes to obtain as part of the transaction when the real property is purchased. Items other than the real property are usually conveyed by a bill of sale, which is essentially the buyer's evidence that ownership of those items was transferred.

The Contract already lists, as part of the standard contract language, many common fixtures and personal property, but you will want to be sure to add the fixtures (for example, air conditioning) and personal property (such as appliances) that are specific to the property being purchased.

§ 5.7 Price and Terms

§ 5.7.1 Earnest Money Deposit

When a buyer makes an offer, the buyer also makes a deposit of money, called "earnest money." The earnest money shows that the buyer is serious about purchasing the property, and it also constitutes "consideration," which is legally required to make a binding contract. Earnest money is most often in the form of a personal check, but it could also be in the form of a promissory note, cash, or a money order.

If the offer is not accepted, then the earnest money will be returned to the buyer. If the parties go under contract (that is, the seller accepts the offer), then the earnest money will be held by the seller (by the seller's agent, the title company, or another designee) pending closing. At closing, the earnest money deposit will be credited against the purchase price or costs due from the buyer.

If the contract is terminated (for example, the parties both agree not to proceed with the contract, or a required condition of the contract is not satisfied), then the earnest money is returned to the buyer.

If the buyer defaults on the Contract, then the buyer has failed to perform as required by the Contract, and the seller may be able to keep the earnest money. The deposit is intended as good-faith evidence that the buyer intends to perform the Contract.

§ 5.8 Contingencies

A "contingency" is a condition in a contract that must be satisfied or else the contract may be terminated. There are several contingencies in the Contract for the benefit of the buyer: inspection, appraisal, loan commitment, and title review.

§ 5.8.1 Inspection

The inspection provision is in Paragraph 10 of the Contract. First, it contains a date for the seller to provide a disclosure statement. The seller does not have to agree to furnish this document. Moreover, the statement, even when it is completely filled out by the seller, does not fully inform the buyer of the condition of the property. Many sellers do not have the knowledge to disclose the condition of the property.

For instance, the form asks the seller to state the age of the included items, if known. Some of the inclusions could have been in place when the seller purchased the property, and the seller may have no idea when they were purchased. For the Seller's Property Disclosure form, see *Appendix 1, Form 7: Seller's Property Disclosure (Residential)*. This form is merely a checklist of what is included, whether the inclusions are currently working, and the age of each item (if known).

Paragraph 10 is a strong provision for the buyer, however. It allows a buyer: (1) to inspect the property and the inclusions; (2) to research any proposed projects (such as road construction), whether on or off the property, that may effect the property; and (3) to terminate the Contract if the buyer finds anything that is unsatisfactory in the buyer's subjective opinion. When the Contract terminates, the buyer is entitled to recover the earnest money deposit (see Paragraph 25.2 of the Contract).

Alternatively, Paragraph 10 says that the buyer can ask the seller to remedy any unsatisfactory conditions. It is common for buyers to hire a professional inspector. Inspectors are listed as "Home and Building Inspectors" in the yellow pages. Unfortunately, Colorado does not license home inspectors, so you want to be careful when you hire one to make sure that he or she is competent and will do the inspection that you require.

A typical inspector will examine all of the mechanics of the property, plumbing, electricity, heat, hot water heater, appliances, the structural conditions, roof, and foundation. Among the items that you may want to include in your inspection are tests for radon, lead-based paint, and mold. The Environmental Protection Agency (EPA) publishes booklets on all three of these hazards. Copies of those booklets are available on the EPA's website at *http://www.epa.gov.*

If the buyer gives the seller a Notice to Correct, which advises the seller of the unsatisfactory conditions that the buyer wants the seller to fix, the seller may agree to make the necessary repairs. Generally, if the repairs relate to health or safety issues, the buyer should expect the seller to make the repairs.

Of course, the seller may refuse to make all or some of the repairs that the buyer requests, and the Contract will continue only if the parties can agree on what will be done. The Notice to Correct is contained within the Inspection Notice, a copy of which can be found at *Appendix 1, Form 9: Inspection Notice.*

The Contract contains a deadline for the buyer to submit any objections to the condition of the property and another deadline for the parties to resolve how those objections will be handled. If the parties cannot reach an agreement to resolve the Notice to Correct by the deadline, then the Contract terminates. If this happens, the buyer is entitled to recover the earnest money deposit (see Paragraph 25.2 of the Contract).

§ 5.8.2 Appraisal

The Contract may be contingent on the outcome of an appraisal. If a lender is involved, the lender will likely require an appraisal of the property. The appraisal is a formal, written opinion of the market value of the property. Appraisers are licensed in Colorado. Usually, the lender hires the appraiser and the buyer pays for the appraisal.[29] The provisions in the Contract (see Paragraph 6 of the Contract) create the right in the buyer to terminate the Contract if the appraised value of the property does not equal or exceed the purchase price.

There are different sections in the appraisal provision in the Contract to track necessary language for whatever type of loan the buyer will be getting.

§ 5.8.3 Loan Commitment

There is a provision in the Contract to protect the buyer in the event the buyer is unable to obtain financing. Paragraph 4.5 of the Contract requires the buyer to inform the seller if the buyer intends to get financing to complete the purchase. If the buyer cannot get a lender to make a loan to the buyer that is acceptable, then the buyer has the right to terminate the Contract (see Paragraph 5.2 of the Contract).

§ 5.8.4 Title Review

It is standard for the seller to provide the buyer with title insurance, which is an insurance policy that provides some protection to the effect that the buyer

---

[29] To help enhance the integrity of the home appraisal process in the mortgage finance industry, in March 2008, the Home Valuation Code of Conduct (HVCC) was enacted to establish standards for solicitation, selection, compensation, conflicts of interest and appraiser independence. It requires a lender to use an appraisal management company (AMC) to get an appraisal. The goal, in part, was to prohibit REALTORS® and mortgage brokers from selecting appraisers.

is actually receiving ownership to the property that the buyer expects. After the parties are under contract, the seller will provide the buyer with a title commitment, which is a statement by a title company confirming that it is prepared to issue title insurance (once all of the requirements listed in the title commitment are satisfied, the premium is paid, and provided that it handles the closing so that it can be sure that all documents are properly created, executed, and recorded). The title commitment generally shows all of the recorded documents affecting title to the property that the title insurance company will not insure against. These are called "exceptions to title." This is the best source of information that the buyer will receive to learn about any exceptions to full ownership of the property the buyer intends to purchase.

The title commitment will list several "standard" exceptions to title. For instance, in Colorado, since property taxes are paid in arrears (e.g., 2011 real property taxes will be paid in 2012), there is always a lien on real property in favor of the county for taxes not yet due and payable. This is a standard exception to title, and all buyers will take title subject to this exception.

There will likely be non-standard exceptions to title as well, which are exceptions specific to the subject property. Common exceptions that are not standard may exist for easements for the placement of lines for public services such as power, electric, cable, and telephone across the property. Over the years, utility companies have acquired rights to use certain portions of properties to bring utility services to the property and through the property to other locations. Another common, but not standard, exception would be one relating to a common-interest property. If common elements are owned and operated by a community of homes or condominiums, the rights and responsibilities of the co-owners are defined by a document that is of record and is an exception to each owner's title.

Exceptions to title must be reviewed carefully. They may or may not be objectionable, but the buyer must review them—and understand them—to determine whether to object to them or buy property that is subject to them.

A good example of a potential title issue to which a buyer might want to object is when a buyer is purchasing a townhome or condominium, and the Declaration of Covenants, Conditions, and Restrictions that governs the use of the property and the maintenance of the common properties states that there shall be no pets on the property. If the buyer has pets, the buyer may have to object to title. If the seller cannot change that provision (and depending on the size of the development, that can be very difficult, if not impossible), then the buyer will have the right to terminate the Contract.

Title problems are not that common, but they do exist. Here are some examples of possible title issues:

- The home to be purchased was owned by the seller's parents. The seller's father died several years ago, and the mother just recently passed away. A title search reveals that the property is titled in the mother's name, but there is no will on file to indicate how she disposed of it.

- You are buying a house to which an addition was made several years ago. The sellers of the home took out a home-improvement loan and did the work themselves. They have repaid the loan, or claim they have repaid the loan, but the lien was never removed from the title.

- The seller of the house added central air conditioning some time ago. The seller and the contractor had a dispute over the workmanship, and the seller withheld the final payment on the contract. The contractor filed a mechanic's lien on the property, which has never been removed.

If you do not review the title commitment or have an attorney review the title commitment for you and timely object to any matters that are not acceptable, you will have to accept title to the property even though there may be problems with it.

§ 5.8.5 Lead-Based Paint Disclosure

If the property was built in 1978 or earlier, the seller has the duty to provide the buyer with a lead-based paint disclosure as well as the Environmental Protection Agency's booklet on lead-based paint hazards. For a copy of the form, see *Appendix 1, Form 8: Lead-Based Paint Disclosure (Sales).* According to federal law, if the lead-based paint disclosure is not signed by both parties to the Contract at the time of or prior to signing the real estate Contract, then the real estate Contract is void. The EPA provides helpful information about lead-based paint and downloadable booklet titled "Protect Your Family From Lead in Your Home" on its website at *http://www.epa.gov/lead/pubs/leadinfo.htm#protect.*

§ 5.8.6 Mold Disclosure

It has become common for sellers in Colorado to provide a mold disclosure. The Environmental Protection Agency (EPA) provides helpful information about mold and a downloadable booklet titled "A Brief Guide to Mold, Moisture, and Your Home" on its website at *http://epa.gov/mold/.* As of the writing of this book, there is no official Colorado Real Estate Commission approved form for mold disclosure.

§ 5.8.7 Property Insurance

Paragraph 10.5 of the Contract makes the Contract contingent on the buyer's ability to secure home owner's insurance. The issue of insurability rarely comes into play in Colorado cities. This provision was added to the Contract at a time when potential buyers of homes in the foothills could not obtain insurance, or could only obtain insurance that was prohibitively expensive, due to fear of forest fires. Insurance can also cost more than one would expect if the property is in a flood zone. If the insurance cost makes the property less attractive to a buyer, the buyer may be able to terminate the Contract.

§ 5.8.8 Survey

Paragraph 9.2 of the Contract gives a buyer the right to terminate the Contract if the survey is unsatisfactory. Surveys are not usually obtained in residential real estate transactions because they are pretty expensive. More often there is an Improvement Location Certificate ("ILC"), which is a document that shows the physical location of the home on the land, and which is defined as a survey for purposes of the Contract. If the ILC shows anything unsatisfactory to the buyer, the buyer may object under Paragraph 9.2. There is a problem if, for instance, the subject property encroaches on other people's land (i.e. the house goes beyond the lines for the lot itself) or a neighbor's home or garage encroaches on the property being purchased.

§ 5.8.9 Methamphetamine Laboratory

There is a contingency in the Contract, in Paragraph 11, that allows a buyer to terminate a contract if there was previously a methamphetamine laboratory on the property. This paragraph requires the seller to acknowledge if the property was used as a methamphetamine laboratory if the property was not remediated in accordance with state standards. The buyer has the right to test the property to learn if it was used as a meth lab. If the buyer's test shows that the property was used as a meth lab and the property was not remediated according to the state standards, the buyer may terminate the contract. The buyer must provide the test results to the seller.

§ 5.9 Paragraph-by-Paragraph Summary of the Contract

Following is a summary of each paragraph of the Contract to Buy and Sell Real Estate (Residential).[30] This section does not discuss any assumable loans or seller carry back loans, and focuses on the standard contract provisions. Hopefully this will help you understand the Contract and how the blanks should be completed.

---

[30] There are actually five forms of contract to buy and sell property. In addition to the Contract to Buy and Sell Real Estate (Residential), there is a contract for: (1) Residential – Colorado Foreclosure Act, (2) Residential – Income, (3) Land, and (4) Commercial.

Paragraph 1 – Is one sentence stating that the buyer agrees to buy, and the seller agrees to sell, the property defined in the Contract.

Paragraph 2 – Identifies the parties to the Contract, states whether the Contract is or is not assignable, and specifies the legal description of the property and the street address. This paragraph lists all of the inclusions (i.e., everything that is being sold with the real property) and exclusions (i.e., items that are at the property but are not being sold pursuant to the contract). This paragraph separates out the fixtures (things attached to the property, such as lighting and heating) and personal property (things included in the sale that are not attached, such as storm windows and blinds). In its boilerplate language, the Contract includes in the sale most common fixtures and personal property, and the buyer will want to supplement those lists if additional items are to be included in the sale. Paragraph 2 also indicates that the personal property will be transferred by a bill of sale free and clear of any taxes, liens, and encumbrances, unless those are specifically identified in this section of the Contract. This paragraph also identifies any parking, storage facilities, or water rights that are being transferred with the property.

Paragraph 3 – States the dates and deadlines for the Contract. This paragraph also defines blank lines or blanks completed with "N/A" or "Deleted means "not applicable" Also, this paragraph defines "MEC" which is "mutual execution of the Contract" and is when both parties have signed the Contract.

Paragraph 4 – Lists the purchase price and terms, including the amount and the form of the earnest money and who will hold it; identifies the deadline for the delivery of the earnest money, and a deadline for return of the earnest money when a contract is terminated. This paragraph also states that the down payment and the closing costs to be paid by the buyer will be paid in cash, electronic transfer of funds, certified check, savings and loan teller's check, or cashier's check ("Good Funds"). Paragraph 4 includes the amount of any concessions from the seller, and the amount of the loans (if any) that the buyer may get, and the amount of the down payment that the buyer will make. If the contract involves the assumption of a mortgage or seller financing, those provisions are also included in Paragraph 4.

Paragraph 5 – Contains the text that creates the deadline for the buyer to submit a full loan application and the deadline for the lender to commit to make the loan. If the buyer notifies the seller in writing by the loan commitment deadline that the buyer is unable to obtain a satisfactory the loan commitment, the Contract will terminate. If no such notice is received by the seller, the buyer waives the loan contingency and the earnest money becomes nonrefundable except pursuant to other provisions of the Contract. If the contingency is waived but the buyer is not able to obtain the loan at the time of closing, the buyer may be in default under the Contract. If the Contract involves the assumption of a mortgage or seller financing, Paragraph 5 also includes the deadline for the buyer to provide credit information and a deadline for buyer to review existing loan documents.

Paragraph 6 – This is the appraisal condition in the Contract, and essentially provides that the buyer may terminate the Contract if the property does not appraise for at least as much as the purchase price. The buyer would have to give the seller written notice of termination and a copy of the appraisal or notice from the lender on or before the appraisal deadline. Either party can pay for the cost of the appraisal, but the buyer typically pays for it. If the lender imposes any requirements or repairs, this paragraph gives the seller the right to terminate the Contract on or before three days after receipt of the lenders requirements.

Paragraph 7 – This is the title section of the Contract. It says that the seller must provide a title commitment to the buyer before the record title deadline. This section of the Contract also specifies the extent of the title insurance, when the commitment must be received, and a deadline for the buyer to ask for copies of documents referenced in the commitment. Paragraph 7 also establishes the deadline for the seller to provide to the buyer the governing documents for the homeowners' association (if there is one), including:

- The association declaration, bylaws, operating agreements, rules and regulations, and party wall agreements.

- Minutes of the most recent annual owners' meeting and minutes of any directors' or managers' meetings during the six months preceding the date of the Contract.

- The most recent financial documents, including the annual balance sheet, annual income and expenditures statement, and annual budget.

This paragraph also establishes the deadline for the buyer to object to those documents.

Paragraph 8 – Establishes the deadline for the buyer to object to the title commitment; the deadline for the seller to provide leases and surveys and other information pertaining to the property that the seller has (and a deadline for the buyer to object to those off-record title matters); and a deadline for the exercise of a right of first refusal or approval of the Contract by a third party. This paragraph also contains the language required of all real estate contracts in Colorado: that the property may be in a special taxing district, and that the surface estate may be owned separately from the underlying mineral estate.

Paragraph 9 – This section of the Contract contains the survey deadline and specifies who will pay for the survey if one is obtained. This is a negotiable item; either the seller or the buyer can pay for the survey or the improvement location certificate.

Paragraph 10 – This is the inspection provision that was discussed earlier in this chapter (see Section 5.8.1). Paragraph 10 provides for a deadline for the Seller's Property Disclosure Statement, a deadline for the buyer's Inspection Objections, and a deadline for the parties to resolve such objections (called the "Inspection Resolution Deadline"). This paragraph requires the seller to disclose, in writing, any latent defects in the property. This paragraph also contains an insurance section, which provides that the buyer may terminate the Contract by written notice to the seller (before the property insurance objection deadline) stating that the buyer cannot get satisfactory property insurance. What is "satisfactory" insurance is up to the buyer's subjective discretion. Paragraph 10 also states that the buyer is responsible for any damage caused by the inspection. This paragraph requires the seller to provide documents to the buyer, Due Diligence Documents, as specified by the buyer. This paragraph also contains a disclosure by the buyer regarding whether the buyer has to sell another property to be able to close this transaction. Also, this paragraph requires the buyer to state whether he or she has received disclosure of the source of potable water from the seller, and in bold print this paragraph advises that you might want to contact the water provider to determine the sufficiency of the water supply. Paragraph 10 also requires the parties to acknowledge that Colorado law requires the seller to have operational carbon monoxide alarms installed within 15 feet of the entrance to each bedroom. If the property was built in 1978 or earlier, the seller has the duty to provide the buyer with a lead-based paint disclosure as well as the Environmental Protection Agency's booklet on lead-based paint hazards. For a copy of the disclosure form, see *Appendix 1, Form 8: Lead-Based Paint Disclosure (Sales)*. A copy of the EPA's booklet, which is titled "Protect Your Family From Lead in Your Home" can be found on the EPA's website at *http://www.epa.gov/lead/pubs/ leadinfo.htm#protect*. By federal law, if the lead-based paint disclosure is not signed by both parties to the Contract before or when they sign the real estate Contract, then the real estate Contract is void. Paragraph 10 also requires the seller to acknowledge if the property was used as a methamphetamine laboratory if the property was not remediated in accordance with state standards. The buyer has the right to test the property to learn whether it was used as a meth lab. If the buyer's test shows that the property was used as a meth lab and was not appropriately remediated, the buyer may terminate the contract by written notice to the seller.

Paragraph 11 – Defines the applicability of the Colorado Foreclosure Protection Act, which requires that: (1) the property is residential, (2) the property is the seller's principal residence, (3) the property will NOT be the buyer's personal residence, and (4) the property is in foreclosure or any loan secured by the property is at least 30 days delinquent or in default. If the transaction is a Short Sale transaction and there is a Short Sale Addendum as part of the contract, the Colorado Foreclosure Protection Act does not apply. The paragraph also advises the parties to consult with their own attorney.

Paragraph 12 – Requires the delivery of closing documents by a date specified. Requires the parties to cooperate with the closing company and to sign all customary or reasonably required documents at or before the closing. Establishes the date for closing and leaves a blank for the place and time. Generally, that blank is filled in with the words "mutual agreement."

Paragraph 13 – Describes the transfer of title. The blank to be filled in is the type of deed to be used. The best form of deed for a buyer to receive is a General Warranty Deed. Deeds are discussed further in Chapter 6.

Paragraph 14 – Allows the seller to pay off his or her loans with the proceeds of the sale to the buyer.

Paragraph 15 – Requires that all payments be Good Funds. It also references some fees and states who will pay them. The first fee is the fee to handle the closing. Currently, that fee is about $250, and it is customary for the seller and the buyer to split it. The other fees, relating to HOA statements and transfers, transfer taxes, private transfer fees (developer or community fees), and sales and use taxes, are negotiable items and either the seller or buyer may pay those.

Paragraph 16 – Describes certain items that will be prorated at the time of closing. Taxes are paid in arrears, so in the year following closing the buyer will have to pay the entire tax bill. At the time of closing, an amount is calculated and charged to the seller for taxes prorated to the day of closing. Other expenses, such as association dues, may have been paid in advance, and the proration will result in a charge to the buyer and a credit to the seller for those amounts. The title company will calculate the required prorations.

Paragraph 17 – States when possession will be transferred from the seller to the buyer.

Paragraph 18 – Explains how to compute days and deadlines.

Paragraph 19 – Addresses what happens if there is damage to the property prior to closing. It provides that the property and inclusions shall be delivered in the condition existing at the date of the Contract, ordinary wear and tear excepted. If there is damage of less than 10%, the seller is obligated to make the required repairs. If the seller fails to make the repairs, the buyer has the right to terminate the Contract or proceed with the Contract and get a credit for the damage. This paragraph also addresses what happens in the event of condemnation (if the seller receives notice prior to closing of a pending action that may result in a taking of all or part of the property or inclusions, and the buyer's right to terminate or the way the condemnation proceeds would be handled if the Contract goes forward. Paragraph 19 also provides that the buyer is entitled to do a walk-through prior to closing.

Paragraph 20 – Recommends that the parties seek legal and tax or other counsel before signing the Contract.

Paragraph 21 – Addresses a default and the remedies available. I always check the box that provides for liquidated damages if the buyer is in default. What that means is that if the buyer defaults on the contract, the seller gets to retain the earnest money and any other payments made by the buyer, and the parties are released from any other obligations under the Contract. The other option is specific performance, which means that the seller can bring a legal action to force the buyer to proceed with the Contract, or sue for damages, or both. There is no box to check to specify remedies in the event of the seller's default; if the seller defaults, the buyer gets to choose from all the remedies available.

Paragraph 22 – Provides that in the event of arbitration or litigation relating to the Contract, the prevailing party must be awarded attorney fees and expenses.

Paragraph 23 – States that the parties will seek to mediate rather than litigate their differences.

Paragraph 24 – Allows the entity that holds the earnest money to avoid getting involved if there is a dispute about who is entitled to the earnest money deposit, by allowing the holder of the deposit to do nothing until there is a proceeding. Alternatively, the holder of the earnest money can give notice that it will return the earnest money to the buyer if the holder does not receive notice of a lawsuit between the buyer and seller within 100 days. The holder may also interplead the funds (which essentially places the parties before the court to determine who is entitled to the deposit, but keeps the holder out of the fray). This paragraph only applies if the holder of the earnest money is one of the brokerage firms involved in the transaction.

Paragraph 25 – States that if the Contract is terminated, the earnest money is returned to the buyer. Termination is different than a default. Termination occurs when one of the contingencies fails and the buyer timely notifies the seller in writing that the buyer is terminating the Contract.

Paragraph 26 – Merely provides that all agreements are contained in the Contract, its exhibits and addenda, and that anything discussed but not included in the written Contract is not part of the agreement. This paragraph also provides that any changes made to the Contract also have to be in writing and signed by the parties.

Paragraph 27 – Repeats that all notices or documents required under the Contract must be in writing. Also, notice to the seller's broker or the buyer's broker is notice to the party. The parties may elect to have delivery by facsimile, e-mail or internet as acceptable forms of notice. Also, this paragraph provides that Colorado law will govern the Contract.

Paragraph 28 – This paragraph spells out the deadline for the seller to accept the offer. Acceptance must be in writing and received by the buyer by the acceptance deadline date and time.

Paragraph 29 – This section is available for the insertion of any additional provisions.

Paragraph 30 – Lists any attachments that are part of the Contract and any disclosure forms that are attached to, but are not part of, the Contract.

§ 5.10 Counteroffer or Counterproposal

If the seller wants to accept the offer, but does not agree with certain provisions in the offer, then the seller will prepare a counteroffer (also called a counterproposal) and submit it to the buyer. The counteroffer accepts all provisions of the offer except those stated in the counteroffer. In other words, the seller does not sign the offer, but instead signs the counteroffer, which incorporates the offer with the changes spelled out in the counteroffer.

The counteroffer is then presented to the buyer to accept or reject. If the buyer accepts the changed terms, the buyer signs the counteroffer, and the counteroffer together with the offer constitute the Contract. For a form of a counteroffer, see *Appendix 1, Form 10: Counterproposal.*

§ 5.11 Amendments

After the contract has been signed by both parties, any changes to the contract must be in writing and signed by both parties to be enforceable. For a form of an amendment, see *Appendix 1, Form 11: Agreement to Amend/Extend Contract.*

§ 5.12 Conclusion

If you have the property under contract and all of the contingencies are satisfied, you are on your way home . . . literally! The last hurdle is the closing, and that is discussed in the Chapter 6.

CHAPTER 6
CLOSING

§ 6.1 Introduction

The contract establishes the date of closing, which is the date when all of the required legal documents are signed, the purchase price is paid, and the title is transferred from the seller to the buyer. In other states, the closing date is sometimes referred to as "settlement." This chapter discusses the buyer's remaining responsibilities before and at closing.

§ 6.2 Pre-Closing Matters

§ 6.2.1 Utility Service

Once all of the contingencies in the Contract have been satisfied so that you know you are going to move, it may be wise to start scheduling the transfer of utilities from the seller to you, and make those changes effective on the date you will take possession of the property.

An unpaid water and sewer bill can become a lien on the property, so the transfer of the water and sewer service and the payment of the seller's water and sewer bill is an issue handled by the title company. Since the title company is going to issue a title insurance policy that will say there is no lien superior to the lien of your lender (in the normal scenario), the title company has to know that any bill for water regarding service that predates the closing will be satisfied. So, the title company generally withholds an amount from the seller at closing that will easily satisfy the outstanding water and sewer bill, and the title company will pay the bill and refund the balance to the seller.

To transfer services of other utilities, you will need to contact the utility companies directly, such as: Xcel Energy (gas and electric); CenturyLink (telephone); Comcast, Dish Network, or Direct TV (cable or satellite television); and the *Denver Post* (newspaper delivery).

Making the call to transfer telephone service if you want a land line should be made as soon as possible, since that tends to take some time to accomplish. Some buyers simply rely on their mobile phone for a period of time so that they do not have to worry about a lack of phone service during a move. Gas and electric can be moved at any time, as the company merely creates a cut-off date and issues a bill to the seller and starts a new bill for you.

Cable cannot be installed if the seller currently has an active cable account, so sometimes the buyer has to wait until the seller cancels his or her account before the buyer can activate the new account.

You may need to find out from the seller what companies provide gas, electric, cable, and trash service to the property so you can call and coordinate the change of those services. In some areas in Colorado, you will have a choice of service providers. Checking with the seller will at least advise you of one (and maybe the only) service provider. In some areas, such as Denver, trash removal is provided by the city.

If you are buying a condominium, the homeowners' association might pay for and obtain some of the services. If that is the case, you do not need to do anything to change the service for your ownership. The title company will gather information for the homeowners' association about the transfer of ownership and will submit it to the HOA.

§ 6.2.2 Change of Address

You will want to advise the post office, as well as your family, friends, and others, of your change of address. The U.S. Postal Service has a free packet available that includes postcards you can use to notify people of your new address. You can also change your address online on the U.S. Postal Service's website at *www.usps.com*. Before the closing, it is wise to gather the addresses of those whom you want to contact so that you can send out the "Just Moved" cards promptly after closing. Don't forget to include credit card companies, your bank, and magazine subscription providers among those to be notified.

§ 6.3 Closing Documents

Quite a few documents have to be signed at closing. Some of the documents must be notarized, meaning that someone has to attest to the fact that it was you who signed them. The person assigned to handle the closing for the title company (the "Closer") will be a notary. You will need to bring evidence that you are who you claim to be. It would be wise to check with the title company and make sure you bring the identification that they require, which may be your passport or driver's license, for instance.

There are two different parts to the closing: the real estate closing and the loan closing. You will pay the Closer a separate fee for each of these closings; generally, the seller and the buyer split the cost of the real estate closing fee and the buyer pays the entire loan closing fee. Each closing fee is about $250. This fee is just for the Closer to handle all the paperwork; it is not the only closing cost that you will pay.

§ 6.3.1 Deeds

A "deed" is a document that is created to transfer an interest in property from the seller (the grantor under the deed) to the buyer (the grantee under the deed). Several forms of deeds are used in Colorado, and they are all discussed in detail below. Appendix 1 contains copies of the different kinds of deeds, including general warranty deed, special warranty deed, personal representative's deed, a bargain and sale deed, and a quitclaim deed. See *Appendix I, Form 12A - Form 12I.*

While it is in the buyer's interest to receive the title (i.e., the ownership) to the property with warranties, sometimes warranties cannot be given. If the property owner does not know the history of the property personally, he or she should not give any warranty or promise with respect to the condition of title. However, in Colorado, property is generally sold with title insurance, which gives the buyer significant protection against adverse claim to the title being obtained.

From the buyer's standpoint, the best form of deed to receive is a General Warranty Deed. In this form of deed, the seller binds himself or herself and his or her heirs and assigns to "warrant and forever defend" to the buyer and his or her heirs and assigns title to the property being conveyed, against the lawful claims of all persons whatsoever. This is a very broad warranty of the status of the title on the property. The warranty deed does not warrant the condition of the house or land in any respect, just ownership of the property.

A Special Warranty Deed, Personal Representative's Deed, Bargain and Sale Deed, and Quitclaim Deed are all legal documents that will transfer title from the seller to the buyer, but these deeds contain limited warranties. With a Special Warranty Deed, the seller agrees to warrant and forever defend the title, but only against all persons claiming "by, through, or under" the seller or his or her heirs. What that means is that the seller is giving assurance to the buyer that no third party is going to claim that they have title to the property or a lien on the property that they obtained from the seller. It does not require the seller to protect the buyer from claims of third parties who claim some right, title, or interest in the property that predates the title held by the seller, but it does "pass through" to the buyer any warranties of title received by the seller when the seller purchased the property. The Special Warranty Deed is fully insurable by title insurance companies, is the most common form of deed used in commercial transactions, and is often used by corporations or other entities in conveying title in residential transactions. It is also used if an individual seller acquired the property in a way that did not include any warranties of title, such as when the seller inherited the property or acquired the property through a foreclosure sale, or if the seller did not obtain title insurance when it purchased the property. The language of this deed basically states that this seller did not convey the property or create any other interests in the property while the seller owned the property.

A Personal Representative's Deed is used to convey title to property that was owned by someone who died; the individual appointed as the personal representative for the deceased owner is conveying the title. If the deed is in fact executed by the personal representative, and the conveyance was authorized by the will or by the court, this deed will convey the deceased's interest in the property as described in the Personal Representative's Deed. Title insurance companies will insure transfers of title by Personal Representative's Deeds. There is no agreement by the personal representative to warrant and defend title, but a buyer has no choice but to accept a Personal Representative's Deed if the buyer wants to purchase that property.

Neither the Bargain and Sale Deed nor the Quitclaim Deed contains any warranty of title. Each is a legal document that effectively conveys whatever title the grantor has; but neither provides any assurance that the grantor has any title, and therefore, they could convey no title. The difference between a Quitclaim Deed and a Bargain and Sale Deed is only that in the event the grantor using a Bargain and Sale Deed obtains any title or interest in the property *after* deeding the property to the buyer, that after-acquired interest will "pass through" to the new buyer by reason of the Bargain and Sale Deed. This will not happen with a Quitclaim Deed. Many title insurance companies will not insure transfers of properties by Quitclaim or Bargain and Sale Deed. Quitclaim Deeds and Bargain and Sale Deeds are used most often when there is some question about the ownership of property. These deeds convey the interest of the seller, if there is any, on the date the deed is executed, but they do not contain any warranty or representation by the seller of ownership to the property described. As a general rule, you should get a General Warranty Deed, not a Quitclaim Deed or a Bargain and Sale Deed, when you purchase real estate.

An example of when a Quitclaim Deed is used and perfectly acceptable may be in a divorce situation where one party quitclaim deeds the property to the other (the party receiving the Quitclaim Deed already has an ownership interest in the property, and has title warranties through his or her existing interest in the property).

§ 6.3.2 Promissory Notes and Deeds of Trust

If the buyer finances any portion of the purchase price, more documents will be required for the transaction. Whenever a borrower seeks a loan, it is customary for the lender to give the borrower the funds in exchange for a promissory note (essentially an IOU from the borrower). The promissory note states the amount of the loan, the interest rate, and the terms for repayment.

When a borrower seeks funds to purchase a home, in addition to giving the lender a promissory note acknowledging the debt owed by the borrower and the agreed-upon terms for its repayment, the borrower also gives the lender an interest in the property being purchased. This is generally referred to as a mortgage, and the nature and extent of the lender's rights obtained from a mortgage can vary.

In Colorado, the form of mortgage most commonly used is a Public Trustee deed of trust. A deed of trust does not transfer the legal ownership of the property (the legal title remains with the buyer/borrower), but it creates a lien or claim against the property for the benefit of the lender.[31] After the deed of trust has been recorded with the clerk and recorder of the county in which the property is located, it gives notice to the world that the lender has a lien on the property.

In every county in Colorado, there is a Public Trustee. The Public Trustee is usually appointed by the governor; in smaller counties, the Country Treasurer may act as the Public Trustee. A deed of trust transfers to the Public Trustee in the county where the property is located certain powers and rights as a means of protecting the lender's ability to collect payment on the note (the debt). The deed of trust spells out that the Public Trustee holds the property *in trust* for the benefit of the lender, and grants the Public Trustee the power to sell the property if the borrower fails to repay the debt for which the deed of trust was given.

The process to enforce the rights granted in a deed of trust is called a foreclosure. In essence, the deed of trust allows a lender to commence a foreclosure when a borrower defaults under the terms of the promissory note or the deed of trust, e.g., if the borrower fails to make payments on the note when due, fails to pay property taxes, or fails to perform any obligation of the borrower under the terms of the promissory note or the deed of trust. The procedure for foreclosure is defined by the deed of trust as well as by statute.[32]

If you are getting your loan from an institution (a bank, savings and loan, or credit union), then the promissory note and deed of trust used will be standard forms. This is because many lenders want to be able to sell notes and deeds of trust. The secondary market for notes and deeds of trust only accepts loans that are "conforming loans" (i.e., are made using standard forms and are made to borrowers who meet standard guidelines). As a result, an individual borrower has little or no ability to negotiate the language on the promissory note and deed of trust forms. For copies of the forms, see *Appendix 1, Form 13: Promissory Note* and *Form 14: Deed of Trust (Due on Transfer - Strict)*.

---

[31] *See* C.R.S. §§ 38-35-117 *et seq.*

[32] *See* C.R.S. §§ 38-38-100.3 *et seq.*

Below is a diagram that summarizes the relationship of the parties and the documents involved in the transaction.

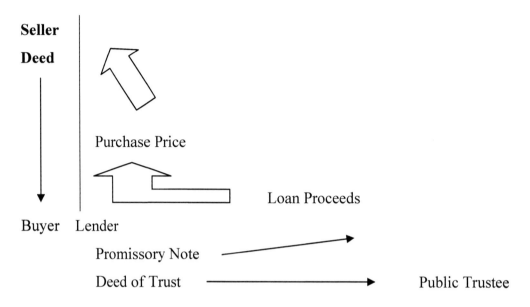

The seller gives the buyer a deed, and the buyer pays the purchase price. The buyer gets a loan from the lender for all or part of the purchase price, and the buyer gives the lender a promissory note and executes a deed of trust to the Public Trustee for the benefit of the lender.

§ 6.3.3 Bill of Sale

The "Bill of Sale" is the document that transfers all the personal property to the buyer. It is effectively the buyer's evidence that the buyer owns those items. For a copy of the form, see *Appendix 1, Form 15: Bill of Sale*.

§ 6.3.4 Other Documents

Real Property Transfer Declaration Form

At the closing, you will be asked to complete a Real Property Transfer Declaration Form, which is a document that is required by the county and describes the real estate transaction. For a copy of the form, see *Appendix 1, Form 16: Real Property Transfer Declaration*. Because this form seeks objective information about the transaction, the title company will complete most of it. However, a few questions will be left blank for you to complete.

One section of the Real Property Transfer Declaration Form asks if any personal property was transferred, and if so, the approximate value of the personal property and a description of it. "Personal property" includes all of the items of sale that are not the land and the structure itself (both of which are referred to as "real property"). So, for instance, any appliances that are sold with the home would be personal property.

Another section of the Real Property Transfer Declaration Form asks about the condition of the property. You will have to indicate if it is excellent, good, average, fair, or poor.

§ 6.4 What to Bring to Closing

You will need to bring two items with you to closing: (1) proof of your identity (since you will be signing documents that have to be recorded and will have to be notarized), and (2) a cashier's check for your closing costs and fees. I recommend that you have the cashier's check made out to you, and you can endorse it over to the title company at closing.

CHAPTER 7
POST-CLOSING MATTERS

§ 7.1 Introduction

After all the papers are signed and the closing is concluded, a few post-closing items regarding your ownership will still require your attention. At the conclusion of the closing, the title company will give you copies of all of the documents that you signed, as well as a copy of the deed. When you leave the closing table, the title company will possess funds that have to be disbursed, documents that have to be recorded, and documents that have to be delivered to different people. Most of the responsibility is with the title company, but you should be aware of what is supposed to happen so that you can follow up if someone else drops the ball. In addition to making sure that the title company properly performs its duties, a few things will be your responsibility.

§ 7.2 Moving

When the time is right, you can change your address with the post office. You can do this online at *www.usps.com*. That website provides some useful information, including a moving guide with hints on packing and moving, as well as the change of address form.

§ 7.3 Recording Documents

The title company has the responsibility to record all of the documents that have to be recorded, such as:

- The release of the seller's deed of trust(s), if any.

- Release of any other liens that were satisfied as part of the transaction.

- The deed that provides public notice that title to the property has been transferred to you.

- The deed of trust that gives your lender a lien on the property.

These documents have to be recorded with the clerk and recorder in the county where the property is located, and the title company should have collected the recording fees at the closing. In most counties in Colorado, it will be some time after the clerk and recorder receives the documents for recording that the documents are actually recorded and sent to their rightful owner.

§ 7.4 Recorded Deed

The original, signed deed should be returned to you after it is recorded with the county. When you receive it, you should check that it was recorded in the correct county. If the deed has been properly recorded, you should file the original deed with your other important papers.

If, within a few weeks, you do not receive the deed reflecting that it was recorded in the correct county, you should contact the title company. It is the title company's responsibility to properly record the documents. The title insurance policy that you will receive from the title company will not be issued until the deed is properly recorded.

§ 7.5 Real Property Transfer Declaration Form

At the closing, you should have been asked to complete a Real Property Transfer Declaration Form, which is a document that is required by the county and describes the real estate transaction. For a copy of the form, see *Appendix 1, Form 16: Real Property Transfer Declaration.*

After the closing, a copy of this same form may be sent to you at the property from the county. If you receive this form, you must complete it and return it within 30 days. Failure to complete this form will result in a fine, so you are wise to complete it upon receipt. Fill it in just as you did at the closing. Your closing file should contain a copy of the one that you completed at closing, so that will be an easy task.

§ 7.6 Title Insurance Policy

Once the deed and the deed of trust have been recorded, the title company will be able to issue the title insurance policy. One copy is sent to you and one to your lender. If you do not receive a copy of your title insurance policy within 60 days of the closing, you should call the title company and check on it.

A broker associate of mine had not received a copy of the recorded deed and did not receive the title insurance policy on the home that she bought, and after a few months, she was concerned. She called the title company and was assured that it takes time, and she was asked to be patient. After another month, she called again and was a bit more insistent. The title company pulled the file and found that the original deed was still sitting in the file and had not been sent to the clerk and recorder for recording. Fortunately, when the title company performs the closing, it is responsible for the period of time between the last review of the recorded documents and the time the deed is recorded. In this case, there had been no intervening matters that affected the title, but even with the protection of title insurance, the failure to record a deed or the delay in recording a deed can cause all sorts of title problems—which can be a real headache for you and time consuming to resolve.

§ 7.7 Damage to the Property Before Transfer of Possession

It is common for the transfer of possession of the property to be delayed for some time after closing—often for two or three days. This allows the seller to obtain the proceeds from the sale of the property, use those proceeds for the purchase of another property, and then move. Problems can occur if there is damage to the property before delivery of possession to the buyer.

A seller of mine, as a favor to the buyers, had the entire home professionally cleaned (including the carpets) after she moved out and before she turned over possession. The standard Colorado Real Estate Commission Contract requires that the property be delivered in "the condition existing as of the date of this Contract, ordinary wear and tear excepted." (See *Appendix 1, Form 6: Contract to Buy and Sell Real Estate (Residential)* at paragraph 19). There is no affirmative duty for the seller to have the carpets and the home professionally cleaned, unless that is added as an additional provision in the Contract. When the buyers took possession the following day, they discovered some water damage in the laundry room. The seller immediately called a plumber upon learning of the problem, and had the pipes repaired. The only people who were in the property were the home cleaner and the carpet cleaners, and it was unknown who or what caused the plumbing to break and result in water damage. The seller paid the plumbing bill, but the buyers sued the seller for the cost of repairs to the property resulting from the water damage. The seller made a settlement offer in an amount that seller believed was reasonable to make the repairs, but the buyers rejected the offer and proceeded with the lawsuit. The court sided with the buyers, and the seller had to pay additional amounts after trial.

The worst story I ever heard involved the sale of a new townhome in Denver. After closing, but before the transfer of possession to the buyers, the entire property burned down. Apparently, there were workers at the property doing some last minute touch-up work, and a cigarette butt was tossed accidentally into a highly flammable product.

You have the right to walk through the property before the closing to make sure that the condition has not changed since you agreed to buy the property. The Contract provides that the seller must deliver the property in the same condition as it was at the time the contract was signed, ordinary wear and tear excepted. If there has been some damage to the property, you may have a claim against the seller for the cost of repairs.

§ 7.8 Monthly Payments

Your first mortgage payment will be due on the date stated in your loan papers. You should receive copies of all the papers you sign at the closing. You may or may not receive a statement or coupon book from your lender, but your payment is still due. Often a temporary coupon book is provided at the closing, just in case.

If you buy property that is governed by a homeowners' association, you will likely owe homeowners' dues. Again, these payments are due even if you do not receive a statement or coupon book.

§ 7.9 Transfer of Servicing of the Loan

It is common for lenders to sell loans, and yours may be sold even before you close. If you are informed that your loan has been sold, you will be required to make your payments to a new location. Do not send payments to a new location unless your initial lender advises you to do so.

There have been some fraudulent schemes where borrowers receive an official-looking letter advising them to send their loan payments to a new address. Keep in mind that the terms of your loan (the date it was created, the amount, the interest rate, etc.) are all included in the deed of trust, and the deed of trust is recorded. That means that anyone can view that information at the clerk and recorder's office, and it is not difficult to make a letter incorporating that information look official. If you have any doubt about the transfer of your loan, contact your original lender directly to confirm the fact.

§ 7.10 Home Maintenance

Now that you have taken care of the business of buying your home, you still have to take care of the business of owning a home. Hopefully, you were able to learn much about your home during your home inspection. If not, there are many good manuals available on home maintenance.[33]

§ 7.11 Conclusion

While there are many advantages to home ownership, like emotional and financial security, with home ownership there are also new responsibilities and liabilities. This book was intended to answer your questions and provide a road map through all of the steps of home ownership.

---

[33] For good information on home maintenance, see ROB LUTES & ANGELIKA GOLLNOW, HOME REPAIR HANDBOOK (Sunset Publishing 1999); BENJAMIN W. ALLEN, HOME IMPROVEMENT 1-2-3: EXPERT ADVICE FROM THE HOME DEPOT (Meredith Publishing 1995).

The first step is finding out how much of a home you can afford. You will want to get pre-qualified for a mortgage early in the home buying process. Finding the right lender and understanding the various loan options available today should be easier now that you have read this book.

Take advantage of using a real estate broker to assist you in finding the right property and negotiating the best deal. Use the guidance provided in this book for selecting a real estate broker and negotiating the appropriate agency relationship with your broker.

Finding the right home can be a challenge, but if you use the checklists and information in this book, it will help you focus your home search. Once you find the right home, you need to get it under contract. You can review the terms of the contract and the form contract itself that are provided in this book.

I hope this book has given you the information and knowledge you need to buy a place to call home. Now take the time to make that place a home by furnishing it, by filling it with visits from family and friends, and by adding decorative touches that give it a personality all its own.

Appendix 1: Forms

1. Good Faith Estimate

GOOD FAITH ESTIMATE

Applicant(s): _____   _____
Property Address: _____
Prepared by: _____

The information provided below reflects estimates of the charges you are likely to incur at the settlement of your loan. The fees listed are estimates – actual charges may be more or less. Your transaction may not involve a fee for every item listed. The numbers listed beside the estimates generally correspond to the numbered lines contained in the HUD-1 settlement statement which you will be receiving at closing. The HUD-1 settlement statement will show you the actual cost for items paid at closing.

Total Loan Amount $_____   Interest Rate _____%   Term/Due in _____months

800	Items payable in connection with loan:	
801	Loan Origination Fee	$_____
802	Discount Points	$_____
803	Appraisal Fee	$_____
804	Credit Report	$_____
808	Mortgage Broker Fee	$_____
809	Tax Service Fee	$_____
810	Processing Fee	$_____
811	Underwriting Fee	$_____
812	Wire Transfer Fee	$_____
Compensation Paid to Broker (Not paid out of Loan Proceeds)		$_____
1100	Title Charges	$_____
1101	Closing Fee	$_____
1105	Document Prep Fee	$_____
1106	Notary Fees	$_____
1107	Attorney Fees	$_____
1108	Title Insurance	$_____
1200	Government Recording & Transfer Charges	
1201	Recording Fees	$_____
1202	City/County Tax/Stamps	$_____
1203	State Tax/Stamps	$_____

Estimated Closing Costs $_____

900	Items Required by Lender to be Paid in Advance		
901	Interest for ___ days @ ____/day		$_____
902	Mortgage Insurance Premium		$_____
903	Hazard Insurance Premium		$_____
1000	Reserves Deposited with Lender		
1001	Hazard Insurance Premium Reserves	____months@____/month	$_____
1002	Mortgage Insurance Premium Reserves	____months@____/month	$_____
1004	Taxes & Assessment Reserves	____months@____/month	$_____
1005	Flood Insurance Reserves	____months@____/month	$_____

Estimated Prepaids/Reserves $_____

Total Estimated Funds Needed to Close: _____   Total Estimated Monthly Payment:

Down Payment	_____	Principal & Interest	_____
Estimated Closing Cost	_____	Hazard Insurance	_____
Estimated Prepaids	_____	Real Estate Taxes	_____
Less Seller Paid Costs	_____	Mortgage Insurance	_____
Total	_____	H.O. A. Dues	_____
		Total	_____

This Good Faith Estimate is being provided by _____, a Mortgage Broker, and no lender has been obtained. These estimates are provided pursuant to the Real Estate Procedures Act of 1974, as amended (RESPA). Additional information can be found in the HUD Special Information Booklet, which is to be provided to you by your mortgage broker or lender, if your application is to purchase residential real property and the lender will take a first lien on the property. The undersigned acknowledges receipt of the booklet "Settlement Costs" and if applicable the Consumer Handbook on ARM Mortgages.

_____   _____
Applicant   Date   Applicant   Date

NOTES ON USE:

For a discussion of good faith estimates and the use of this form, see § 2.2.5.

2. Uniform Residential Loan Application

Uniform Residential Loan Application

This application is designed to be completed by the applicant(s) with the Lender's assistance. Applicants should complete this form as "Borrower" or "Co-Borrower", as applicable. Co-Borrower information must also be provided (and the appropriate box checked) when [ ] the income or assets of a person other than the "Borrower" (including the Borrower's spouse) will be used as a basis for loan qualification or [ ] the income or assets of the Borrower's spouse will not be used as a basis for loan qualification, but his or her liabilities must be considered because the Borrower resides in a community property state, the security property is located in a community property state, or the Borrower is relying on other property located in a community property state as a basis for repayment of the loan.

I. TYPE OF MORTGAGE AND TERMS OF LOAN

Mortgage Applied for:	[ ] VA [ ] Conventional [ ] Other:	[ ] FHA [ ] USDA/Rural Housing Service	Agency Case Number	Lender Case Number

Amount	Interest Rate	No. of Months	Amortization Type:	[ ] Fixed Rate [ ] Other (explain):
$	%			[ ] GPM [ ] ARM (type):

II. PROPERTY INFORMATION AND PURPOSE OF LOAN

Subject Property Address (street, city, state & ZIP)	No. of Units

Legal Description of Subject Property (attach description if necessary)	Year Built

Purpose of Loan: [ ] Purchase [ ] Construction [ ] Other (explain): [ ] Refinance [ ] Construction-Permanent	Property will be: [ ] Primary Residence [ ] Secondary Residence [ ] Investment

Complete this line if construction or construction-permanent loan.

Year Lot Acquired	Original Cost	Amount Existing Liens	(a) Present Value of Lot	(b) Cost of Improvements	Total (a + b)
	$	$	$	$	$

Complete this line if this is a refinance loan.

Year Acquired	Original Cost	Amount Existing Liens	Purpose of Refinance	Describe Improvements [ ] made [ ] to be made
	$	$		Cost: $

Title will be held in what Name(s)	Manner in which Title will be held	Estate will be held in: [ ] Fee Simple
Source of Down Payment, Settlement Charges and/or Subordinate Financing (explain)		[ ] Leasehold (show expiration date)

III. BORROWER INFORMATION

Borrower	Co-Borrower
Borrower's Name (include Jr. or Sr. if applicable)	Co-Borrower's Name (include Jr. or Sr. if applicable)

Social Security Number	Home Phone (incl. area code)	DOB (MM/DD/YYYY)	Yrs. School	Social Security Number	Home Phone (incl. area code)	DOB (MM/DD/YYYY)	Yrs. School

[ ] Married [ ] Separated	[ ] Unmarried (include single, divorced, widowed)	Dependents (not listed by Co-Borrower) no. ages	[ ] Married [ ] Separated	[ ] Unmarried (include single, divorced, widowed)	Dependents (not listed by Borrower) no. ages

Present Address (street, city, state, ZIP) [ ] Own [ ] Rent No. Yrs:	Present Address (street, city, state, ZIP) [ ] Own [ ] Rent No. Yrs:

Mailing Address, if different from Present Address	Mailing Address, if different from Present Address

If residing at present address for less than two years, complete the following:

Former Address (street, city, state, ZIP) [ ] Own [ ] Rent No. Yrs:	Former Address (street, city, state, ZIP) [ ] Own [ ] Rent No. Yrs:

IV. EMPLOYMENT INFORMATION

Borrower	Co-Borrower
Name & Address of Employer [ ] Self Employed	Yrs. in this job	Name & Address of Employer [ ] Self Employed	Yrs. in this job
	Yrs. employed in this line of work/profession		Yrs. employed in this line of work/profession

Position/Title/Type of Business	Business Phone (incl. area code)	Position/Title/Type of Business	Business Phone (incl. area code)

If employed in current position for less than two years or if currently employed in more than one position, complete the following:

Name & Address of Employer [ ] Self Employed	Dates (from - to)	Name & Address of Employer [ ] Self Employed	Dates (from - to)
	Monthly Income $		Monthly Income $

Position/Title/Type of Business	Business Phone (incl. area code)	Position/Title/Type of Business	Business Phone (incl. area code)

Name & Address of Employer [ ] Self Employed	Dates (from - to)	Name & Address of Employer [ ] Self Employed	Dates (from - to)
	Monthly Income $		Monthly Income $

Position/Title/Type of Business	Business Phone (incl. area code)	Position/Title/Type of Business	Business Phone (incl. area code)

Freddie Mac Form 65 01/04 1003PG1 08/03	Page 1 of 4 Printed by The Loan Handler from Contour Software, Inc. (408) 370-1700 www.contoursoft.com	Fannie Mae Form 1003 01/04

NOTES ON USE:

For a discussion on completing the loan application, see § 2.4.1.

V. MONTHLY INCOME AND COMBINED HOUSING EXPENSE INFORMATION

Gross Monthly Income	Borrower	Co-Borrower	Total	Combined Monthly Housing Expense	Present	Proposed
Base Empl. Income *	$	$	$	Rent	$	
Overtime				First Mortgage (P&I)		$
Bonuses				Other Financing (P&I)		
Commissions				Hazard Insurance		
Dividends/Interest				Real Estate Taxes		
Net Rental Income				Mortgage Insurance		
Other (before completing see the notice in "describe other income," below)				Homeowner Assn. Dues		
				Other:		
Total	$	$	$	Total	$	$

* Self Employed Borrower(s) may be required to provide additional documentation such as tax returns and financial statements.

B/C	Describe Other Income Notice: Alimony, child support, or separate maintenance income need not be revealed if the Borrower (B) or Co-Borrower (C) does not choose to have it considered for repaying this loan.	Monthly Amount
		$

VI. ASSETS AND LIABILITIES

This Statement and any applicable supporting schedules may be completed jointly by both married and unmarried Co-Borrowers if their assets and liabilities are sufficiently joined so that the Statement can be meaningfully and fairly presented on a combined basis; otherwise, separate Statements and Schedules are required. If the Co-Borrower section was completed about a spouse, this Statement and supporting schedules must be completed about that spouse also.   Completed ☐ Jointly ☐ Not Jointly

ASSETS Description	Cash or Market Value	Liabilities and Pledged Assets. List the creditor's name, address and account number for all outstanding debts, including automobile loans, revolving charge accounts, real estate loans, alimony, child support, stock pledges, etc. Use continuation sheet, if necessary. Indicate by (*) those liabilities which will be satisfied upon sale of real estate owned or upon refinancing of the subject property.	Monthly Payment & Months Left to Pay	Unpaid Balance
Cash deposit toward purchase held by:	$	**LIABILITIES**		
List checking and savings accounts below		Name and address of Company	$ Payment/Months	$
Name and address of Bank, S&L, or Credit Union				
		Acct. no.		
Acct. no.	$	Name and address of Company	$ Payment/Months	$
Name and address of Bank, S&L, or Credit Union				
		Acct. no.		
Acct. no.	$	Name and address of Company	$ Payment/Months	$
Name and address of Bank, S&L, or Credit Union				
		Acct. no.		
Acct. no.	$	Name and address of Company	$ Payment/Months	$
Name and address of Bank, S&L, or Credit Union				
		Acct. no.		
Acct. no.	$	Name and address of Company	$ Payment/Months	$
Stocks & Bonds (Company name/number & description)	$			
		Acct. no.		
		Name and address of Company	$ Payment/Months	$
Life insurance net cash value	$			
Face amount: $				
Subtotal Liquid Assets	$	Acct. no.		
Real estate owned (enter market value from schedule of real estate owned)	$	Name and address of Company	$ Payment/Months	$
Vested interest in retirement fund	$			
Net worth of business(es) owned (attach financial statement)	$	Acct. no.		
Automobiles owned (make and year)	$	Alimony/Child Support/Separate Maintenance Payments Owed to:	$	
Other Assets (itemize)	$	Job-Related Expense (child care, union dues, etc.)	$	
		Total Monthly Payments	$	
Total Assets a.	$	**Net Worth (a minus b)** $	**Total Liabilities b.**	$

Freddie Mac 65 01/04
1003PG2 08/03

Printed by The Loan Handler from Contour Software, Inc. (408) 370-1700

Fannie Mae Form 1003 01/04

VI. ASSETS AND LIABILITIES (cont.)

Schedule of Real Estate Owned (If additional properties are owned, use continuation sheet.)

Property Address (enter S if sold, PS if pending sale or R if rental being held for income)	Type of Property	Present Market Value	Amount of Mortgages & Liens	Gross Rental Income	Mortgage Payments	Insurance, Maintenance, Taxes & Misc.	Net Rental Income
		$	$	$	$	$	$
Totals		$	$	$	$	$	$

List any additional names under which credit has previously been received and indicate appropriate creditor name(s) and account number(s):

Alternate Name	Creditor Name	Account Number

VII. DETAILS OF TRANSACTION

a. Purchase price	$
b. Alterations, improvements, repairs	
c. Land (if acquired separately)	
d. Refinance (incl. debts to be paid off)	
e. Estimated prepaid items	
f. Estimated closing costs	
g. PMI, MIP, Funding Fee	
h. Discount (if Borrower will pay)	
i. Total costs (add items a through h)	
j. Subordinate financing	
k. Borrower's closing costs paid by Seller	
l. Other Credits (explain)	
m. Loan amount (exclude PMI, MIP, Funding Fee financed)	
n. PMI, MIP, Funding Fee financed	
o. Loan amount (add m & n)	
p. Cash from / to Borrower (subtract j, k, l & o from i)	

VIII. DECLARATIONS

If you answer "Yes" to any questions a through i, please use continuation sheet for explanation.

	Borrower Yes	Borrower No	Co-Borrower Yes	Co-Borrower No
a. Are there any outstanding judgments against you?	☐	☐	☐	☐
b. Have you been declared bankrupt within the past 7 years?	☐	☐	☐	☐
c. Have you had property foreclosed upon or given title or deed in lieu thereof in the last 7 years?	☐	☐	☐	☐
d. Are you a party to a lawsuit?	☐	☐	☐	☐
e. Have you directly or indirectly been obligated on any loan which resulted in foreclosure, transfer of title in lieu of foreclosure, or judgment? (This would include such loans as home mortgage loans, SBA loans, home improvement loans, educational loans, manufactured (mobile) home loans, any mortgage, financial obligation, bond, or loan guarantee. If "Yes," provide details, including date, name and address of Lender, FHA or VA case number, if any, and reasons for the action.)	☐	☐	☐	☐
f. Are you presently delinquent or in default on any Federal debt or any other loan, mortgage, financial obligation, bond, or loan guarantee? If "Yes," give details as described in the preceding question.	☐	☐	☐	☐
g. Are you obligated to pay alimony, child support, or separate maintenance?	☐	☐	☐	☐
h. Is any part of the down payment borrowed?	☐	☐	☐	☐
i. Are you a co-maker or endorser on a note?	☐	☐	☐	☐
j. Are you a U.S. citizen?	☐	☐	☐	☐
k. Are you a permanent resident alien?	☐	☐	☐	☐
l. Do you intend to occupy the property as your primary residence? If "Yes," complete question m below.	☐	☐	☐	☐
m. Have you had an ownership interest in a property in the last three years?	☐	☐	☐	☐
(1) What type of property did you own -- principal residence (PR), second home (SH), or investment property (IP)?				
(2) How did you hold title to the home -- solely by yourself (S), jointly with your spouse (SP), or jointly with another person (O)?				

IX. ACKNOWLEDGMENT AND AGREEMENT

Each of the undersigned specifically represents to Lender and to Lender's actual or potential agents, brokers, processors, attorneys, insurers, servicers, successors and assigns and agrees and acknowledges that: (1) the information provided in this application is true and correct as of the date set forth opposite my signature and that any intentional or negligent misrepresentation of this information contained in this application may result in civil liability, including monetary damages, to any person who may suffer any loss due to reliance upon any misrepresentation that I have made on this application, and/or in criminal penalties including, but not limited to, fine or imprisonment or both under the provisions of Title 18, United States Code, Sec. 1001, et seq.; (2) the loan requested pursuant to this application (the "Loan") will be secured by a mortgage or deed of trust on the property described herein; (3) the property will not be used for any illegal or prohibited purpose or use; (4) all statements made in this application are made for the purpose of obtaining a residential mortgage loan; (5) the property will be occupied as indicated herein; (6) any owner or servicer of the Loan may verify or reverify any information contained in the application from any source named in this application, and Lender, its successors or assigns may retain the original and/or electronic record of this application, even if the Loan is not approved; (7) the Lender and its agents, brokers, insurers, servicers, successors and assigns may continuously rely on the information contained in the application, and I am obligated to amend and/or supplement the information provided in this application if any of the material facts that I have represented herein should change prior to closing of the Loan; (8) in the event that my payments on the Loan become delinquent, the owner or servicer of the Loan may, in addition to any other rights and remedies that it may have relating to such delinquency, report my name and account information to one or more consumer credit reporting agencies; (9) ownership of the Loan and/or administration of the Loan account may be transferred with such notice as may be required by law; (10) neither Lender nor its agents, brokers, insurers, servicers, successors or assigns has made any representation or warranty express or implied, to me regarding the property or the condition or value of the property; and (11) my transmission of this application as an "electronic record" containing my "electronic signature," as those terms are defined in applicable federal and/or state laws (excluding audio and video recordings), or my facsimile transmission of this application containing a facsimile of my signature, shall be as effective, enforceable and valid as if a paper version of this application were delivered containing my original written signature.

Borrower's Signature	Date	Co-Borrower's Signature	Date
X		X	

X. INFORMATION FOR GOVERNMENT MONITORING PURPOSES

The following information is requested by the Federal Government for certain types of loans related to a dwelling in order to monitor the lender's compliance with equal credit opportunity, fair housing and home mortgage disclosure laws. You are not required to furnish this information, but are encouraged to do so. The law provides that a lender may discriminate neither on the basis of this information, nor on whether you choose to furnish it. If you furnish the information, please provide both ethnicity and race. For race, you may check more than one designation. If you do not furnish ethnicity, race, or sex, under Federal regulations, this lender is required to note the information on the basis of visual observation or surname. If you do not wish to furnish the information, please check the box below. (Lender must review the above material to assure that the disclosures satisfy all requirements to which the lender is subject under applicable state law for the particular type of loan applied for.)

BORROWER ☐ I do not wish to furnish this information.   **CO-BORROWER** ☐ I do not wish to furnish this information.

	BORROWER	CO-BORROWER
Ethnicity	☐ Hispanic or Latino ☐ Not Hispanic or Latino	☐ Hispanic or Latino ☐ Not Hispanic or Latino
Race:	☐ American Indian or Alaska Native ☐ Asian ☐ Black or African American ☐ Native Hawaiian or Other Pacific Islander ☐ White	☐ American Indian or Alaska Native ☐ Asian ☐ Black or African American ☐ Native Hawaiian or Other Pacific Islander ☐ White
Sex:	☐ Female ☐ Male	☐ Female ☐ Male

To be Completed by Interviewer

This application was taken by:
☐ Face-to-face interview
☐ Mail
☐ Telephone
☐ Internet

Interviewer's Name (print or type)	Name and Address of Interviewer's Employer
Interviewer's Signature Date	
Interviewer's Phone Number (incl. area code)	

Freddie Mac 65 01/04
1003PG3 03/04   Page 3 of 4   Fannie Mae Form 1003 01/04
Printed by The Loan Handler from Contour Software, Inc. (408) 370-1700

95

Continuation Sheet/Residential Loan Application

Use this continuation sheet if you need more space to complete the Residential Loan Application. Mark B for Borrower or C for Co-Borrower.	Borrower:	Agency Case Number:
	Co-Borrower:	Lender Case Number:

I/We fully understand that it is a Federal crime punishable by fine or imprisonment, or both, to knowingly make any false statements concerning any of the above facts as applicable under the provisions of Title 18, United States Code, Section 1001, et seq.

Borrower's Signature	Date	Co-Borrower's Signature	Date
X		X	

Freddie Mac Form 65 01/04
1003PG4 08/03

Page 4 of 4

Fannie Mae Form 1003 01/04

Printed by The Loan Handler from Contour Software, Inc. (408) 370-1700 www.contoursoft.com

3. Closing Statement

The printed portions of this form, except differentiated additions, have been approved by the Colorado Real Estate Commission. (SS60-9-08) (Mandatory 1-09)

☐ **ESTIMATE**   ☐ **FINAL**

CLOSING STATEMENT
☐ **SELLER'S** ☐ **BUYER'S**

PROPERTY ADDRESS_____

_____

SELLER _____   BUYER _____

SETTLEMENT DATE _____   DATE OF PRORATION _____

LEGAL DESCRIPTION:

	Debits	Credits
1. Purchase Price		
2. Deposit (Earnest Money) Paid to		
3. Principal amount of new 1st Loan Payable to		
4. Principal amount of new 2nd Loan Payable to		
5. 1st Loan Payoff to		
6. 2nd Loan Payoff to		
7. Taxes for Preceding Year(s)		
8. Taxes for Current Year		
9. Personal Property Taxes		
10. Transaction Fee		
11. Loan Origination Fee		
12. Loan Discount Fee		
13. Appraisal Fee		
14. Appraisal Fee		
15. Loan Processing Fee		
16. Tax Service Fee		
17. Flood Certification		
18. Loan Document Preparation Fee		
19. Loan Underwriting Fee		
20. Interest on New Loan		
21. Mortgage Insurance Premium/PMI		
22. Premium for new Hazard Insurance		
23. Reserves Deposited with Lender		
23a. Hazard Insurance Reserve		
23b. Mortgage Insurance Reserve		
23c. County Property Tax Reserve		
24. Aggregate Adjustment		
25. Real Estate Closing Fee		
26. Loan Closing Fee		
27. Title Insurance Premium – Owner's		
28. Owner's Extended Coverage		
29. Title Insurance Premium – Lender's Policy		
30. Endorsements:		

No. SS60-9-08. CLOSING STATEMENT (Page 1 of 2)

Bradford Publishing, 1743 Wazee St., Denver, CO 80202 — (303) 292-2590 — www.bradfordpublishing.com

NOTES ON USE:

For a discussion of the closing statement and closing fees, see § 2.7.5.

	Debits	Credits
31. Certificate of Taxes Due		
32. Overnight Delivery Fee		
33. E-Doc Fee (Loan)		
34. Release Facilitation Fee		
35. Cashier's Check/Wire Fee		
36. Recording:		
36a. Warranty Deed		
36b. Deed of Trust		
36c. Release		
36d. Other		
37. Survey		
38. Documentary Fee		
39. Transfer Fee		
40. Sales and Use Tax		
41. HOA–CIC Document Procurement Fee		
42. HOA Transfer/Status Letter Fee		
43. HOA Dues		
44. HOA Working Capital		
45. Water and/or Sewer Escrow		
46. Homeowner Warranty		
47. 2% Colorado Withholding		
48. Foreign Investment in Real Property Tax Act (FIRPTA) – 10%		
49. Propane/Fuel Oil Proration		
50. Rents/Rent Proration		
51. Security Deposits		
52. Seller Concessions:		
53. Broker's Fee		
54. Other:		
Subtotals		
Balance due to/from Seller		
Balance due to/from Buyer		
TOTALS		

APPROVED AND ACCEPTED

Buyer/Seller _____   Buyer/Seller _____

Brokerage Firm's Name: _____

_____
Broker

No. SS60-9-08. CLOSING STATEMENT (Page 2 of 2)

4. Exclusive Right-to-Buy Listing Contract (All Types of Properties)

> The printed portions of this form, except differentiated additions, have been approved by the Colorado Real Estate Commission. (BC60-8-10) (Mandatory 1-11)

THIS IS A BINDING CONTRACT. THIS FORM HAS IMPORTANT LEGAL CONSEQUENCES AND THE PARTIES SHOULD CONSULT LEGAL AND TAX OR OTHER COUNSEL BEFORE SIGNING.

Compensation charged by brokerage firms is not set by law. Such charges are established by each real estate brokerage firm.

DIFFERENT BROKERAGE RELATIONSHIPS ARE AVAILABLE WHICH INCLUDE BUYER AGENCY, SELLER AGENCY, OR TRANSACTION-BROKERAGE.

EXCLUSIVE RIGHT-TO-BUY LISTING CONTRACT

☐ **BUYER AGENCY** ☐ **TRANSACTION-BROKERAGE**

Date: _____

1. AGREEMENT. Buyer and Brokerage Firm enter into this exclusive, irrevocable contract (Buyer Listing Contract) as of the date set forth above.

2. BROKER AND BROKERAGE FIRM.
☐ **2.1. Multiple-Person Firm.** If this box is checked, the individual designated by Brokerage Firm to serve as the broker of Buyer and to perform the services for Buyer required by this Buyer Listing Contract is called Broker. If more than one individual is so designated, then references in this Buyer Listing Contract to Broker shall include all persons so designated, including substitute or additional brokers. The brokerage relationship exists only with Broker and does not extend to the employing broker, Brokerage Firm or to any other brokers employed or engaged by Brokerage Firm who are not so designated.
☐ **2.2. One-Person Firm.** If this box is checked, Broker is a real estate brokerage firm with only one licensed natural person. References in this Buyer Listing Contract to Broker or Brokerage Firm mean both the licensed natural person and brokerage firm, who serve as the broker of Buyer and perform the services for Buyer required by this Buyer Listing Contract.

3. DEFINED TERMS.
   3.1. Buyer: _____
and any other person or entity on whose behalf the named party acts, directly or indirectly, to Purchase the Property.

   3.2. Brokerage Firm: _____

   3.3. Broker: _____

   3.4. Property. Property means real estate which substantially meets the following requirements or similar real estate acceptable to Buyer:

   3.5. Purchase.
      3.5.1. Purchase means the acquisition of any interest in the Property or the creation of the right to acquire any interest in the Property (including a contract or lease). It also includes an agreement to acquire any ownership interest in an entity that owns the Property.
      ☐ **3.5.2.** If this box is checked, Buyer authorizes Broker to negotiate a lease of the Property. Lease of the Property or Lease means any lease of an interest in the Property.
   3.6. Term. The Term of this Buyer Listing Contract shall begin on _____, and shall continue through the earlier of (1) completion of the Purchase of the Property or Lease of the Property or (2) _____. Broker shall continue to assist in the completion of any purchase or lease for which compensation is payable to Brokerage Firm under § 7 of this Buyer Listing Contract.
   3.7. Applicability of Terms. A check or similar mark in a box means that such provision is applicable. The abbreviation "N/A" or the word "Deleted" means not applicable. The abbreviation "MEC" (mutual execution of this contract) means the date upon which both parties have signed this Buyer Listing Contract.
   3.8. Day; Computation of Period of Days, Deadline.
      3.8.1. Day. As used in this Buyer Listing Contract, the term "day" shall mean the entire day ending at 11:59 p.m., United States Mountain Time (Standard or Daylight Savings as applicable).
      3.8.2. Computation of Period of Days, Deadline. In computing a period of days, when the ending date is not specified, the first day is excluded and the last day is included, e.g., three days after MEC. If any deadline falls on a Saturday,

---

NOTES ON USE:

For information about hiring a real estate agent, see §§ 3.4 and 3.5. For a discussion on negotiating the contract with your real estate agent and using this form, see § 3.6.

53 Sunday or federal or Colorado state holiday (Holiday), such deadline ☐ **Shall** ☐ **Shall Not** be extended to the next day that is
54 not a Saturday, Sunday or Holiday. Should neither box be checked, the deadline shall not be extended.

55 **4. BROKERAGE RELATIONSHIP.**
56 **4.1.** If the Buyer Agency box at the top of page 1 is checked, Broker shall represent Buyer as a Buyer's limited agent
57 (Buyer's Agent). If the Transaction-Brokerage box at the top of page 1 is checked, Broker shall act as a Transaction-Broker.
58 **4.2. In-Company Transaction – Different Brokers.** When the seller and Buyer in a transaction are working with different
59 brokers, those brokers continue to conduct themselves consistent with the brokerage relationships they have established. Buyer
60 acknowledges that Brokerage Firm is allowed to offer and pay compensation to brokers within Brokerage Firm working with a
61 seller.
62 **4.3. In-Company Transaction – One Broker.** If the seller and Buyer are both working with the same Broker, Broker shall
63 function as:
64   **4.3.1. Buyer's Agent.** If the Buyer Agency box at the top of page 1 is checked, the parties agree the following applies:
65   **4.3.1.1. Buyer Agency Only.** Unless the box in § 4.3.1.2 (**Buyer Agency Unless Brokerage Relationship
66 with Both**) is checked, Broker shall represent Buyer as Buyer's Agent and shall treat the seller as a customer. A customer is a
67 party to a transaction with whom Broker has no brokerage relationship. Broker shall disclose to such customer Broker's
68 relationship with Buyer.
69   ☐ **4.3.1.2. Buyer Agency Unless Brokerage Relationship with Both.** If this box is checked, Broker shall
70 represent Buyer as Buyer's Agent and shall treat the seller as a customer, unless Broker currently has or enters into an agency or
71 Transaction-Brokerage relationship with the seller, in which case Broker shall act as a Transaction-Broker.
72   **4.3.2. Transaction-Broker.** If the Transaction-Brokerage box at the top of page 1 is checked, or in the event neither
73 box is checked, Broker shall work with Buyer as a Transaction-Broker. A Transaction-Broker shall perform the duties described in
74 § 5 and facilitate purchase transactions without being an advocate or agent for either party. If the seller and Buyer are working
75 with the same broker, Broker shall continue to function as a Transaction-Broker.

76 **5. BROKERAGE DUTIES.** Brokerage Firm, acting through Broker, as either a Transaction-Broker or a Buyer's Agent, shall
77 perform the following **Uniform Duties** when working with Buyer:
78 **5.1.** Broker shall exercise reasonable skill and care for Buyer, including but not limited to the following:
79   **5.1.1.** Performing the terms of any written or oral agreement with Buyer;
80   **5.1.2.** Presenting all offers to and from Buyer in a timely manner regardless of whether Buyer is already a party to a
81 contract to Purchase the Property;
82   **5.1.3.** Disclosing to Buyer adverse material facts actually known by Broker;
83   **5.1.4.** Advising Buyer regarding the transaction and advising Buyer to obtain expert advice as to material matters
84 about which Broker knows but the specifics of which are beyond the expertise of Broker;
85   **5.1.5.** Accounting in a timely manner for all money and property received; and
86   **5.1.6.** Keeping Buyer fully informed regarding the transaction.
87 **5.2.** Broker shall not disclose the following information without the informed consent of Buyer:
88   **5.2.1.** That Buyer is willing to pay more than the purchase price offered for the Property;
89   **5.2.2.** What Buyer's motivating factors are;
90   **5.2.3.** That Buyer will agree to financing terms other than those offered;
91   **5.2.4.** Any material information about Buyer unless disclosure is required by law or failure to disclose such
92 information would constitute fraud or dishonest dealing; or
93   **5.2.5.** Any facts or suspicions regarding circumstances that could psychologically impact or stigmatize the Property.
94 **5.3.** Buyer consents to Broker's disclosure of Buyer's confidential information to the supervising broker or designee for the
95 purpose of proper supervision, provided such supervising broker or designee shall not further disclose such information without
96 consent of Buyer, or use such information to the detriment of Buyer.
97 **5.4.** Broker may show properties in which the Buyer is interested to other prospective buyers without breaching any duty or
98 obligation to such Buyer. Broker shall not be prohibited from showing competing buyers the same property and from assisting
99 competing buyers in attempting to purchase a particular property.
100 **5.5.** Broker shall not be obligated to seek other properties while Buyer is already a party to a contract to purchase property.
101 **5.6.** Broker has no duty to conduct an independent inspection of the Property for the benefit of Buyer and has no duty to
102 independently verify the accuracy or completeness of statements made by a seller or independent inspectors. Broker has no duty to
103 conduct an independent investigation of Buyer's financial condition or to verify the accuracy or completeness of any statement
104 made by Buyer.
105 **5.7.** Broker shall disclose to any prospective seller all adverse material facts actually known by Broker, including but not
106 limited to adverse material facts concerning Buyer's financial ability to perform the terms of the transaction and whether Buyer
107 intends to occupy the Property as a principal residence.
108 **5.8.** Buyer understands that Buyer shall not be liable for Broker's acts or omissions that have not been approved, directed,
109 or ratified by Buyer.

No. BC60-8-10. **EXCLUSIVE RIGHT-TO-BUY LISTING CONTRACT**   Page 2 of 5

110 **6. ADDITIONAL DUTIES OF BUYER'S AGENT.** If the Buyer Agency box at the top of page 1 is checked, Broker is
111 Buyer's Agent, with the following additional duties:
112   **6.1.** Promoting the interests of Buyer with the utmost good faith, loyalty and fidelity;
113   **6.2.** Seeking a price and terms that are acceptable to Buyer; and
114   **6.3.** Counseling Buyer as to any material benefits or risks of a transaction that are actually known by Broker.

115 **7. COMPENSATION TO BROKERAGE FIRM.** In consideration of the services to be performed by Broker, Brokerage Firm
116 shall be paid as set forth in this section, with no discount or allowance for any efforts made by Buyer or any other person.
117 Brokerage Firm shall be entitled to receive additional compensation, bonuses, and incentives paid by listing brokerage firm or
118 seller. Broker shall inform Buyer of the fee to be paid to Brokerage Firm and, if there is a written agreement, Broker shall supply a
119 copy to Buyer, upon written request of Buyer.

120 **Check Compensation Arrangement:**
121 ☐ **7.1. Listing Brokerage Firm or Seller May Pay. Buyer IS Obligated to Pay.** Broker is authorized and instructed to request
122 payment of the Brokerage Firm's fee from the listing brokerage firm or seller. Buyer shall be obligated to pay any portion of
123 Brokerage Firm's fee as described in § 7.2 which is not paid by the listing brokerage firm or seller.
124 ☐ **7.2. Buyer Will Pay.** Buyer shall be obligated to pay the Brokerage Firm's fee as described in § 7.2.1 (**Success Fee**) unless
125 the box in § 7.3 (**Listing Brokerage Firm or Seller May Pay. Buyer is NOT Obligated to Pay**) is checked.
126   ☐ **7.2.1. Success Fee.** Brokerage Firm shall be paid by Buyer as follows:
127   **7.2.1.1. Amount.** A fee equal to _____% of the purchase price, but not less than \$_____, except
128 as provided in § 7.2.1.2.
129   **7.2.1.2. Adjusted Amount.** ☐ **See Section 18. Additional Provisions or** ☐ **Other** _____
130   **7.2.1.3. When Earned.** The Success Fee is earned by the Brokerage Firm upon the Purchase of the Property
131 and is payable upon closing of the transaction. If any transaction fails to close as a result of the seller's default, with no fault on the
132 part of Buyer, the Success Fee shall be waived. If any transaction fails to close as a result of Buyer's default, in whole or in part,
133 the Success Fee shall not be waived; such fee shall be payable upon Buyer's default, but in any event not later than the date that
134 the closing of the transaction was to have occurred.
135   ☐ **7.2.2. Hourly Fee.** Brokerage Firm shall be paid \$_____ per hour for time spent by Broker pursuant to this
136 Buyer Listing Contract, up to a maximum total fee of \$_____. This hourly fee shall be paid to Brokerage Firm upon receipt
137 of an invoice from Brokerage Firm.
138   ☐ **7.2.3. Retainer Fee.** Buyer shall pay Brokerage Firm a nonrefundable retainer fee of \$_____ due and payable
139 upon signing of this Buyer Listing Contract. This amount ☐ **Shall** ☐ **Shall Not** be credited against other fees payable to
140 Brokerage Firm under this section.
141   ☐ **7.2.4. Other Compensation.** _____
142 ☐ **7.3. Listing Brokerage Firm or Seller May Pay. Buyer is NOT Obligated to Pay.** Broker is authorized to obtain payment
143 of the Brokerage Firm's fee from the listing brokerage firm or seller. Provided Buyer has fulfilled Buyer's obligations in this Buyer
144 Listing Contract, Buyer shall **not** be obligated to pay Brokerage Firm's fee. If no box is checked above, then § 7.2 (**Buyer Will Pay**)
145 shall apply.
146 ☐ **7.4. Lease Fee.** If the box in § 3.5.2 is checked and if Brokerage Firm is unable to obtain payment of Brokerage Firm's
147 entire fee from listing brokerage firm or landlord, Buyer shall pay the Brokerage Firm a fee as follows, less any amounts paid by
148 the listing brokerage firm or landlord:
149   **7.4.1. Amount.** \$_____ **Per Square Foot** per _____, up to a maximum of _____; or _____%
150 of the ☐ **Net** ☐ **Gross** amount of rent payable under the lease up to a maximum of _____.
151   **7.4.2. Adjusted Amount.** ☐ **See Section 18. Additional Provisions or** ☐ **Other** _____.
152   **7.4.3. Other.** _____
153   **7.4.4. When Earned.** This lease fee is earned upon the execution of the Lease. One-half of this lease fee shall be
154 paid upon mutual execution of the Lease and one-half upon possession of the premises by tenant or as follows: _____
155 _____. If the Lease, executed after the date of this Buyer Listing Contract, contains an option to extend or
156 renew, Brokerage Firm ☐ **Shall** ☐ **Shall Not** be paid a fee upon exercise of such extension or renewal option. If Brokerage Firm
157 is to be paid a fee for such extension or renewal, the amount of such fee and its payment shall be as follows: _____
158 _____.
159 **7.5. Holdover Period.** Brokerage Firm's fee shall apply to Property contracted for (or leased if § 3.5.2 is checked) during
160 the Term of this Buyer Listing Contract or any extensions and shall also apply to Property contracted for or leased within _____
161 calendar days after this Buyer Listing Contract expires or is terminated (Holdover Period) (1) if the Property is one on which
162 Broker negotiated and (2) if Broker submitted its address or other description in writing to Buyer during the Term, (Submitted
163 Property). Provided, however, Buyer ☐ **Shall** ☐ **Shall Not** owe the compensation to Broker under §§ 7.2.1, 7.2.2, 7.2.4 and 7.4
164 as indicated, if a commission is earned by another real estate brokerage firm acting pursuant to an exclusive agreement with Buyer
165 entered into during the Holdover Period, and a Sale or Lease of the Submitted Property is consummated. If no box is checked
166 above in this § 7.5, then Buyer shall not owe the commission to Brokerage Firm.

No. BC60-8-10. **EXCLUSIVE RIGHT-TO-BUY LISTING CONTRACT**   **Page 3 of 5**

167 **8. LIMITATION ON THIRD-PARTY COMPENSATION.** Neither Broker nor Brokerage Firm, except as set forth in § 7,
168 shall accept compensation from any other person or entity in connection with the Property without the written consent of Buyer.
169 Additionally, neither Broker nor Brokerage Firm shall be permitted to assess and receive mark-ups or other compensation for
170 services performed by any third party or affiliated business entity unless Buyer signs a separate written consent for such services.

171 **9. BUYER'S OBLIGATIONS TO BROKER.** Buyer agrees to conduct all negotiations for the Property only through Broker,
172 and to refer to Broker all communications received in any form from real estate brokers, prospective sellers, or any other source
173 during the Term of this Buyer Listing Contract. Buyer represents that Buyer ☐ **Is** ☐ **Is Not** currently a party to any agreement
174 with any other broker to represent or assist Buyer in the location or purchase of property.

175 **10. COST OF SERVICES OR PRODUCTS OBTAINED FROM OUTSIDE SOURCES.** Broker will not obtain or order
176 products or services from outside sources unless Buyer has agreed to pay for them promptly when due (examples: surveys, radon
177 tests, soil tests, title reports, engineering studies, property inspections). Neither Broker nor Brokerage Firm shall be obligated to
178 advance funds for Buyer. Buyer shall reimburse Brokerage Firm for payments made by Brokerage Firm for other products or
179 services authorized by Buyer.

180 **11. BROKERAGE SERVICES: SHOWING PREMISES.**
181   **11.1. Brokerage Services.** The Broker shall provide brokerage services to Buyer. The following additional tasks shall be
182 performed by Broker:
183
184
185
186   **11.2. Showing Properties.** Buyer acknowledges that Broker has explained the possible methods used by listing brokers and
187 sellers to show properties, and the limitations (if any) on Buyer and Broker being able to access properties due to such methods.
188 Broker's limitations on accessing premises are as follows: _____.
189 Broker, through Brokerage Firm, has access to the following multiple listing services and property information services:
190 _____.

191 **12. DISCLOSURE OF BUYER'S IDENTITY.** Broker ☐ **Does** ☐ **Does Not** have Buyer's permission to disclose Buyer's
192 identity to third parties without prior written consent of Buyer.

193 **13. DISCLOSURE OF SETTLEMENT SERVICE COSTS.** Buyer acknowledges that costs, quality, and extent of service vary
194 between different settlement service providers (e.g., attorneys, lenders, inspectors and title companies).

195 **14. NONDISCRIMINATION.** The parties agree not to discriminate unlawfully against any prospective seller because of the
196 race, creed, color, sex, sexual orientation, marital status, familial status, physical or mental disability, handicap, religion, national
197 origin or ancestry of such person.

198 **15. RECOMMENDATION OF LEGAL AND TAX COUNSEL.** By signing this document, Buyer acknowledges that Broker has
199 advised that this document has important legal consequences and has recommended consultation with legal and tax or other counsel,
200 before signing this Buyer Listing Contract.

201 **16. MEDIATION.** If a dispute arises relating to this Buyer Listing Contract, prior to or after closing, and is not resolved, the
202 parties shall first proceed in good faith to submit the matter to mediation. Mediation is a process in which the parties meet with an
203 impartial person who helps to resolve the dispute informally and confidentially. Mediators cannot impose binding decisions. The
204 parties to the dispute must agree, in writing, before any settlement is binding. The parties will jointly appoint an acceptable
205 mediator and will share equally in the cost of such mediation. The mediation, unless otherwise agreed, shall terminate in the event
206 the entire dispute is not resolved within 30 calendar days of the date written notice requesting mediation is delivered by one party
207 to the other at the party's last known address.

208 **17. ATTORNEY FEES.** In the event of any arbitration or litigation relating to this Buyer Listing Contract, the arbitrator or court
209 shall award to the prevailing party all reasonable costs and expenses, including attorney and legal fees.

210 **18. ADDITIONAL PROVISIONS.** (The following additional provisions have not been approved by the Colorado Real Estate Commission.)
211
212
213
214
215

No. BC60-8-10. **EXCLUSIVE RIGHT-TO-BUY LISTING CONTRACT**   **Page 4 of 5**

216 **19. ATTACHMENTS.** The following are a part of this Buyer Listing Contract:
217
218
219

220 **20. NOTICE, DELIVERY AND CHOICE OF LAW.**
221   **20.1. Physical Delivery.** All notices must be in writing, except as provided in § 20.2. Any document, including a signed
222 document or notice, delivered to the other party to this Buyer Listing Contract, is effective upon physical receipt. Delivery to
223 Buyer shall be effective when physically received by Buyer, any signator on behalf of Buyer, any named individual of Buyer or
224 representative of Buyer.
225   **20.2. Electronic Delivery.** As an alternative to physical delivery, any document, including any signed document or written
226 notice may be delivered in electronic form only by the following indicated methods: ☐ **Facsimile** ☐ **Email** ☐ **Internet** ☐ **No**
227 **Electronic Delivery.** Documents with original signatures shall be provided upon request of any party.
228   **20.3. Choice of Law.** This Buyer Listing Contract and all disputes arising hereunder shall be governed by and construed in
229 accordance with the laws of the State of Colorado that would be applicable to Colorado residents who sign a contract in this state
230 for property located in Colorado.

231 **21. MODIFICATION OF THIS CONTRACT.** No subsequent modification of any of the terms of this Buyer Listing Contract
232 shall be valid, binding upon the parties, or enforceable unless in writing and signed by the parties.

233 **22. COUNTERPARTS.** If more than one person is named as a Buyer herein, this Buyer Listing Contract may be executed by
234 each Buyer, separately, and when so executed, such copies taken together with one executed by Broker on behalf of Brokerage
235 Firm shall be deemed to be a full and complete contract between the parties.

236 **23. ENTIRE AGREEMENT.** This agreement constitutes the entire contract between the parties and any prior agreements,
237 whether oral or written, have been merged and integrated into this Buyer Listing Contract.

238 **24. COPY OF CONTRACT.** Buyer acknowledges receipt of a copy of this Buyer Listing Contract signed by Broker, including
239 all attachments.

240 **25. MEGAN'S LAW.** If the presence of a registered sex offender is a matter of concern to Buyer, Buyer understands that Buyer
241 must contact local law enforcement officials regarding obtaining such information.

242 Brokerage Firm authorizes Broker to execute this Buyer Listing Contract on behalf of Brokerage Firm.

Buyer's Name: _____   Broker's Name: _____

Buyer's Signature _____ Date   Broker's Signature _____ Date

Address: _____   Address: _____

Phone No.: _____   Phone No.: _____
Fax No: _____   Fax No: _____
Electronic Address: _____   Electronic Address: _____

    Brokerage
    Firm's Name: _____
    Address: _____

    Phone No.: _____
    Fax No.: _____
    Electronic Address: _____

243

No. BC60-8-10. **EXCLUSIVE RIGHT-TO-BUY LISTING CONTRACT**   Page 5 of 5

5. Exclusive Right-to-Sell Listing Contract (All Types of Properties)

<table>
<tr><td>1
2</td><td>The printed portions of this form, except differentiated additions, have been approved by the Colorado Real Estate Commission.
(LC50-8-10) (Mandatory 1-11)</td></tr>
</table>

3

4 **THIS IS A BINDING CONTRACT. THIS FORM HAS IMPORTANT LEGAL CONSEQUENCES AND THE PARTIES SHOULD**
5 **CONSULT LEGAL AND TAX OR OTHER COUNSEL BEFORE SIGNING.**

6 Compensation charged by brokerage firms is not set by law. Such charges are established by each real estate brokerage firm.

7 **DIFFERENT BROKERAGE RELATIONSHIPS ARE AVAILABLE WHICH INCLUDE BUYER AGENCY, SELLER AGENCY, OR**
8 **TRANSACTION-BROKERAGE.**
9

10 ## EXCLUSIVE RIGHT-TO-SELL LISTING CONTRACT

11 ☐ **SELLER AGENCY**   ☐ **TRANSACTION-BROKERAGE**
12
13 Date: _____

14 **1.   AGREEMENT.** Seller and Brokerage Firm enter into this exclusive, irrevocable contract (Seller Listing Contract) as of the
15 date set forth above.

16 **2.   BROKER AND BROKERAGE FIRM.**
17 ☐ **2.1.   Multiple-Person Firm.** If this box is checked, the individual designated by Brokerage Firm to serve as the broker of
18 Seller and to perform the services for Seller required by this Seller Listing Contract is called Broker. If more than one individual is
19 so designated, then references in this Seller Listing Contract to Broker shall include all persons so designated, including substitute
20 or additional brokers. The brokerage relationship exists only with Broker and does not extend to the employing broker, Brokerage
21 Firm or to any other brokers employed or engaged by Brokerage Firm who are not so designated.
22 ☐ **2.2.   One-Person Firm.** If this box is checked, Broker is a real estate brokerage firm with only one licensed natural person.
23 References in this Seller Listing Contract to Broker or Brokerage Firm mean both the licensed natural person and brokerage firm
24 who shall serve as the broker of Seller and perform the services for Seller required by this Seller Listing Contract.

25 **3.   DEFINED TERMS.**
26 **3.1.   Seller:** _____
27 **3.2.   Brokerage Firm:** _____
28 **3.3.   Broker:** _____
29 **3.4.   Property.** The Property is the following legally described real estate in the County of _____, Colorado:
30
31
32
33 known as No. _____,
34   Street Address   City   State   Zip
35 together with the interests, easements, rights, benefits, improvements and attached fixtures appurtenant thereto, and all interest of
36 Seller in vacated streets and alleys adjacent thereto, except as herein excluded.
37 **3.5.   Sale.**
38 **3.5.1.** A Sale is the voluntary transfer or exchange of any interest in the Property or the voluntary creation of the
39 obligation to convey any interest in the Property, including a contract or lease. It also includes an agreement to transfer any
40 ownership interest in an entity which owns the Property.
41 ☐ **3.5.2.** If this box is checked, Seller authorizes Broker to negotiate leasing the Property. Lease of the Property or
42 Lease means any lease of an interest in the Property.
43 **3.6.   Listing Period.** The Listing Period of this Seller Listing Contract shall begin on _____, and
44 shall continue through the earlier of (1) completion of the Sale of the Property or (2) _____.
45 Broker shall continue to assist in the completion of any sale or lease for which compensation is payable to Brokerage Firm under
46 § 7 of this Seller Listing Contract.
47 **3.7.   Applicability of Terms.** A check or similar mark in a box means that such provision is applicable. The abbreviation
48 "N/A" or the word "Deleted" means not applicable. The abbreviation "MEC" (mutual execution of this contract) means the date upon
49 which both parties have signed this Seller Listing Contract.

---

50   **3.8.**   **Day; Computation of Period of Days, Deadline.**
51   **3.8.1.**   **Day.** As used in this Seller Listing Contract, the term "day" shall mean the entire day ending at 11:59 p.m.,
52 United States Mountain Time (Standard or Daylight Savings as applicable).
53   **3.8.2.**   **Computation of Period of Days, Deadline.** In computing a period of days, when the ending date is not
54 specified, the first day is excluded and the last day is included, e.g., three days after MEC. If any deadline falls on a Saturday,
55 Sunday or federal or Colorado state holiday (Holiday), such deadline ☐ **Shall** ☐ **Shall Not** be extended to the next day that is
56 not a Saturday, Sunday or Holiday. Should neither box be checked, the deadline shall not be extended.

57 **4.**   **BROKERAGE RELATIONSHIP.**
58   **4.1.**   If the Seller Agency box at the top of page 1 is checked, Broker shall represent Seller as a Seller's limited agent
59 (Seller's Agent). If the Transaction-Brokerage box at the top of page 1 is checked, Broker shall act as a Transaction-Broker.
60   **4.2.**   **In-Company Transaction – Different Brokers.** When Seller and buyer in a transaction are working with different
61 brokers, those brokers continue to conduct themselves consistent with the brokerage relationships they have established. Seller
62 acknowledges that Brokerage Firm is allowed to offer and pay compensation to brokers within Brokerage Firm working with a
63 buyer.
64   **4.3.**   **In-Company Transaction – One Broker.** If Seller and buyer are both working with the same broker, Broker shall
65 function as:
66   **4.3.1.**   **Seller's Agent.** If the Seller Agency box at the top of page 1 is checked, the parties agree the following applies:
67   **4.3.1.1.**   **Seller Agency Only.** Unless the box in § 4.3.1.2 (**Seller Agency Unless Brokerage Relationship**
68 **with Both**) is checked, Broker shall represent Seller as Seller's Agent and shall treat the buyer as a customer. A customer is a
69 party to a transaction with whom Broker has no brokerage relationship. Broker shall disclose to such customer Broker's
70 relationship with Seller.
71   ☐   **4.3.1.2.**   **Seller Agency Unless Brokerage Relationship with Both.** If this box is checked, Broker shall
72 represent Seller as Seller's Agent and shall treat the buyer as a customer, unless Broker currently has or enters into an agency or
73 Transaction-Brokerage relationship with the buyer, in which case Broker shall act as a Transaction-Broker.
74   **4.3.2.**   **Transaction-Broker.** If the Transaction-Brokerage box at the top of page 1 is checked, or in the event neither
75 box is checked, Broker shall work with Seller as a Transaction-Broker. A Transaction-Broker shall perform the duties described in
76 § 5 and facilitate sales transactions without being an advocate or agent for either party. If Seller and buyer are working with the
77 same broker, Broker shall continue to function as a Transaction-Broker.

78 **5.**   **BROKERAGE DUTIES.** Brokerage Firm, acting through Broker, as either a Transaction-Broker or a Seller's Agent, shall
79 perform the following **Uniform Duties** when working with Seller:
80   **5.1.**   Broker shall exercise reasonable skill and care for Seller, including, but not limited to the following:
81   **5.1.1.**   Performing the terms of any written or oral agreement with Seller;
82   **5.1.2.**   Presenting all offers to and from Seller in a timely manner regardless of whether the Property is subject to a
83 contract for Sale;
84   **5.1.3.**   Disclosing to Seller adverse material facts actually known by Broker;
85   **5.1.4.**   Advising Seller regarding the transaction and advising Seller to obtain expert advice as to material matters
86 about which Broker knows but the specifics of which are beyond the expertise of Broker;
87   **5.1.5.**   Accounting in a timely manner for all money and property received; and
88   **5.1.6.**   Keeping Seller fully informed regarding the transaction.
89   **5.2.**   Broker shall not disclose the following information without the informed consent of Seller:
90   **5.2.1.**   That Seller is willing to accept less than the asking price for the Property;
91   **5.2.2.**   What the motivating factors are for Seller to sell the Property;
92   **5.2.3.**   That Seller will agree to financing terms other than those offered;
93   **5.2.4.**   Any material information about Seller unless disclosure is required by law or failure to disclose such
94 information would constitute fraud or dishonest dealing; or
95   **5.2.5.**   Any facts or suspicions regarding circumstances that could psychologically impact or stigmatize the Property.
96   **5.3.**   Seller consents to Broker's disclosure of Seller's confidential information to the supervising broker or designee for the
97 purpose of proper supervision, provided such supervising broker or designee shall not further disclose such information without
98 consent of Seller, or use such information to the detriment of Seller.
99   **5.4.**   Brokerage Firm may have agreements with other sellers to market and sell their property. Broker may show alternative
100 properties not owned by Seller to other prospective buyers and list competing properties for sale.
101   **5.5.**   Broker shall not be obligated to seek additional offers to purchase the Property while the Property is subject to a
102 contract for Sale.
103   **5.6.**   Broker has no duty to conduct an independent inspection of the Property for the benefit of a buyer and has no duty to
104 independently verify the accuracy or completeness of statements made by Seller or independent inspectors. Broker has no duty to
105 conduct an independent investigation of a buyer's financial condition or to verify the accuracy or completeness of any statement
106 made by a buyer.

LC50-8-10. EXCLUSIVE RIGHT-TO-SELL LISTING CONTRACT   Page 2 of 7

107   **5.7.**   Seller understands that Seller shall not be liable for Broker's acts or omissions that have not been approved, directed, or
108   ratified by Seller.
109   **5.8.**   When asked, Broker ☐ **Shall** ☐ **Shall Not** disclose to prospective buyers and cooperating brokers the existence of
110   offers on the Property and whether the offers were obtained by Broker, a broker within Brokerage Firm or by another broker.

111   **6.   ADDITIONAL DUTIES OF SELLER'S AGENT.** If the Seller Agency box at the top of page 1 is checked, Broker is
112   Seller's Agent, with the following additional duties:
113   **6.1.**   Promoting the interests of Seller with the utmost good faith, loyalty and fidelity;
114   **6.2.**   Seeking a price and terms that are set forth in this Seller Listing Contract; and
115   **6.3.**   Counseling Seller as to any material benefits or risks of a transaction that are actually known by Broker.

116   **7.   COMPENSATION TO BROKERAGE FIRM; COMPENSATION TO COOPERATIVE BROKER.** Seller agrees that
117   any Brokerage Firm compensation that is conditioned upon the Sale of the Property shall be earned by Brokerage Firm as set forth
118   herein without any discount or allowance for any efforts made by Seller or by any other person in connection with the Sale of the
119   Property.
120   **7.1.**   **Amount.** In consideration of the services to be performed by Broker, Seller agrees to pay Brokerage Firm as follows:
121   **7.1.1.**   **Sale Commission.** (1) _____% of the gross purchase price or (2) _____,
122   in U.S. dollars.
123   **7.1.2.**   **Lease Commission.** If the box in § 3.5.2 is checked, Brokerage Firm shall be paid a fee equal to (1) _____%
124   of the gross rent under the lease, or (2) _____, in U.S. dollars, payable
125   as follows: _____.
126   **7.2.**   **When Earned.** Such commission shall be earned upon the occurrence of any of the following:
127   **7.2.1.**   Any Sale of the Property within the Listing Period by Seller, by Broker or by any other person;
128   **7.2.2.**   Broker finding a buyer who is ready, willing and able to complete the sale or lease as specified in this Seller
129   Listing Contract; or
130   **7.2.3.**   Any Sale (or Lease if § 3.5.2 is checked) of the Property within _____ calendar days subsequent to the
131   expiration of the Listing Period (Holdover Period) (1) to anyone with whom Broker negotiated and (2) whose name was submitted,
132   in writing, to Seller by Broker during the Listing Period, including any extensions thereof, (Submitted Prospect). Provided,
133   however, Seller ☐ **Shall** ☐ **Shall Not** owe the commission to Brokerage Firm under this § 7.2.3 if a commission is earned by
134   another licensed real estate brokerage firm acting pursuant to an exclusive agreement entered into during the Holdover Period and
135   a Sale or Lease to a Submitted Prospect is consummated. If no box is checked above in this § 7.2.3, then Seller shall not owe the
136   commission to Brokerage Firm.
137   **7.3.**   **When Applicable and Payable.** The commission obligation shall apply to a Sale made during the Listing Period or
138   any extension of such original or extended term. The commission described in § 7.1.1 shall be payable at the time of the closing of
139   the Sale, or, if there is no closing (due to the refusal or neglect of Seller) then on the contracted date of closing, as contemplated by
140   § 7.2.1 or § 7.2.3, or upon fulfillment of § 7.2.2 where the offer made by such buyer is not accepted by Seller.
141   **7.4.**   **Other Compensation.** _____
142   **7.5.**   **Cooperative Broker Compensation.** Broker shall seek assistance from, and Brokerage Firm offers compensation to,
143   outside brokerage firms, whose brokers are acting as:
144   ☐ **Buyer Agents:** _____% of the gross sales price or _____, in U.S. dollars.
145   ☐ **Transaction-Brokers:** _____% of the gross sales price or _____, in U.S. dollars.

146   **8.   LIMITATION ON THIRD-PARTY COMPENSATION.** Neither Broker nor the Brokerage Firm, except as set forth in
147   § 7, shall accept compensation from any other person or entity in connection with the Property without the written consent of
148   Seller. Additionally, neither Broker nor Brokerage Firm shall assess or receive mark-ups or other compensation for services
149   performed by any third party or affiliated business entity unless Seller signs a separate written consent.

150   **9.   OTHER BROKERS' ASSISTANCE, MULTIPLE LISTING SERVICES AND MARKETING.** Seller has been advised
151   by Broker of the advantages and disadvantages of various marketing methods, including advertising and the use of multiple listing
152   services (MLS) and various methods of making the Property accessible by other brokerage firms (e.g., using lock boxes, by-
153   appointment-only showings, etc.), and whether some methods may limit the ability of another broker to show the Property. After
154   having been so advised, Seller has chosen the following (check all that apply):
155   **9.1.**   **MLS/Information Exchange.**
156   **9.1.1.**   The Property ☐ **Shall** ☐ **Shall Not** be submitted to one or more MLS and ☐ **Shall** ☐ **Shall Not** be
157   submitted to one or more property information exchanges. If submitted, Seller authorizes Broker to provide timely notice of any
158   status change to such MLS and information exchanges. Upon transfer of deed from Seller to buyer, Seller authorizes Broker to
159   provide sales information to such MLS and information exchanges.
160   **9.1.2.**   Seller authorizes the use of electronic and all other marketing methods except: _____.
161   **9.1.3.**   Seller further authorizes use of the data by MLS and property information exchanges, if any.

162   **9.1.4.** The Property Address ☐ **Shall** ☐ **Shall Not** be displayed on the Internet.

163   **9.1.5.** The Property Listing ☐ **Shall** ☐ **Shall Not** be displayed on the Internet.

164   **9.2.** **Property Access.** Access to the Property may be by:

165   ☐ Lock Box

166   ☐ _____

167   Other instructions: _____

168   **9.3.** **Broker Marketing.** The following specific marketing tasks shall be performed by Broker:

169

170

171   **9.4.** **Brokerage Services.** The Broker shall provide brokerage services to Seller.

172 **10. SELLER'S OBLIGATIONS TO BROKER; DISCLOSURES AND CONSENT.**

173   **10.1. Negotiations and Communication.** Seller agrees to conduct all negotiations for the Sale of the Property only through
174 Broker, and to refer to Broker all communications received in any form from real estate brokers, prospective buyers, tenants or any
175 other source during the Listing Period of this Seller Listing Contract.

176   **10.2. Advertising.** Seller agrees that any advertising of the Property by Seller (e.g., Internet, print and signage) shall first be
177 approved by Broker.

178   **10.3. No Existing Listing Agreement.** Seller represents that Seller ☐ **Is** ☐ **Is Not** currently a party to any listing
179 agreement with any other broker to sell the Property.

180   **10.4. Ownership of Materials and Consent.** Seller represents that all materials (including all photographs, renderings,
181 images or other creative items) supplied to Broker by or on behalf of Seller are owned by Seller, except as Seller has disclosed in
182 writing to Broker. Seller is authorized to and grants to Broker, Brokerage Firm and any MLS (that Broker submits the Property to)
183 a nonexclusive irrevocable, royalty-free license to use such material for marketing of the Property, reporting as required and the
184 publishing, display and reproduction of such material, compilation and data. This license shall survive the termination of this
185 Seller Listing Contract.

186   **10.5. Colorado Foreclosure Protection Act.** The Colorado Foreclosure Protection Act (Act) generally applies if (1) the
187 Property is residential (2) Seller resides in the Property as Seller's principal residence (3) Buyer's purpose in purchase of the
188 Property is not to use the Property as Buyer's personal residence and (4) the Property is in foreclosure or Buyer has notice that any
189 loan secured by the Property is at least thirty days delinquent or in default. If all requirements 1, 2, 3 and 4 are met and the Act
190 otherwise applies, then a contract, between Buyer and Seller for the sale of the Property, that complies with the provisions of the
191 Act is required. If the transaction is a Short Sale transaction and a Short Sale Addendum is part of the Contract between Seller and
192 Buyer, the Act does not apply. It is recommended that Seller consult with an attorney.

193 **11. PRICE AND TERMS.** The following Price and Terms are acceptable to Seller:

194   **11.1. Price.** U.S. $_____

195   **11.2. Terms.** ☐ **Cash** ☐ **Conventional** ☐ **FHA** ☐ **VA** ☐ **Other:** _____

196   **11.3. Loan Discount Points.** _____

197   **11.4. Buyer's Closing Costs (FHA/VA).** Seller shall pay closing costs and fees, not to exceed $_____, that Buyer
198 is not allowed by law to pay, for tax service and _____.

199   **11.5. Earnest Money.** Minimum amount of earnest money deposit U.S. $_____ in the form of _____

200   **11.6. Seller Proceeds.** Seller will receive net proceeds of closing as indicated: ☐ **Cashier's Check** at Seller's expense;
201 ☐ **Funds Electronically Transferred (Wire Transfer)** to an account specified by Seller, at Seller's expense; or ☐ **Closing**
202 **Company's Trust Account Check.**

203   **11.7. Advisory: Tax Withholding.** The Internal Revenue Service and the Colorado Department of Revenue may require
204 closing company to withhold a substantial portion of the proceeds of this Sale when Seller either (1) is a foreign person or (2) will
205 not be a Colorado resident after closing. Seller should inquire of Seller's tax advisor to determine if withholding applies or if an
206 exemption exists.

207 **12. DEPOSITS.** Brokerage Firm is authorized to accept earnest money deposits received by Broker pursuant to a proposed Sale
208 contract. Brokerage Firm is authorized to deliver the earnest money deposit to the closing agent, if any, at or before the closing of
209 the Sale contract.

210 **13. INCLUSIONS AND EXCLUSIONS.**

211   **13.1. Inclusions.** The Purchase Price includes the following items (Inclusions):

212   **13.1.1. Fixtures.** If attached to the Property on the date of this Seller Listing Contract, lighting, heating, plumbing,
213 ventilating, and air conditioning fixtures, TV antennas, inside telephone, network and coaxial (cable) wiring and connecting
214 blocks/jacks, plants, mirrors, floor coverings, intercom systems, built-in kitchen appliances, sprinkler systems and controls, built-in
215 vacuum systems (including accessories), garage door openers including _____ remote controls; and

216

217   **13.1.2. Personal Property.** If on the Property whether attached or not on the date of this Seller Listing Contract:
218 storm windows, storm doors, window and porch shades, awnings, blinds, screens, window coverings, curtain rods, drapery rods,
219 fireplace inserts, fireplace screens, fireplace grates, heating stoves, storage sheds, and all keys. If checked, the following are
220 included: ☐ **Water Softeners** ☐ **Smoke/Fire Detectors** ☐ **Security Systems** ☐ **Satellite Systems** (including satellite
221 dishes); and
222
223
224   The Personal Property to be conveyed at closing shall be conveyed by Seller free and clear of all taxes (except personal
225 property taxes for the year of closing), liens and encumbrances, except _____ .
226 Conveyance shall be by bill of sale or other applicable legal instrument.
227   **13.1.3. Trade Fixtures.** The following trade fixtures: _____
228   The Trade Fixtures to be conveyed at closing shall be conveyed by Seller, free and clear of all taxes (except personal property
229 taxes for the year of closing), liens and encumbrances, except _____ .
230 Conveyance shall be by bill of sale or other applicable legal instrument.
231   **13.1.4. Parking and Storage Facilities.** ☐ **Use Only** ☐ **Ownership** of the following parking facilities: _____
232 _____; and ☐ **Use Only** ☐ **Ownership** of the following storage facilities: _____ .
233   **13.1.5. Water Rights.** The following legally described water rights: _____
234
235
236   Any water rights shall be conveyed by _____ deed or other applicable legal instrument. The Well
237 Permit # is _____ .
238   **13.1.6. Growing Crops.** The following growing crops: _____
239
240
241   **13.2. Exclusions.** The following are excluded (Exclusions): _____

242 **14. TITLE AND ENCUMBRANCES.** Seller represents to Broker that title to the Property is solely in Seller's name. Seller shall
243 deliver to Broker true copies of all relevant title materials, leases, improvement location certificates and surveys in Seller's
244 possession and shall disclose to Broker all easements, liens and other encumbrances, if any, on the Property, of which Seller has
245 knowledge. Seller authorizes the holder of any obligation secured by an encumbrance on the Property to disclose to Broker the
246 amount owing on said encumbrance and the terms thereof. In case of Sale, Seller agrees to convey, by a _____
247 deed, only that title Seller has in the Property. Property shall be conveyed free and clear of all taxes, except the general taxes for
248 the year of closing.
249   All monetary encumbrances (such as mortgages, deeds of trust, liens, financing statements) shall be paid by Seller and released
250 except as Seller and buyer may otherwise agree. Existing monetary encumbrances are as follows: _____ .
251   The Property is subject to the following leases and tenancies: _____ .
252   If the Property has been or will be subject to any governmental liens for special improvements installed at the time of signing
253 a Sale contract, Seller shall be responsible for payment of same, unless otherwise agreed. Brokerage Firm may terminate this Seller
254 Listing Contract upon written notice to Seller that title is not satisfactory to Brokerage Firm.

255 **15. EVIDENCE OF TITLE.** Seller agrees to furnish buyer, at Seller's expense, a current commitment and an owner's title
256 insurance policy in an amount equal to the Purchase Price in the form specified in the Sale contract, or if this box is checked,
257 ☐ **An Abstract of Title** certified to a current date.

258 **16. ASSOCIATION ASSESSMENTS.** Seller represents that the amount of the regular owners' association assessment is
259 currently payable at $_____ per _____ and that there are no unpaid regular or special assessments against
260 the Property except the current regular assessments and except _____ . Seller agrees to promptly
261 request the owners' association to deliver to buyer before date of closing a current statement of assessments against the Property.

262 **17. POSSESSION.** Possession of the Property shall be delivered to buyer as follows: _____ ,
263 subject to leases and tenancies as described in § 14.

264 **18. MATERIAL DEFECTS, DISCLOSURES AND INSPECTION.**
265   **18.1. Broker's Obligations.** Colorado law requires a broker to disclose to any prospective buyer all adverse material facts
266 actually known by such broker including but not limited to adverse material facts pertaining to the title to the Property and the
267 physical condition of the Property, any material defects in the Property, and any environmental hazards affecting the Property which
268 are required by law to be disclosed. These types of disclosures may include such matters as structural defects, soil conditions,
269 violations of health, zoning or building laws, and nonconforming uses and zoning variances. Seller agrees that any buyer may have
270 the Property and Inclusions inspected and authorizes Broker to disclose any facts actually known by Broker about the Property.

LC50-8-10. EXCLUSIVE RIGHT-TO-SELL LISTING CONTRACT   Page 5 of 7

271 **18.2. Seller's Obligations.**
272   **18.2.1. Seller's Property Disclosure Form.** A seller is not required by law to provide a written disclosure of adverse
273 matters regarding the Property. However, disclosure of known material latent (not obvious) defects is required by law. Seller
274 ☐ **Agrees** ☐ **Does Not Agree** to provide a Seller's Property Disclosure form completed to Seller's current, actual knowledge.
275   **18.2.2. Lead-Based Paint.** Unless exempt, if the improvements on the Property include one or more residential
276 dwellings for which a building permit was issued prior to January 1, 1978, a completed Lead-Based Paint Disclosure (Sales) form
277 must be signed by Seller and the real estate licensees, and given to any potential buyer in a timely manner.
278   **18.2.3. Carbon Monoxide Alarms.** Note: If the improvements on the Property have a fuel-fired heater or appliance, a
279 fireplace, or an attached garage and one or more rooms lawfully used for sleeping purposes (Bedroom), Seller understands that
280 Colorado law requires that Seller assure the Property has an operational carbon monoxide alarm installed within fifteen feet of the
281 entrance to each Bedroom or in a location as required by the applicable building code, prior to offering the Property for sale or lease.
282   **18.3. Right of Broker to Terminate.** Although Broker has no obligation to investigate or inspect the Property, and no duty
283 to verify statements made, Broker shall have the right to terminate this Seller Listing Contract if the physical condition of the
284 Property, Inclusions, any proposed or existing transportation project, road, street or highway, or any other activity, odor or noise
285 (whether on or off the Property) and its effect or expected effect on the Property or its occupants, or if any facts or suspicions
286 regarding circumstances that could psychologically impact or stigmatize the Property are unsatisfactory to Broker.

287 **19. FORFEITURE OF PAYMENTS.** In the event of a forfeiture of payments made by a buyer, the sums received shall be
288 divided between Brokerage Firm and Seller, one-half thereof to Brokerage Firm but not to exceed the Brokerage Firm
289 compensation agreed upon herein, and the balance to Seller. Any forfeiture of payment under this section shall not reduce any
290 Brokerage Firm compensation owed, earned and payable under § 7.

291 **20. COST OF SERVICES AND REIMBURSEMENT.** Unless otherwise agreed upon in writing, Brokerage Firm shall bear all
292 expenses incurred by Brokerage Firm, if any, to market the Property and to compensate cooperating brokerage firms, if any.
293 Neither Broker nor Brokerage Firm shall obtain or order any other products or services unless Seller agrees in writing to pay for
294 them promptly when due (examples: surveys, radon tests, soil tests, title reports, engineering studies). Unless otherwise agreed,
295 neither Broker nor Brokerage Firm shall be obligated to advance funds for the benefit of Seller in order to complete a closing.
296 Seller shall reimburse Brokerage Firm for payments made by Brokerage Firm for such products or services authorized by Seller.

297 **21. DISCLOSURE OF SETTLEMENT COSTS.** Seller acknowledges that costs, quality, and extent of service vary between
298 different settlement service providers (e.g., attorneys, lenders, inspectors and title companies).

299 **22. MAINTENANCE OF THE PROPERTY.** Neither Broker nor Brokerage Firm shall be responsible for maintenance of the
300 Property nor shall they be liable for damage of any kind occurring to the Property, unless such damage shall be caused by their
301 negligence or intentional misconduct.

302 **23. NONDISCRIMINATION.** The parties agree not to discriminate unlawfully against any prospective buyer because of the
303 race, creed, color, sex, sexual orientation, marital status, familial status, physical or mental disability, handicap, religion, national
304 origin or ancestry of such person.

305 **24. RECOMMENDATION OF LEGAL AND TAX COUNSEL.** By signing this document, Seller acknowledges that Broker
306 has advised that this document has important legal consequences and has recommended consultation with legal and tax or other
307 counsel before signing this Seller Listing Contract.

308 **25. MEDIATION.** If a dispute arises relating to this Seller Listing Contract, prior to or after closing, and is not resolved, the
309 parties shall first proceed in good faith to submit the matter to mediation. Mediation is a process in which the parties meet with an
310 impartial person who helps to resolve the dispute informally and confidentially. Mediators cannot impose binding decisions. The
311 parties to the dispute must agree, in writing, before any settlement is binding. The parties will jointly appoint an acceptable
312 mediator and will share equally in the cost of such mediation. The mediation, unless otherwise agreed, shall terminate in the event
313 the entire dispute is not resolved within 30 calendar days of the date written notice requesting mediation is delivered by one party
314 to the other at the party's last known address.

315 **26. ATTORNEY FEES.** In the event of any arbitration or litigation relating to this Seller Listing Contract, the arbitrator or court
316 shall award to the prevailing party all reasonable costs and expenses, including attorney and legal fees.

317 **27. ADDITIONAL PROVISIONS.** (The following additional provisions have not been approved by the Colorado Real Estate Commission.)
318
319
320

LC50-8-10. EXCLUSIVE RIGHT-TO-SELL LISTING CONTRACT   Page 6 of 7

321 **28. ATTACHMENTS.** The following are a part of this Seller Listing Contract:
322
323

324 **29. NO OTHER PARTY OR INTENDED BENEFICIARIES.** Nothing in this Seller Listing Contract shall be deemed to inure
325 to the benefit of any person other than Seller, Broker and Brokerage Firm.

326 **30. NOTICE, DELIVERY AND CHOICE OF LAW.**
327   **30.1. Physical Delivery.** All notices must be in writing, except as provided in § 30.2. Any document, including a signed
328 document or notice, delivered to the other party to this Seller Listing Contract, is effective upon physical receipt. Delivery to Seller
329 shall be effective when physically received by Seller, any signator on behalf of Seller, any named individual of Seller or
330 representative of Seller.
331   **30.2. Electronic Delivery.** As an alternative to physical delivery, any document, including any signed document or written
332 notice may be delivered in electronic form only by the following indicated methods: ☐ **Facsimile** ☐ **Email** ☐ **Internet** ☐ **No**
333 **Electronic Delivery.** Documents with original signatures shall be provided upon request of any party.
334   **30.3. Choice of Law.** This Seller Listing Contract and all disputes arising hereunder shall be governed by and construed in
335 accordance with the laws of the State of Colorado that would be applicable to Colorado residents who sign a contract in this state
336 for property located in Colorado.

337 **31. MODIFICATION OF THIS SELLER LISTING CONTRACT.** No subsequent modification of any of the terms of this
338 Seller Listing Contract shall be valid, binding upon the parties, or enforceable unless made in writing and signed by the parties.

339 **32. COUNTERPARTS.** If more than one person is named as a Seller herein, this Seller Listing Contract may be executed by
340 each Seller, separately, and when so executed, such copies taken together with one executed by Broker on behalf of Brokerage
341 Firm shall be deemed to be a full and complete contract between the parties.

342 **33. ENTIRE AGREEMENT.** This agreement constitutes the entire contract between the parties, and any prior agreements,
343 whether oral or written, have been merged and integrated into this Seller Listing Contract.

344 **34. COPY OF CONTRACT.** Seller acknowledges receipt of a copy of this Seller Listing Contract signed by Broker, including
345 all attachments.

346 Brokerage Firm authorizes Broker to execute this Seller Listing Contract on behalf of Brokerage Firm.

Seller's Name: _____ Broker's Name: _____

Seller's Signature   Date Broker's Signature   Date
Address: _____ Address: _____

Phone No.: _____ Phone No.: _____
Fax No: _____ Fax No: _____
Electronic Address: _____ Electronic Address: _____

Brokerage
Firm's Name: _____
Address: _____

Phone No.: _____
Fax No.: _____
Electronic Address: _____

347

6. Contract to Buy and Sell Real Estate (All Types of Properties)

1	The printed portions of this form, except differentiated additions, have been approved by the Colorado Real Estate Commission.
2	(CBS1-10-11) (Mandatory 1-12)

3
4 **THIS FORM HAS IMPORTANT LEGAL CONSEQUENCES AND THE PARTIES SHOULD CONSULT LEGAL AND TAX OR**
5 **OTHER COUNSEL BEFORE SIGNING.**

6
7 ## CONTRACT TO BUY AND SELL REAL ESTATE
8 ## (RESIDENTIAL)
9
10 Date: _____

11
$$\boxed{\textbf{AGREEMENT}}$$

12 **1. AGREEMENT.** Buyer, identified in § 2.1, agrees to buy, and Seller, identified in § 2.3, agrees to sell, the Property
13 described below on the terms and conditions set forth in this contract (Contract).

14 **2. PARTIES AND PROPERTY.**
15 **2.1. Buyer.** Buyer, _____, will take title to the Property
16 described below as ☐ **Joint Tenants** ☐ **Tenants In Common** ☐ **Other** _____.
17 **2.2. Assignability and Inurement.** This Contract ☐ **Shall** ☐ **Shall Not** be assignable by Buyer without Seller's prior
18 written consent. Except as so restricted, this Contract shall inure to the benefit of and be binding upon the heirs, personal
19 representatives, successors and assigns of the parties.
20 **2.3. Seller.** Seller, _____, is the current owner of the
21 Property described below.
22 **2.4. Property.** The Property is the following legally described real estate in the County of _____, Colorado:
23
24
25
26
27 known as No. _____,
28   Street Address   City   State   Zip
29 together with the interests, easements, rights, benefits, improvements and attached fixtures appurtenant thereto, and all interest of
30 Seller in vacated streets and alleys adjacent thereto, except as herein excluded (Property).
31 **2.5. Inclusions.** The Purchase Price includes the following items (Inclusions):
32   **2.5.1. Fixtures.** If attached to the Property on the date of this Contract: lighting, heating, plumbing, ventilating
33 and air conditioning fixtures, TV antennas, inside telephone, network and coaxial (cable) wiring and connecting blocks/jacks,
34 plants, mirrors, floor coverings, intercom systems, built-in kitchen appliances, sprinkler systems and controls, built-in vacuum
35 systems (including accessories), garage door openers including _____ remote controls.
36 **Other Fixtures:**
37
38
39 If any fixtures are attached to the Property after the date of this Contract, such additional fixtures are also included in the Purchase
40 Price.
41   **2.5.2. Personal Property.** If on the Property whether attached or not on the date of this Contract: storm windows,
42 storm doors, window and porch shades, awnings, blinds, screens, window coverings, curtain rods, drapery rods, fireplace inserts,
43 fireplace screens, fireplace grates, heating stoves, storage sheds, and all keys. If checked, the following are included: ☐ **Water**
44 **Softeners** ☐ **Smoke/Fire Detectors** ☐ **Security Systems** ☐ **Satellite Systems** (including satellite dishes).
45 **Other Personal Property:**
46
47
48   The Personal Property to be conveyed at Closing shall be conveyed by Seller free and clear of all taxes (except
49 personal property taxes for the year of Closing), liens and encumbrances, except _____.
50 Conveyance shall be by bill of sale or other applicable legal instrument.
51   **2.5.3. Parking and Storage Facilities.** ☐ **Use Only** ☐ **Ownership** of the following parking facilities:
52 _____; and ☐ **Use Only** ☐ **Ownership** of the following storage facilities: _____.

NOTES ON USE:
For a detailed discussion of this contract, including a paragraph-by-paragraph explanation of its terms, see Chapter 5.

53   **2.5.4.**   **Water Rights, Water and Sewer Taps.**
54   **2.5.4.1. Deeded Water Rights.** The following legally described water rights:
55
56
57   Any water rights shall be conveyed by ☐ _____ **Deed** ☐ **Other** applicable legal instrument.
58   ☐   **2.5.4.2. Well Rights.** If any water well is to be transferred to Buyer, Seller agrees to supply required
59 information about such well to Buyer. Buyer understands that if the well to be transferred is a Small Capacity Well or a Domestic
60 Exempt Water Well used for ordinary household purposes, Buyer shall, prior to or at Closing, complete a Change in Ownership
61 form for the well. If an existing well has not been registered with the Colorado Division of Water Resources in the Department of
62 Natural Resources (Division), Buyer shall complete a registration of existing well form for the well and pay the cost of
63 registration. If no person will be providing a closing service in connection with the transaction, Buyer shall file the form with the
64 Division within sixty days after Closing. The Well Permit # is _____.
65   **2.5.4.3.** ☐ **Water Stock Certificates:**
66
67
68   **2.5.4.4.** ☐ **Water Tap**   ☐ **Sewer Tap**

69 **Note: Buyer is advised to obtain, from the provider, written confirmation of the amount remaining to be paid, if any, time**
70 **and other restrictions for transfer and use of the tap.**
71   **2.5.4.5. Other Rights:**
72
73
74   **2.6.**   **Exclusions.** The following items are excluded (Exclusions):
75
76

77 **3.**   **DATES AND DEADLINES.**

Item No.	Reference	Event	Date or Deadline
1	§ 4.2	Alternative Earnest Money Deadline	
		Title and Association	
2	§ 7.1	Record Title Deadline	
3	§ 7.2	Exceptions Request Deadline	
4	§ 8.1	Record Title Objection Deadline	
5	§ 8.2	Off-Record Title Deadline	
6	§ 8.2	Off-Record Title Objection Deadline	
7	§ 8.3	Title Resolution Deadline	
8	§ 7.3	Association Documents Deadline	
9	§ 7.3	Association Documents Objection Deadline	
10	§ 8.5	Right of First Refusal Deadline	
		Seller's Property Disclosure	
11	§ 10.1	Seller's Property Disclosure Deadline	
		Loan and Credit	
12	§ 5.1	Loan Application Deadline	
13	§ 5.2	Loan Conditions Deadline	
14	§ 5.3	Buyer's Credit Information Deadline	
15	§ 5.3	Disapproval of Buyer's Credit Information Deadline	
16	§ 5.4	Existing Loan Documents Deadline	
17	§ 5.4	Existing Loan Documents Objection Deadline	
18	§ 5.4	Loan Transfer Approval Deadline	
		Appraisal	
19	§ 6.2	Appraisal Deadline	
20	§ 6.2	Appraisal Objection Deadline	
		Survey	
21	§ 9.1	Current Survey Deadline	
22	§ 9.2	Current Survey Objection Deadline	
		Inspection and Due Diligence	
23	§ 10.2	Inspection Objection Deadline	
24	§ 10.3	Inspection Resolution Deadline	

CBS1-10-11. CONTRACT TO BUY AND SELL REAL ESTATE (RESIDENTIAL)   Page 2 of 15

25	§ 10.5	Property Insurance Objection Deadline		
26	§ 10.6	Due Diligence Documents Delivery Deadline		
27	§ 10.7	Due Diligence Documents Objection Deadline		
		Closing and Possession		
28	§ 12.3	**Closing Date**		
29	§ 17	Possession Date		
30	§ 17	Possession Time		
31	§ 28	**Acceptance Deadline Date**		
32	§ 28	**Acceptance Deadline Time**		

78 **Note: Applicability of Terms.**
79 Any box, blank or line in this Contract left blank or completed with the abbreviation "N/A", or the word "Deleted" means such
80 provision in **Dates and Deadlines** (§ 3), including any deadline, is not applicable and the corresponding provision of this Contract
81 to which reference is made is deleted.

82 The abbreviation "MEC" (mutual execution of this Contract) means the date upon which both parties have signed this Contract.

83 **Note:** If **FHA** or **VA** loan boxes are checked in § 4.5.3 (Loan Limitations), the **Appraisal Deadline** (§ 3) does **Not** apply to **FHA**
84 insured or **VA** guaranteed loans.

85 **4.   PURCHASE PRICE AND TERMS.**
86   **4.1.   Price and Terms.** The Purchase Price set forth below shall be payable in U.S. Dollars by Buyer as follows:

Item No.	Reference	Item	Amount	Amount
1	§ 4.1	Purchase Price	$	
2	§ 4.2	Earnest Money		$
3	§ 4.5	New Loan		
4	§ 4.6	Assumption Balance		
5	§ 4.7	Seller or Private Financing		
6				
7				
8	§ 4.3	Cash at Closing		
9		**TOTAL**	$	$

87   **4.2.   Earnest Money.** The Earnest Money set forth in this section, in the form of _____, shall be
88 payable to and held by _____ (Earnest Money Holder), in its trust account, on behalf of
89 both Seller and Buyer. The Earnest Money deposit shall be tendered with this Contract unless the parties mutually agree to an
90 **Alternative Earnest Money Deadline** (§ 3) for its payment. If Earnest Money Holder is other than the Brokerage Firm identified
91 in § 33 or § 34, Closing Instructions signed by Buyer, Seller and Earnest Money Holder must be obtained on or before delivery of
92 Earnest Money to Earnest Money Holder. The parties authorize delivery of the Earnest Money deposit to the company conducting
93 the Closing (Closing Company), if any, at or before Closing. In the event Earnest Money Holder has agreed to have interest on
94 Earnest Money deposits transferred to a fund established for the purpose of providing affordable housing to Colorado residents,
95 Seller and Buyer acknowledge and agree that any interest accruing on the Earnest Money deposited with the Earnest Money
96 Holder in this transaction shall be transferred to such fund.
97   **4.2.1.   Alternative Earnest Money Deadline.** The deadline for delivering the Earnest Money, if other than at the
98 time of tender of this Contract is as set forth as the **Alternative Earnest Money Deadline** (§ 3).
99   **4.2.2.   Return of Earnest Money.** If Buyer has a Right to Terminate and timely terminates, Buyer shall be
100 entitled to the return of Earnest Money as provided in this Contract. If this Contract is terminated as set forth in § 25 and, except as
101 provided in § 24, if the Earnest Money has not already been returned following receipt of a Notice to Terminate, Seller agrees to
102 execute and return to Buyer or Broker working with Buyer, written mutual instructions, i.e., Earnest Money Release form, within
103 three days of Seller's receipt of such form.
104   **4.3.   Form of Funds; Time of Payment; Funds Available.**
105   **4.3.1.   Good Funds.** All amounts payable by the parties at Closing, including any loan proceeds, Cash at Closing
106 and closing costs, shall be in funds that comply with all applicable Colorado laws, including electronic transfer funds, certified
107 check, savings and loan teller's check and cashier's check (Good Funds).
108   **4.3.2.   Available Funds.** All funds required to be paid at Closing or as otherwise agreed in writing between the
109 parties shall be timely paid to allow disbursement by Closing Company at Closing **OR SUCH PARTY SHALL BE IN DEFAULT.**

110 Buyer represents that Buyer, as of the date of this Contract, ☐ **Does** ☐ **Does Not** have funds that are immediately verifiable and
111 available in an amount not less than the amount stated as Cash at Closing in § 4.1.
112   **4.4.**   **Seller Concession.** Seller, at Closing, shall credit, as directed by Buyer, an amount of $_____ to assist
113 with Buyer's closing costs, loan discount points, loan origination fees, prepaid items (including any amounts that Seller agrees to
114 pay because Buyer is not allowed to pay due to FHA, CHFA, VA, etc.), and any other fee, cost, charge, expense or expenditure
115 related to Buyer's New Loan or other allowable Seller concession (collectively, Seller Concession). Seller Concession is in
116 addition to any sum Seller has agreed to pay or credit Buyer elsewhere in this Contract. Seller Concession shall be reduced to the
117 extent it exceeds the amount allowed by Buyer's lender as set forth in the Closing Statement or HUD-1, at Closing.
118   **4.5.**   **New Loan.**
119   **4.5.1.**   **Buyer to Pay Loan Costs.** Buyer, except as provided in § 4.4, if applicable, shall timely pay Buyer's loan
120 costs, loan discount points, prepaid items and loan origination fees, as required by lender.
121   **4.5.2.**   **Buyer May Select Financing.** Buyer may pay in cash or select financing appropriate and acceptable to
122 Buyer, including a different loan than initially sought, except as restricted in § 4.5.3 or § 30 (Additional Provisions).
123   **4.5.3.**   **Loan Limitations.** Buyer may purchase the Property using any of the following types of loan:
124 ☐ **Conventional** ☐ **FHA** ☐ **VA** ☐ **Bond** ☐ **Other** _____.
125   **4.5.4.**   **Good Faith Estimate – Monthly Payment and Loan Costs.** Buyer is advised to review the terms, conditions
126 and costs of Buyer's New Loan carefully. If Buyer is applying for a residential loan, the lender generally must provide Buyer with
127 a good faith estimate of Buyer's closing costs within three days after Buyer completes a loan application. Buyer should also obtain
128 an estimate of the amount of Buyer's monthly mortgage payment. If the New Loan is unsatisfactory to Buyer, Buyer shall have the
129 Right to Terminate under § 25.1, on or before **Loan Conditions Deadline** (§ 3).
130   **4.6.**   **Assumption.** Buyer agrees to assume and pay an existing loan in the approximate amount of the Assumption
131 Balance set forth in § 4.1, presently payable at $_____ per _____ including principal and interest
132 presently at the rate of _____% per annum, and also including escrow for the following as indicated: ☐ **Real Estate Taxes**
133 ☐ **Property Insurance Premium** ☐ **Mortgage Insurance Premium** and ☐ _____.
134   Buyer agrees to pay a loan transfer fee not to exceed $_____. At the time of assumption, the new interest rate shall
135 not exceed _____% per annum and the new payment shall not exceed $_____ per _____ principal and
136 interest, plus escrow, if any. If the actual principal balance of the existing loan at Closing is less than the Assumption Balance,
137 which causes the amount of cash required from Buyer at Closing to be increased by more than $_____, then Buyer shall
138 have the Right to Terminate under § 25.1, on or before **Closing Date** (§ 3), based on the reduced amount of the actual principal
139 balance.
140   Seller ☐ **Shall** ☐ **Shall Not** be released from liability on said loan. If applicable, compliance with the requirements for
141 release from liability shall be evidenced by delivery ☐ **on or before Loan Transfer Approval Deadline** (§ 3) ☐ **at Closing** of
142 an appropriate letter of commitment from lender. Any cost payable for release of liability shall be paid by _____
143 in an amount not to exceed $_____.
144   **4.7.**   **Seller or Private Financing.** Buyer agrees to execute a promissory note payable to _____,
145 as ☐ **Joint Tenants** ☐ **Tenants In Common** ☐ **Other** _____, on the note form as indicated:
146 ☐ **(Default Rate)** NTD81-10-06 ☐ **Other** _____ secured by a _____
147 (1st, 2nd, etc.) deed of trust encumbering the Property, using the form as indicated:
148 ☐ **Due on Transfer – Strict** (TD72-8-10) ☐ **Due on Transfer – Creditworthy** (TD73-8-10) ☐ **Assumable – Not Due on**
149 **Transfer** (TD74-8-10) ☐ **Other** _____.
150   The promissory note shall be amortized on the basis of _____ ☐ **Years** ☐ **Months**, payable at $_____
151 per _____ including principal and interest at the rate of _____% per annum. Payments shall commence
152 _____ and shall be due on the _____ day of each succeeding _____. If not sooner
153 paid, the balance of principal and accrued interest shall be due and payable _____ after Closing.
154 Payments ☐ **Shall** ☐ **Shall Not** be increased by _____ of estimated annual real estate taxes, and ☐ **Shall** ☐ **Shall**
155 **Not** be increased by _____ of estimated annual property insurance premium. The loan shall also contain the following
156 terms: (1) if any payment is not received within _____ days after its due date, a late charge of _____% of such payment
157 shall be due; (2) interest on lender disbursements under the deed of trust shall be _____% per annum; (3) default interest rate
158 shall be _____% per annum; (4) Buyer may prepay without a penalty except _____;
159 and (5) Buyer ☐ **Shall** ☐ **Shall Not** execute and deliver, at Closing, a Security Agreement and UCC-1 Financing Statement
160 granting the holder of the promissory note a _____ (1st, 2nd, etc.) lien on the personal property included in this sale.
161   Buyer ☐ **Shall** ☐ **Shall Not** provide a mortgagee's title insurance policy, at Buyer's expense.

162 | **TRANSACTION PROVISIONS**

163 **5. FINANCING CONDITIONS AND OBLIGATIONS.**
164   **5.1.**   **Loan Application.** If Buyer is to pay all or part of the Purchase Price by obtaining one or more new loans (New
165 Loan), or if an existing loan is not to be released at Closing, Buyer, if required by such lender, shall make an application verifiable
166 by such lender, on or before **Loan Application Deadline** (§ 3) and exercise reasonable efforts to obtain such loan or approval.
167   **5.2.**   **Loan Conditions.** If Buyer is to pay all or part of the Purchase Price with a New Loan, this Contract is conditional
168 upon Buyer determining, in Buyer's sole subjective discretion, whether the New Loan is satisfactory to Buyer, including its
169 availability, payments, interest rate, terms, conditions, and cost of such New Loan. This condition is for the benefit of Buyer.
170 Buyer shall have the Right to Terminate under § 25.1, on or before **Loan Conditions Deadline** (§ 3), if the New Loan is not
171 satisfactory to Buyer, in Buyer's sole subjective discretion. **IF SELLER DOES NOT TIMELY RECEIVE WRITTEN NOTICE**
172 **TO TERMINATE, BUYER'S EARNEST MONEY SHALL BE NONREFUNDABLE,** except as otherwise provided in this
173 Contract (e.g., Appraisal, Title, Survey).
174   **5.3.**   **Credit Information and Buyer's New Senior Loan.** If Buyer is to pay all or part of the Purchase Price by
175 executing a promissory note in favor of Seller, or if an existing loan is not to be released at Closing, this Contract is conditional
176 (for the benefit of Seller) upon Seller's approval of Buyer's financial ability and creditworthiness, which approval shall be at
177 Seller's sole subjective discretion. In such case: (1) Buyer shall supply to Seller by **Buyer's Credit Information Deadline** (§ 3),
178 at Buyer's expense, information and documents (including a current credit report) concerning Buyer's financial, employment and
179 credit condition and Buyer's New Senior Loan, defined below, if any; (2) Buyer consents that Seller may verify Buyer's financial
180 ability and creditworthiness; (3) any such information and documents received by Seller shall be held by Seller in confidence, and
181 not released to others except to protect Seller's interest in this transaction; and (4) in the event Buyer is to execute a promissory
182 note secured by a deed of trust in favor of Seller, this Contract is conditional (for the benefit of Seller) upon Seller's approval of
183 the terms and conditions of any New Loan to be obtained by Buyer if the deed of trust to Seller is to be subordinate to Buyer's
184 New Loan (Buyer's New Senior Loan). If the Cash at Closing is less than as set forth in § 4.1 of this Contract or Buyer's New
185 Senior Loan changes from that approved by Seller, Seller shall have the Right to Terminate under § 25.1, at or before Closing. If
186 Seller disapproves of Buyer's financial ability, creditworthiness or Buyer's New Senior Loan, in Seller's sole subjective discretion,
187 Seller shall have the Right to Terminate under § 25.1, on or before **Disapproval of Buyer's Credit Information Deadline** (§ 3).
188   **5.4.**   **Existing Loan Review.** If an existing loan is not to be released at Closing, Seller shall deliver copies of the loan
189 documents (including note, deed of trust, and any modifications) to Buyer by **Existing Loan Documents Deadline** (§ 3). For the
190 benefit of Buyer, this Contract is conditional upon Buyer's review and approval of the provisions of such loan documents. Buyer
191 shall have the Right to Terminate under § 25.1, on or before **Existing Loan Documents Objection Deadline** (§ 3), based on any
192 unsatisfactory provision of such loan documents, in Buyer's sole subjective discretion. If the lender's approval of a transfer of the
193 Property is required, this Contract is conditional upon Buyer's obtaining such approval without change in the terms of such loan,
194 except as set forth in § 4.6. If lender's approval is not obtained by **Loan Transfer Approval Deadline** (§ 3), this Contract shall
195 terminate on such deadline. Seller shall have the Right to Terminate under § 25.1, on or before Closing, in Seller's sole subjective
196 discretion, if Seller is to be released from liability under such existing loan and Buyer does not obtain such compliance as set forth
197 in § 4.6.

198 **6. APPRAISAL PROVISIONS.**
199   **6.1.**   **Lender Property Requirements.** If the lender imposes any requirements or repairs (Requirements) to be made to
200 the Property (e.g., roof repair, repainting), beyond those matters already agreed to by Seller in this Contract, Seller shall have the
201 Right to Terminate under § 25.1, (notwithstanding § 10 of this Contract), on or before three days following Seller's receipt of
202 Requirements, based on any unsatisfactory Requirements, in Seller's sole subjective discretion. Seller's Right to Terminate in this
203 § 6.1 shall not apply if, on or before any termination by Seller pursuant to this § 6.1: (1) the parties enter into a written agreement
204 regarding the Requirements; or (2) the Requirements have been completed; or (3) the satisfaction of the Requirements is waived in
205 writing by Buyer.
206   **6.2.**   **Appraisal Condition.** The applicable Appraisal provision set forth below shall apply to the respective loan type set
207 forth in § 4.5.3, or if a cash transaction, i.e. no financing, § 6.2.1 shall apply.
208   **6.2.1.**   **Conventional/Other.** Buyer shall have the sole option and election to terminate this Contract if the
209 Property's valuation is less than the Purchase Price determined by an appraiser engaged on behalf of _____.
210 The appraisal shall be received by Buyer or Buyer's lender on or before **Appraisal Deadline** (§ 3). Buyer shall have the Right to
211 Terminate under § 25.1, on or before **Appraisal Objection Deadline** (§ 3), if the Property's valuation is less than the Purchase
212 Price and Seller's receipt of either a copy of such appraisal or written notice from lender that confirms the Property's valuation is
213 less than the Purchase Price.
214   **6.2.2.**   **FHA.** It is expressly agreed that, notwithstanding any other provisions of this Contract, the Purchaser
215 (Buyer) shall not be obligated to complete the purchase of the Property described herein or to incur any penalty by forfeiture of
216 Earnest Money deposits or otherwise unless the Purchaser (Buyer) has been given in accordance with HUD/FHA or VA
217 requirements a written statement issued by the Federal Housing Commissioner, Department of Veterans Affairs, or a Direct

218   Endorsement lender, setting forth the appraised value of the Property of not less than $_____. The Purchaser (Buyer)
219   shall have the privilege and option of proceeding with the consummation of this Contract without regard to the amount of the
220   appraised valuation. The appraised valuation is arrived at to determine the maximum mortgage the Department of Housing and
221   Urban Development will insure. HUD does not warrant the value nor the condition of the Property. The Purchaser (Buyer) should
222   satisfy himself/herself that the price and condition of the Property are acceptable.
223   **6.2.3.**   **VA.** It is expressly agreed that, notwithstanding any other provisions of this Contract, the purchaser (Buyer)
224   shall not incur any penalty by forfeiture of Earnest Money or otherwise or be obligated to complete the purchase of the Property
225   described herein, if the Contract Purchase Price or cost exceeds the reasonable value of the Property established by the Department
226   of Veterans Affairs. The purchaser (Buyer) shall, however, have the privilege and option of proceeding with the consummation of
227   this Contract without regard to the amount of the reasonable value established by the Department of Veterans Affairs.
228   **6.3.**   **Cost of Appraisal.** Cost of any appraisal to be obtained after the date of this Contract shall be timely paid by
229   ☐ **Buyer** ☐ **Seller**.

230   **7.**   **EVIDENCE OF TITLE AND ASSOCIATION DOCUMENTS.**
231   **7.1.**   **Evidence of Title.** On or before **Record Title Deadline** (§ 3), Seller shall cause to be furnished to Buyer, at Seller's
232   expense, a current commitment for owner's title insurance policy (Title Commitment) in an amount equal to the Purchase Price, or
233   if this box is checked, ☐ **An Abstract** of title certified to a current date. If title insurance is furnished, Seller shall also deliver to
234   Buyer copies of any abstracts of title covering all or any portion of the Property (Abstract) in Seller's possession. At Seller's
235   expense, Seller shall cause the title insurance policy to be issued and delivered to Buyer as soon as practicable at or after Closing.
236   The title insurance commitment ☐ **Shall** ☐ **Shall Not** commit to delete or insure over the standard exceptions which relate to:
237   (1) parties in possession, (2) unrecorded easements, (3) survey matters, (4) unrecorded mechanics' liens, (5) gap period (effective
238   date of commitment to date deed is recorded), and (6) unpaid taxes, assessments and unredeemed tax sales prior to the year of
239   Closing. Any additional premium expense to obtain this additional coverage shall be paid by ☐ **Buyer** ☐ **Seller**.
240   **Note:** The title insurance company may not agree to delete or insure over any or all of the standard exceptions. Buyer shall have
241   the right to review the Title Commitment, its provisions and Title Documents (defined in § 7.2), and if not satisfactory to Buyer,
242   Buyer may exercise Buyer's rights pursuant to § 8.1.
243   **7.2.**   **Copies of Exceptions.** On or before **Record Title Deadline** (§ 3), Seller, at Seller's expense, shall furnish to Buyer
244   and _____, (1) copies of any plats, declarations, covenants, conditions and restrictions burdening
245   the Property, and (2) if a Title Commitment is required to be furnished, and if this box is checked ☐ **Copies of any Other**
246   **Documents** (or, if illegible, summaries of such documents) listed in the schedule of exceptions (Exceptions). Even if the box is not
247   checked, Seller shall have the obligation to furnish these documents pursuant to this section if requested by Buyer any time on or
248   before **Exceptions Request Deadline** (§ 3). This requirement shall pertain only to documents as shown of record in the office of
249   the clerk and recorder in the county where the Property is located. The Abstract or Title Commitment, together with any copies or
250   summaries of such documents furnished pursuant to this section, constitute the title documents (collectively, Title Documents).
251   **7.3.**   **Homeowners' Association Documents.** The term Association Documents consists of all owners' associations
252   (Association) declarations, bylaws, operating agreements, rules and regulations, party wall agreements, minutes of most recent
253   annual owners' meeting and minutes of any directors' or managers' meetings during the six-month period immediately preceding
254   the date of this Contract, if any (Governing Documents), most recent financial documents consisting of (1) annual balance sheet,
255   (2) annual income and expenditures statement, and (3) annual budget (Financial Documents), if any (collectively, Association
256   Documents).
257   **7.3.1.**   **Common Interest Community Disclosure. THE PROPERTY IS LOCATED WITHIN A COMMON**
258   **INTEREST COMMUNITY AND IS SUBJECT TO THE DECLARATION FOR SUCH COMMUNITY. THE OWNER**
259   **OF THE PROPERTY WILL BE REQUIRED TO BE A MEMBER OF THE OWNER'S ASSOCIATION FOR THE**
260   **COMMUNITY AND WILL BE SUBJECT TO THE BYLAWS AND RULES AND REGULATIONS OF THE**
261   **ASSOCIATION. THE DECLARATION, BYLAWS, AND RULES AND REGULATIONS WILL IMPOSE FINANCIAL**
262   **OBLIGATIONS UPON THE OWNER OF THE PROPERTY, INCLUDING AN OBLIGATION TO PAY**
263   **ASSESSMENTS OF THE ASSOCIATION. IF THE OWNER DOES NOT PAY THESE ASSESSMENTS, THE**
264   **ASSOCIATION COULD PLACE A LIEN ON THE PROPERTY AND POSSIBLY SELL IT TO PAY THE DEBT. THE**
265   **DECLARATION, BYLAWS, AND RULES AND REGULATIONS OF THE COMMUNITY MAY PROHIBIT THE**
266   **OWNER FROM MAKING CHANGES TO THE PROPERTY WITHOUT AN ARCHITECTURAL REVIEW BY THE**
267   **ASSOCIATION (OR A COMMITTEE OF THE ASSOCIATION) AND THE APPROVAL OF THE ASSOCIATION.**
268   **PURCHASERS OF PROPERTY WITHIN THE COMMON INTEREST COMMUNITY SHOULD INVESTIGATE THE**
269   **FINANCIAL OBLIGATIONS OF MEMBERS OF THE ASSOCIATION. PURCHASERS SHOULD CAREFULLY**
270   **READ THE DECLARATION FOR THE COMMUNITY AND THE BYLAWS AND RULES AND REGULATIONS OF**
271   **THE ASSOCIATION.**
272   **7.3.2.**   **Association Documents to Buyer.**
273   ☐   **7.3.2.1. Seller to Provide Association Documents.** Seller shall cause the Association Documents to be
274   provided to Buyer, at Seller's expense, on or before **Association Documents Deadline** (§ 3).

---

275   ☐   **7.3.2.2. Seller Authorizes Association.** Seller authorizes the Association to provide the Association
276   Documents to Buyer, at Seller's expense.
277   **7.3.2.3. Seller's Obligation.** Seller's obligation to provide the Association Documents shall be fulfilled
278   upon Buyer's receipt of the Association Documents, regardless of who provides such documents.
279   **Note:** If neither box in this § 7.3.2 is checked, the provisions of § 7.3.2.1 shall apply.
280   **7.3.3.   Conditional on Buyer's Review.** If the box in either § 7.3.2.1 or § 7.3.2.2 is checked, the provisions of this
281   § 7.3.3 shall apply. Buyer shall have the Right to Terminate under § 25.1, on or before **Association Documents Objection**
282   **Deadline** (§ 3), based on any unsatisfactory provision in any of the Association Documents, in Buyer's sole subjective discretion.
283   Should Buyer receive the Association Documents after **Association Documents Deadline** (§ 3), Buyer, at Buyer's option, shall
284   have the Right to Terminate under § 25.1 by Buyer's Notice to Terminate received by Seller on or before ten days after Buyer's
285   receipt of the Association Documents. If Buyer does not receive the Association Documents, or if Buyer's Notice to Terminate
286   would otherwise be required to be received by Seller after **Closing Date** (§ 3), Buyer's Notice to Terminate shall be received by
287   Seller on or before three days prior to **Closing Date** (§ 3). If Seller does not receive Buyer's Notice to Terminate within such time,
288   Buyer accepts the provisions of the Association Documents as satisfactory, and Buyer waives any Right to Terminate under this
289   provision, notwithstanding the provisions of § 8.5.

290   **8.   RECORD TITLE AND OFF-RECORD TITLE MATTERS.**
291   **8.1.   Record Title Matters.** Buyer has the right to review and object to any of the Title Documents (Right to Object,
292   Resolution) as set forth in § 8.3. Buyer's objection may be based on any unsatisfactory form or content of Title Commitment,
293   notwithstanding § 13, or any other unsatisfactory title condition, in Buyer's sole subjective discretion. If Buyer objects to any of
294   the Title Documents, Buyer shall cause Seller to receive Buyer's Notice to Terminate or Notice of Title Objection on or before
295   **Record Title Objection Deadline** (§ 3). If Title Documents are not received by Buyer, on or before the **Record Title Deadline**
296   (§ 3), or if there is an endorsement to the Title Commitment that adds a new Exception to title, a copy of the new Exception to title
297   and the modified Title Commitment shall be delivered to Buyer. Buyer shall cause Seller to receive Buyer's Notice to Terminate
298   or Notice of Title Objection on or before ten days after receipt by Buyer of the following documents: (1) any required Title
299   Document not timely received by Buyer, (2) any change to the Title Documents, or (3) endorsement to the Title Commitment. If
300   Seller receives Buyer's Notice to Terminate or Notice of Title Objection, pursuant to this § 8.1 (Record Title Matters), any title
301   objection by Buyer and this Contract shall be governed by the provisions set forth in § 8.3 (Right to Object, Resolution). If Seller
302   does not receive Buyer's Notice to Terminate or Notice of Title Objection by the applicable deadline specified above, Buyer
303   accepts the condition of title as disclosed by the Title Documents as satisfactory.
304   **8.2.   Off-Record Title Matters.** Seller shall deliver to Buyer, on or before **Off-Record Title Deadline** (§ 3), true copies
305   of all existing surveys in Seller's possession pertaining to the Property and shall disclose to Buyer all easements, liens (including,
306   without limitation, governmental improvements approved, but not yet installed) or other title matters (including, without
307   limitation, rights of first refusal and options) not shown by public records, of which Seller has actual knowledge. Buyer shall have
308   the right to inspect the Property to investigate if any third party has any right in the Property not shown by public records (such as
309   an unrecorded easement, unrecorded lease, boundary line discrepancy or water rights). Buyer's Notice to Terminate or Notice of
310   Title Objection of any unsatisfactory condition (whether disclosed by Seller or revealed by such inspection, notwithstanding § 13),
311   in Buyer's sole subjective discretion, shall be received by Seller on or before **Off-Record Title Objection Deadline** (§ 3). If Seller
312   receives Buyer's Notice to Terminate or Notice of Title Objection pursuant to this § 8.2 (Off-Record Title Matters), any title
313   objection by Buyer and this Contract shall be governed by the provisions set forth in § 8.3 (Right to Object, Resolution). If Seller
314   does not receive Buyer's Notice to Terminate or Notice of Title Objection, on or before **Off-Record Title Objection Deadline**
315   (§ 3), Buyer accepts title subject to such rights, if any, of third parties of which Buyer has actual knowledge.
316   **8.3.   Right to Object, Resolution.** Buyer's right to object to any title matters shall include, but not be limited to those
317   matters set forth in §§ 8.1 (Record Title Matters), 8.2 (Off-Record Title Matters) and 13 (Transfer of Title), in Buyer's sole
318   subjective discretion (collectively, Notice of Title Objection). If Buyer objects to any title matter, on or before the applicable
319   deadline, Buyer shall have the choice to either (1) object to the condition of title, or (2) terminate this Contract.
320   **8.3.1.   Title Resolution.** If Seller receives Buyer's Notice of Title Objection, as provided in § 8.1 (Record Title
321   Matters) or § 8.2 (Off-Record Title Matters), on or before the applicable deadline, and if Buyer and Seller have not agreed to a
322   written settlement thereof on or before **Title Resolution Deadline** (§ 3), this Contract shall terminate on the expiration of **Title**
323   **Resolution Deadline** (§ 3), unless Seller receives Buyer's written withdrawal of Buyer's Notice of Title Objection (i.e., Buyer's
324   written notice to waive objection to such items and waives the Right to Terminate for that reason), on or before expiration of **Title**
325   **Resolution Deadline** (§ 3).
326   **8.3.2.   Right to Terminate – Title Objection.** Buyer shall have the Right to Terminate under § 25.1, on or before
327   the applicable deadline, based on any unsatisfactory title matter, in Buyer's sole subjective discretion.
328   **8.4.   Special Taxing Districts.** **SPECIAL TAXING DISTRICTS MAY BE SUBJECT TO GENERAL OBLIGATION**
329   **INDEBTEDNESS THAT IS PAID BY REVENUES PRODUCED FROM ANNUAL TAX LEVIES ON THE TAXABLE**
330   **PROPERTY WITHIN SUCH DISTRICTS. PROPERTY OWNERS IN SUCH DISTRICTS MAY BE PLACED AT RISK**
331   **FOR INCREASED MILL LEVIES AND TAX TO SUPPORT THE SERVICING OF SUCH DEBT WHERE**
332   **CIRCUMSTANCES ARISE RESULTING IN THE INABILITY OF SUCH A DISTRICT TO DISCHARGE SUCH**

333 INDEBTEDNESS WITHOUT SUCH AN INCREASE IN MILL LEVIES. BUYERS SHOULD INVESTIGATE THE
334 SPECIAL TAXING DISTRICTS IN WHICH THE PROPERTY IS LOCATED BY CONTACTING THE COUNTY
335 TREASURER, BY REVIEWING THE CERTIFICATE OF TAXES DUE FOR THE PROPERTY, AND BY OBTAINING
336 FURTHER INFORMATION FROM THE BOARD OF COUNTY COMMISSIONERS, THE COUNTY CLERK AND
337 RECORDER, OR THE COUNTY ASSESSOR.
338   Buyer shall have the Right to Terminate under § 25.1, on or before **Off-Record Title Objection Deadline** (§ 3), based on
339 any unsatisfactory effect of the Property being located within a special taxing district, in Buyer's sole subjective discretion.
340   **8.5.**   **Right of First Refusal or Contract Approval.** If there is a right of first refusal on the Property, or a right to
341 approve this Contract, Seller shall promptly submit this Contract according to the terms and conditions of such right. If the holder
342 of the right of first refusal exercises such right or the holder of a right to approve disapproves this Contract, this Contract shall
343 terminate. If the right of first refusal is waived explicitly or expires, or the Contract is approved, this Contract shall remain in full
344 force and effect. Seller shall promptly notify Buyer in writing of the foregoing. If expiration or waiver of the right of first refusal
345 or Contract approval has not occurred on or before **Right of First Refusal Deadline** (§ 3), this Contract shall then terminate.
346   **8.6.**   **Title Advisory.** The Title Documents affect the title, ownership and use of the Property and should be reviewed
347 carefully. Additionally, other matters not reflected in the Title Documents may affect the title, ownership and use of the Property,
348 including, without limitation, boundary lines and encroachments, area, zoning, unrecorded easements and claims of easements,
349 leases and other unrecorded agreements, and various laws and governmental regulations concerning land use, development and
350 environmental matters. **The surface estate may be owned separately from the underlying mineral estate, and transfer of the**
351 **surface estate does not necessarily include transfer of the mineral rights or water rights. Third parties may hold interests in**
352 **oil, gas, other minerals, geothermal energy or water on or under the Property, which interests may give them rights to**
353 **enter and use the Property.** Such matters may be excluded from or not covered by the title insurance policy. Buyer is advised to
354 timely consult legal counsel with respect to all such matters as there are strict time limits provided in this Contract [e.g., **Record**
355 **Title Objection Deadline** (§ 3) and **Off-Record Title Objection Deadline** (§ 3)].

356 **9.   CURRENT SURVEY REVIEW.**
357   **9.1.**   **Current Survey Conditions.** If the box in § 9.1.1 or § 9.1.2 is checked, Buyer, the issuer of the Title Commitment
358 or the provider of the opinion of title if an abstract, and _____ shall receive a Current Survey, i.e.,
359 Improvement Location Certificate, Improvement Survey Plat or other form of survey set forth in § 9.1.2 (collectively, Current
360 Survey), on or before **Current Survey Deadline** (§ 3). The Current Survey shall be certified by the surveyor to all those who are
361 to receive the Current Survey.
362   ☐   **9.1.1.**   **Improvement Location Certificate.** If the box in this § 9.1.1 is checked, ☐ **Seller** ☐ **Buyer** shall order
363 or provide, and pay, on or before Closing, the cost of an **Improvement Location Certificate**.
364   ☐   **9.1.2.**   **Other Survey.** If the box in this § 9.1.2 is checked, a Current Survey, other than an Improvement Location
365 Certificate, shall be an ☐ **Improvement Survey Plat** ☐ _____. The parties agree that payment of the cost of
366 the Current Survey and obligation to order or provide the Current Survey shall be as follows:
367
368
369
370   **9.2.**   **Survey Objection.** Buyer shall have the right to review and object to the Current Survey. Buyer shall have the Right
371 to Terminate under § 25.1, on or before the **Current Survey Objection Deadline** (§ 3), if the Current Survey is not timely
372 received by Buyer or based on any unsatisfactory matter with the Current Survey, notwithstanding § 8.2 or § 13.

373 | DISCLOSURE, INSPECTION AND DUE DILIGENCE |
---

374 **10.   PROPERTY DISCLOSURE, INSPECTION, INDEMNITY, INSURABILITY, DUE DILIGENCE, BUYER**
375 **DISCLOSURE AND SOURCE OF WATER.**
376   **10.1.**   **Seller's Property Disclosure Deadline.** On or before **Seller's Property Disclosure Deadline** (§ 3), Seller agrees to
377 deliver to Buyer the most current version of the applicable Colorado Real Estate Commission's Seller's Property Disclosure form
378 completed by Seller to Seller's actual knowledge, current as of the date of this Contract.
379   **10.2.**   **Inspection Objection Deadline.** Unless otherwise provided in this Contract, Buyer acknowledges that Seller is
380 conveying the Property to Buyer in an "as is" condition, "where is" and "with all faults". Seller shall disclose to Buyer, in writing,
381 any latent defects actually known by Seller. Buyer, acting in good faith, shall have the right to have inspections (by one or more
382 third parties, personally or both) of the Property and Inclusions (Inspection), at Buyer's expense. If (1) the physical condition of
383 the Property, including, but not limited to, the roof, walls, structural integrity of the Property, the electrical, plumbing, HVAC and
384 other mechanical systems of the Property, (2) the physical condition of the Inclusions, (3) service to the Property (including
385 utilities and communication services), systems and components of the Property, e.g. heating and plumbing, (4) any proposed or
386 existing transportation project, road, street or highway, or (5) any other activity, odor or noise (whether on or off the Property) and

---

387 its effect or expected effect on the Property or its occupants is unsatisfactory, in Buyer's sole subjective discretion, Buyer shall, on
388 or before **Inspection Objection Deadline** (§ 3):
389   **10.2.1.   Notice to Terminate.** Notify Seller in writing that this Contract is terminated; or
390   **10.2.2.   Inspection Objection.** Deliver to Seller a written description of any unsatisfactory physical condition that
391 Buyer requires Seller to correct.
392   Buyer shall have the Right to Terminate under § 25.1, on or before **Inspection Objection Deadline** (§ 3), based on any
393 unsatisfactory physical condition of the Property or Inclusions, in Buyer's sole subjective discretion.
394   **10.3.   Inspection Resolution Deadline.** If an Inspection Objection is received by Seller, on or before **Inspection**
395 **Objection Deadline** (§ 3), and if Buyer and Seller have not agreed in writing to a settlement thereof on or before **Inspection**
396 **Resolution Deadline** (§ 3), this Contract shall terminate on **Inspection Resolution Deadline** (§ 3), unless Seller receives Buyer's
397 written withdrawal of the Inspection Objection before such termination, i.e., on or before expiration of **Inspection Resolution**
398 **Deadline** (§ 3).
399   **10.4.   Damage, Liens and Indemnity.** Buyer, except as otherwise provided in this Contract or other written agreement
400 between the parties, is responsible for payment for all inspections, tests, surveys, engineering reports, or any other work performed
401 at Buyer's request (Work) and shall pay for any damage that occurs to the Property and Inclusions as a result of such Work. Buyer
402 shall not permit claims or liens of any kind against the Property for Work performed on the Property at Buyer's request. Buyer
403 agrees to indemnify, protect and hold Seller harmless from and against any liability, damage, cost or expense incurred by Seller
404 and caused by any such Work, claim, or lien. This indemnity includes Seller's right to recover all costs and expenses incurred by
405 Seller to defend against any such liability, damage, cost or expense, or to enforce this section, including Seller's reasonable
406 attorney fees, legal fees and expenses. The provisions of this section shall survive the termination of this Contract.
407   **10.5.   Insurability.** Buyer shall have the right to review and object to the availability, terms and conditions of and
408 premium for property insurance (Property Insurance). Buyer shall have the Right to Terminate under § 25.1, on or before **Property**
409 **Insurance Objection Deadline** (§ 3), based on any unsatisfactory provision of the Property Insurance, in Buyer's sole subjective
410 discretion.
411   **10.6.   Due Diligence Documents.** Seller agrees to deliver copies of the following documents and information pertaining to
412 the Property (Due Diligence Documents) to Buyer on or before **Due Diligence Documents Delivery Deadline** (§ 3) to the extent
413 such Due Diligence Documents exist and are in Seller's possession:
414   **10.6.1.** All current leases, including any amendments or other occupancy agreements, pertaining to the Property
415 (Leases).
416   **10.6.2.** Other documents and information:
417
418
419
420
421
422   **10.7.   Due Diligence Documents Conditions.** Buyer shall have the right to review and object to Due Diligence Documents,
423 in Buyer's sole subjective discretion, or Seller's failure to deliver to Buyer all Due Diligence Documents. Buyer shall also have the
424 unilateral right to waive any condition herein.
425   **10.7.1.   Due Diligence Documents Objection.** Buyer shall have the Right to Terminate under § 25.1, on or before
426 **Due Diligence Documents Objection Deadline** (§ 3), based on any unsatisfactory matter with the Due Diligence Documents, in
427 Buyer's sole subjective discretion. If, however, Due Diligence Documents are not timely delivered under § 10.6, or if Seller fails
428 to deliver all Due Diligence Documents to Buyer, then Buyer shall have the Right to Terminate under § 25.1 on or before the
429 earlier of ten days after **Due Diligence Documents Objection Deadline** (§ 3) or Closing.
430   **10.8.   Buyer Disclosure.** Buyer represents that Buyer ☐ **Does** ☐ **Does Not** need to sell and close a property to complete
431 this transaction.
432 **Note:** Any property sale contingency should appear in **Additional Provisions** (§ 30).
433   **10.9.   Source of Potable Water (Residential Land and Residential Improvements Only).** Buyer ☐ **Does** ☐ **Does Not**
434 acknowledge receipt of a copy of Seller's Property Disclosure or Source of Water Addendum disclosing the source of potable water
435 for the Property. Buyer ☐ **Does** ☐ **Does Not** acknowledge receipt of a copy of the current well permit. ☐ There is **No Well.**
436 **Note to Buyer: SOME WATER PROVIDERS RELY, TO VARYING DEGREES, ON NONRENEWABLE GROUND**
437 **WATER. YOU MAY WISH TO CONTACT YOUR PROVIDER (OR INVESTIGATE THE DESCRIBED SOURCE) TO**
438 **DETERMINE THE LONG-TERM SUFFICIENCY OF THE PROVIDER'S WATER SUPPLIES.**
439   **10.10.   Carbon Monoxide Alarms. Note:** If the improvements on the Property have a fuel-fired heater or appliance, a
440 fireplace, or an attached garage and include one or more rooms lawfully used for sleeping purposes (Bedroom), the parties
441 acknowledge that Colorado law requires that Seller assure the Property has an operational carbon monoxide alarm installed within
442 fifteen feet of the entrance to each Bedroom or in a location as required by the applicable building code.
443   **10.11.   Lead-Based Paint.** Unless exempt, if the improvements on the Property include one or more residential dwellings
444 for which a building permit was issued prior to January 1, 1978, this Contract shall be void unless (1) a completed Lead-Based
445 Paint Disclosure (Sales) form is signed by Seller, the required real estate licensees and Buyer, and (2) Seller receives the

446 completed and fully executed form prior to the time when this Contract is signed by all parties. Buyer acknowledges timely receipt
447 of a completed Lead-Based Paint Disclosure (Sales) form signed by Seller and the real estate licensees.
448   **10.12. Methamphetamine Disclosure.** If Seller knows that methamphetamine was ever manufactured, processed, cooked,
449 disposed of, used or stored at the Property, Seller is required to disclose such fact. No disclosure is required if the Property was
450 remediated in accordance with state standards and other requirements are fulfilled pursuant to § 25-18.5-102, C.R.S. Buyer further
451 acknowledges that Buyer has the right to engage a certified hygienist or industrial hygienist to test whether the Property has ever
452 been used as a methamphetamine laboratory. Buyer shall have the Right to Terminate under § 25.1, upon Seller's receipt of
453 Buyer's written notice to terminate, notwithstanding any other provision of this Contract, based on Buyer's test results that indicate
454 the Property has been contaminated with methamphetamine, but has not been remediated to meet the standards established by rules
455 of the State Board of Health promulgated pursuant to § 25-18.5-102, C.R.S. Buyer shall promptly give written notice to Seller of
456 the results of the test.

457 **11. COLORADO FORECLOSURE PROTECTION ACT.** The Colorado Foreclosure Protection Act (Act) generally applies
458 if: (1) the Property is residential, (2) Seller resides in the Property as Seller's principal residence, (3) Buyer's purpose in purchase
459 of the Property is not to use the Property as Buyer's personal residence, and (4) the Property is in foreclosure or Buyer has notice
460 that any loan secured by the Property is at least thirty days delinquent or in default. If the transaction is a Short Sale transaction
461 and a Short Sale Addendum is part of this Contract, the Act does not apply. Each party is further advised to consult an attorney.

462   **CLOSING PROVISIONS**

463 **12. CLOSING DOCUMENTS, INSTRUCTIONS AND CLOSING.**
464   **12.1. Closing Documents and Closing Information.** Seller and Buyer shall cooperate with the Closing Company to
465 enable the Closing Company to prepare and deliver documents required for Closing to Buyer and Seller and their designees. If
466 Buyer is obtaining a new loan to purchase the Property, Buyer acknowledges Buyer's lender shall be required to provide the
467 Closing Company in a timely manner all required loan documents and financial information concerning Buyer's new loan. Buyer
468 and Seller will furnish any additional information and documents required by Closing Company that will be necessary to complete
469 this transaction. Buyer and Seller shall sign and complete all customary or reasonably required documents at or before Closing.
470   **12.2. Closing Instructions.** Buyer and Seller agree to execute the Colorado Real Estate Commission's Closing Instructions.
471 Such Closing Instructions ☐ **Are** ☐ **Are Not** executed with this Contract. Upon mutual execution, ☐ **Seller** ☐ **Buyer** shall
472 deliver such Closing Instructions to the Closing Company.
473   **12.3. Closing.** Delivery of deed from Seller to Buyer shall be at closing (Closing). Closing shall be on the date specified
474 as the **Closing Date** (§ 3) or by mutual agreement at an earlier date. The hour and place of Closing shall be as designated
475 by_____.
476   **12.4. Disclosure of Settlement Costs.** Buyer and Seller acknowledge that costs, quality, and extent of service vary
477 between different settlement service providers (e.g., attorneys, lenders, inspectors and title companies).

478 **13. TRANSFER OF TITLE.** Subject to tender of payment at Closing as required herein and compliance by Buyer with the
479 other terms and provisions hereof, Seller shall execute and deliver a good and sufficient _____ deed
480 to Buyer, at Closing, conveying the Property free and clear of all taxes except the general taxes for the year of Closing. Except as
481 provided herein, title shall be conveyed free and clear of all liens, including any governmental liens for special improvements
482 installed as of the date of Buyer's signature hereon, whether assessed or not. Title shall be conveyed subject to:
483   **13.1.** Those specific Exceptions described by reference to recorded documents as reflected in the Title Documents
484 accepted by Buyer in accordance with **Record Title Matters** (§ 8.1),
485   **13.2.** Distribution utility easements (including cable TV),
486   **13.3.** Those specifically described rights of third parties not shown by the public records of which Buyer has actual
487 knowledge and which were accepted by Buyer in accordance with **Off-Record Title Matters** (§ 8.2) and **Current Survey Review**
488 (§ 9),
489   **13.4.** Inclusion of the Property within any special taxing district, and
490   **13.5.** Other_____.

491 **14. PAYMENT OF ENCUMBRANCES.** Any encumbrance required to be paid shall be paid at or before Closing from the
492 proceeds of this transaction or from any other source.

493 **15. CLOSING COSTS, CLOSING FEE, ASSOCIATION FEES AND TAXES.**
494   **15.1. Closing Costs.** Buyer and Seller shall pay, in Good Funds, their respective closing costs and all other items required
495 to be paid at Closing, except as otherwise provided herein.
496   **15.2. Closing Services Fee.** The fee for real estate closing services shall be paid at Closing by ☐ **Buyer** ☐ **Seller**
497 ☐ **One-Half by Buyer and One-Half by Seller** ☐ **Other**_____.

498   **15.3. Status Letter and Transfer Fees.** Any fees incident to the issuance of Association's statement of assessments
499 (Status Letter) shall be paid by ☐ **Buyer** ☐ **Seller** ☐ **One-Half by Buyer and One-Half by Seller** ☐ **None**. Any transfer
500 fees assessed by the Association including, but not limited to, any record change fee, regardless of name or title of such fee
501 (Association's Transfer Fee) shall be paid by ☐ **Buyer** ☐ **Seller** ☐ **One-Half by Buyer and One-Half by Seller** ☐ **None**.
502   **15.4. Local Transfer Tax.** ☐ **The Local Transfer Tax** of _____ % of the Purchase Price shall be paid at Closing by
503 ☐ **Buyer** ☐ **Seller** ☐ **One-Half by Buyer and One-Half by Seller** ☐ **None**.
504   **15.5. Private Transfer Fee.** Private transfer fees and other fees due to a transfer of the Property, payable at Closing, such
505 as community association fees, developer fees and foundation fees, shall be paid at Closing by ☐ **Buyer** ☐ **Seller** ☐ **One-Half**
506 **by Buyer and One-Half by Seller** ☐ **None**.
507   **15.6. Sales and Use Tax.** Any sales and use tax that may accrue because of this transaction shall be paid when due by
508 ☐ **Buyer** ☐ **Seller** ☐ **One-Half by Buyer and One-Half by Seller** ☐ **None**.

509 **16. PRORATIONS.** The following shall be prorated to **Closing Date** (§ 3), except as otherwise provided:
510   **16.1. Taxes.** Personal property taxes, if any, special taxing district assessments, if any, and general real estate taxes for the
511 year of Closing, based on ☐ **Taxes for the Calendar Year Immediately Preceding Closing** ☐ **Most Recent Mill Levy and**
512 **Most Recent Assessed Valuation**, adjusted by any applicable qualifying seniors property tax exemption, or ☐ **Other** _____.
513   **16.2. Rents.** Rents based on ☐ **Rents Actually Received** ☐ **Accrued**. At Closing, Seller shall transfer or credit to
514 Buyer the security deposits for all Leases assigned, or any remainder after lawful deductions, and notify all tenants in writing of
515 such transfer and of the transferee's name and address. Seller shall assign to Buyer all Leases in effect at Closing and Buyer shall
516 assume Seller's obligations under such Leases.
517   **16.3. Association Assessments.** Current regular Association assessments and dues (Association Assessments) paid in
518 advance shall be credited to Seller at Closing. Cash reserves held out of the regular Association Assessments for deferred
519 maintenance by the Association shall not be credited to Seller except as may be otherwise provided by the Governing Documents.
520 Buyer acknowledges that Buyer may be obligated to pay the Association, at Closing, an amount for reserves or working capital.
521 Any special assessment assessed prior to **Closing Date** (§ 3) by the Association shall be the obligation of ☐ **Buyer** ☐ **Seller**.
522 Except however, any special assessment by the Association for improvements that have been installed as of the date of Buyer's
523 signature hereon, whether assessed prior to or after Closing, shall be the obligation of Seller. Seller represents that the Association
524 Assessments are currently payable at $_____ per _____ and that there are no unpaid regular or special
525 assessments against the Property except the current regular assessments and _____. Such
526 assessments are subject to change as provided in the Governing Documents. Seller agrees to promptly request the Association to
527 deliver to Buyer before **Closing Date** (§ 3) a current Status Letter.
528   **16.4. Other Prorations.** Water and sewer charges, interest on continuing loan, and _____.
529   **16.5. Final Settlement.** Unless otherwise agreed in writing, these prorations shall be final.

530 **17. POSSESSION.** Possession of the Property shall be delivered to Buyer on **Possession Date** (§ 3) at **Possession Time** (§ 3),
531 subject to the following Leases or tenancies:
532
533
534   If Seller, after Closing, fails to deliver possession as specified, Seller shall be subject to eviction and shall be additionally
535 liable to Buyer for payment of $_____ per day (or any part of a day notwithstanding § 18.1) from **Possession Date**
536 (§ 3) and **Possession Time** (§ 3) until possession is delivered.
537   Buyer ☐ **Does** ☐ **Does Not** represent that Buyer will occupy the Property as Buyer's principal residence.

538 | **GENERAL PROVISIONS** |

539 **18. DAY; COMPUTATION OF PERIOD OF DAYS, DEADLINE.**
540   **18.1. Day.** As used in this Contract, the term "day" shall mean the entire day ending at 11:59 p.m., United States
541 Mountain Time (Standard or Daylight Savings as applicable).
542   **18.2. Computation of Period of Days, Deadline.** In computing a period of days, when the ending date is not specified,
543 the first day is excluded and the last day is included, e.g., three days after MEC. If any deadline falls on a Saturday, Sunday or
544 federal or Colorado state holiday (Holiday), such deadline ☐ **Shall** ☐ **Shall Not** be extended to the next day that is not a
545 Saturday, Sunday or Holiday. Should neither box be checked, the deadline shall not be extended.

546 **19. CAUSES OF LOSS, INSURANCE; CONDITION OF, DAMAGE TO PROPERTY AND INCLUSIONS AND**
547 **WALK-THROUGH.** Except as otherwise provided in this Contract, the Property, Inclusions or both shall be delivered in the
548 condition existing as of the date of this Contract, ordinary wear and tear excepted.
549   **19.1. Causes of Loss, Insurance.** In the event the Property or Inclusions are damaged by fire, other perils or causes of
550 loss prior to Closing in an amount of not more than ten percent of the total Purchase Price (Property Damage), Seller shall be

551 obligated to repair the same before **Closing Date** (§ 3). In the event such damage is not repaired within said time or if the damage
552 exceeds such sum, this Contract may be terminated at the option of Buyer. Buyer shall have the Right to Terminate under § 25.1,
553 on or before **Closing Date** (§ 3), based on any Property Damage not repaired before **Closing Date** (§ 3). Should Buyer elect to
554 carry out this Contract despite such Property Damage, Buyer shall be entitled to a credit at Closing for all insurance proceeds that
555 were received by Seller (but not the Association, if any) resulting from such damage to the Property and Inclusions, plus the
556 amount of any deductible provided for in such insurance policy. Such credit shall not exceed the Purchase Price. In the event Seller
557 has not received such insurance proceeds prior to Closing, the parties may agree to extend the **Closing Date** (§ 3) or, at the option
558 of Buyer, Seller shall assign such proceeds at Closing, plus credit Buyer the amount of any deductible provided for in such
559 insurance policy, but not to exceed the total Purchase Price.
560   **19.2. Damage, Inclusions and Services.** Should any Inclusion or service (including utilities and communication
561 services), systems and components of the Property, e.g., heating or plumbing, fail or be damaged between the date of this Contract
562 and Closing or possession, whichever shall be earlier, then Seller shall be liable for the repair or replacement of such Inclusion,
563 service, system, component or fixture of the Property with a unit of similar size, age and quality, or an equivalent credit, but only
564 to the extent that the maintenance or replacement of such Inclusion, service, system, component or fixture is not the responsibility
565 of the Association, if any, less any insurance proceeds received by Buyer covering such repair or replacement. Seller and Buyer
566 are aware of the existence of pre-owned home warranty programs that may be purchased and may cover the repair or replacement
567 of such Inclusions.
568   **19.3. Condemnation.** In the event Seller receives actual notice prior to Closing that a pending condemnation action may
569 result in a taking of all or part of the Property or Inclusions, Seller shall promptly notify Buyer, in writing, of such condemnation
570 action. Buyer shall have the Right to Terminate under § 25.1, on or before **Closing Date** (§ 3), based on such condemnation action,
571 in Buyer's sole subjective discretion. Should Buyer elect to consummate this Contract despite such diminution of value to the
572 Property and Inclusions, Buyer shall be entitled to a credit at Closing for all condemnation proceeds awarded to Seller for the
573 diminution in the value of the Property or Inclusions but such credit shall not include relocation benefits or expenses, or exceed the
574 Purchase Price.
575   **19.4. Walk-Through and Verification of Condition.** Buyer, upon reasonable notice, shall have the right to walk through
576 the Property prior to Closing to verify that the physical condition of the Property and Inclusions complies with this Contract.

577 **20. RECOMMENDATION OF LEGAL AND TAX COUNSEL.** By signing this document, Buyer and Seller acknowledge
578 that the respective broker has advised that this document has important legal consequences and has recommended the examination
579 of title and consultation with legal and tax or other counsel before signing this Contract.

580 **21. TIME OF ESSENCE, DEFAULT AND REMEDIES.** Time is of the essence hereof. If any note or check received as
581 Earnest Money hereunder or any other payment due hereunder is not paid, honored or tendered when due, or if any obligation
582 hereunder is not performed or waived as herein provided, there shall be the following remedies:
583   **21.1. If Buyer is in Default:**
584   ☐   **21.1.1. Specific Performance.** Seller may elect to treat this Contract as canceled, in which case all Earnest Money
585 (whether or not paid by Buyer) shall be paid to Seller and retained by Seller; and Seller may recover such damages as may be
586 proper; or Seller may elect to treat this Contract as being in full force and effect and Seller shall have the right to specific
587 performance or damages, or both.
588   **21.1.2. Liquidated Damages, Applicable.** This § 21.1.2 shall apply <u>unless the box in § 21.1.1. is checked</u>. All
589 Earnest Money (whether or not paid by Buyer) shall be paid to Seller, and retained by Seller. Both parties shall thereafter be
590 released from all obligations hereunder. It is agreed that the Earnest Money specified in § 4.1 is LIQUIDATED DAMAGES, and
591 not a penalty, which amount the parties agree is fair and reasonable and (except as provided in §§ 10.4, 22, 23 and 24), said
592 payment of Earnest Money shall be SELLER'S SOLE AND ONLY REMEDY for Buyer's failure to perform the obligations of
593 this Contract. Seller expressly waives the remedies of specific performance and additional damages.
594   **21.2. If Seller is in Default:** Buyer may elect to treat this Contract as canceled, in which case all Earnest Money received
595 hereunder shall be returned and Buyer may recover such damages as may be proper, or Buyer may elect to treat this Contract as
596 being in full force and effect and Buyer shall have the right to specific performance or damages, or both.

597 **22. LEGAL FEES, COST AND EXPENSES.** Anything to the contrary herein notwithstanding, in the event of any arbitration
598 or litigation relating to this Contract, prior to or after **Closing Date** (§ 3), the arbitrator or court shall award to the prevailing party
599 all reasonable costs and expenses, including attorney fees, legal fees and expenses.

600 **23. MEDIATION.** If a dispute arises relating to this Contract, prior to or after Closing, and is not resolved, the parties shall first
601 proceed in good faith to submit the matter to mediation. Mediation is a process in which the parties meet with an impartial person
602 who helps to resolve the dispute informally and confidentially. Mediators cannot impose binding decisions. The parties to the
603 dispute must agree, in writing, before any settlement is binding. The parties will jointly appoint an acceptable mediator and will
604 share equally in the cost of such mediation. The mediation, unless otherwise agreed, shall terminate in the event the entire dispute

605 is not resolved within thirty days of the date written notice requesting mediation is delivered by one party to the other at the party's
606 last known address. This section shall not alter any date in this Contract, unless otherwise agreed.

607 **24. EARNEST MONEY DISPUTE.** Except as otherwise provided herein, Earnest Money Holder shall release the Earnest
608 Money as directed by written mutual instructions, signed by both Buyer and Seller. In the event of any controversy regarding the
609 Earnest Money (notwithstanding any termination of this Contract), Earnest Money Holder shall not be required to take any action.
610 Earnest Money Holder, at its option and sole subjective discretion, may (1) await any proceeding, (2) interplead all parties and
611 deposit Earnest Money into a court of competent jurisdiction and shall recover court costs and reasonable attorney and legal fees,
612 or (3) provide notice to Buyer and Seller that unless Earnest Money Holder receives a copy of the Summons and Complaint or
613 Claim (between Buyer and Seller) containing the case number of the lawsuit (Lawsuit) within one hundred twenty days of Earnest
614 Money Holder's notice to the parties, Earnest Money Holder shall be authorized to return the Earnest Money to Buyer. In the event
615 Earnest Money Holder does receive a copy of the Lawsuit, and has not interpled the monies at the time of any Order, Earnest
616 Money Holder shall disburse the Earnest Money pursuant to the Order of the Court. The parties reaffirm the obligation of
617 **Mediation** (§ 23). The provisions of this § 24 apply only if the Earnest Money Holder is one of the Brokerage Firms named in
618 § 33 or § 34.

619 **25. TERMINATION.**
620 　　**25.1. Right to Terminate.** If a party has a right to terminate, as provided in this Contract (Right to Terminate), the
621 termination shall be effective upon the other party's receipt of a written notice to terminate (Notice to Terminate), provided such
622 written notice was received on or before the applicable deadline specified in this Contract. If the Notice to Terminate is not
623 received on or before the specified deadline, the party with the Right to Terminate shall have accepted the specified matter,
624 document or condition as satisfactory and waived the Right to Terminate under such provision.
625 　　**25.2. Effect of Termination.** In the event this Contract is terminated, all Earnest Money received hereunder shall be
626 returned and the parties shall be relieved of all obligations hereunder, subject to §§ 10.4, 22, 23 and 24.

627 **26. ENTIRE AGREEMENT, MODIFICATION, SURVIVAL.** This Contract, its exhibits and specified addenda, constitute
628 the entire agreement between the parties relating to the subject hereof, and any prior agreements pertaining thereto, whether oral or
629 written, have been merged and integrated into this Contract. No subsequent modification of any of the terms of this Contract shall
630 be valid, binding upon the parties, or enforceable unless made in writing and signed by the parties. Any obligation in this Contract
631 that, by its terms, is intended to be performed after termination or Closing shall survive the same.

632 **27. NOTICE, DELIVERY, AND CHOICE OF LAW.**
633 　　**27.1. Physical Delivery.** All notices must be in writing, except as provided in § 27.2. Any document, including a signed
634 document or notice, from or on behalf of Seller, and delivered to Buyer shall be effective when physically received by Buyer, any
635 signatory on behalf of Buyer, any named individual of Buyer, any representative of Buyer, or Brokerage Firm of Broker working
636 with Buyer (except for delivery, after Closing, of the notice requesting mediation described in § 23) and except as provided in
637 § 27.2. Any document, including a signed document or notice, from or on behalf of Buyer, and delivered to Seller shall be
638 effective when physically received by Seller, any signatory on behalf of Seller, any named individual of Seller, any representative
639 of Seller, or Brokerage Firm of Broker working with Seller (except for delivery, after Closing, of the notice requesting mediation
640 described in § 23) and except as provided in § 27.2.
641 　　**27.2. Electronic Delivery.** As an alternative to physical delivery, any document, including any signed document or
642 written notice, may be delivered in electronic form only by the following indicated methods: ☐ **Facsimile** ☐ **Email** ☐ **Internet**
643 ☐ **No Electronic Delivery.** If the box "No Electronic Delivery" is checked, this § 27.2 shall not be applicable and § 27.1 shall
644 govern notice and delivery. Documents with original signatures shall be provided upon request of any party.
645 　　**27.3. Choice of Law.** This Contract and all disputes arising hereunder shall be governed by and construed in accordance
646 with the laws of the State of Colorado that would be applicable to Colorado residents who sign a contract in Colorado for property
647 located in Colorado.

648 **28. NOTICE OF ACCEPTANCE, COUNTERPARTS.** This proposal shall expire unless accepted in writing, by Buyer and
649 Seller, as evidenced by their signatures below, and the offering party receives notice of such acceptance pursuant to § 27 on or
650 before **Acceptance Deadline Date** (§ 3) and **Acceptance Deadline Time** (§ 3). If accepted, this document shall become a contract
651 between Seller and Buyer. A copy of this document may be executed by each party, separately, and when each party has executed
652 a copy thereof, such copies taken together shall be deemed to be a full and complete contract between the parties.

653 **29. GOOD FAITH.** Buyer and Seller acknowledge that each party has an obligation to act in good faith including, but not
654 limited to, exercising the rights and obligations set forth in the provisions of **Financing Conditions and Obligations** (§ 5),
655 **Record Title and Off-Record Title Matters** (§ 8), **Current Survey Review** (§ 9) and **Property Disclosure, Inspection,**
656 **Indemnity, Insurability, Due Diligence, Buyer Disclosure and Source of Water** (§ 10).

---

657 | **ADDITIONAL PROVISIONS AND ATTACHMENTS**

658 **30. ADDITIONAL PROVISIONS.** (The following additional provisions have not been approved by the Colorado Real Estate
659 Commission.)
660
661
662
663

664 **31. ATTACHMENTS.** The following are a part of this Contract:
665
666
667
668 **Note:** The following disclosure forms **are attached** but are **not** a part of this Contract:
669
670
671

672 | **SIGNATURES**

673
Buyer's Name: _____   Buyer's Name: _____

Buyer's Signature _____ Date   Buyer's Signature _____ Date

Address: _____   Address: _____

Phone No.: _____   Phone No.: _____
Fax No.: _____   Fax No.: _____
Electronic Address: _____   Electronic Address: _____

674 **[NOTE: If this offer is being countered or rejected, do not sign this document. Refer to § 32]**

Seller's Name: _____   Seller's Name: _____

Seller's Signature _____ Date   Seller's Signature _____ Date

Address: _____   Address: _____

Phone No.: _____   Phone No.: _____
Fax No.: _____   Fax No.: _____
Electronic Address: _____   Electronic Address: _____
675

676 **32. COUNTER; REJECTION.** This offer is ☐ **Countered** ☐ **Rejected**.
677 **Initials only of party (Buyer or Seller) who countered or rejected offer** _____

678 | **END OF CONTRACT TO BUY AND SELL REAL ESTATE**

33. BROKER'S ACKNOWLEDGMENTS AND COMPENSATION DISCLOSURE.
(To be completed by Broker working with Buyer)

Broker ☐ **Does** ☐ **Does Not** acknowledge receipt of Earnest Money deposit and, while not a party to the Contract, agrees to cooperate upon request with any mediation concluded under § 23. Broker agrees that if Brokerage Firm is the Earnest Money Holder and, except as provided in § 24, if the Earnest Money has not already been returned following receipt of a Notice to Terminate or other written notice of termination, Earnest Money Holder shall release the Earnest Money as directed by the written mutual instructions. Such release of Earnest Money shall be made within five days of Earnest Money Holder's receipt of the executed written mutual instructions, provided the Earnest Money check has cleared. Broker agrees that if Earnest Money Holder is other than the Brokerage Firm identified in § 33 or § 34, Closing Instructions signed by Buyer, Seller, and Earnest Money Holder must be obtained on or before delivery of Earnest Money to Earnest Money Holder.

Broker is working with Buyer as a ☐ **Buyer's Agent** ☐ **Seller's Agent** ☐ **Transaction-Broker** in this transaction.
☐ This is a **Change of Status**.

Brokerage Firm's compensation or commission is to be paid by ☐ **Listing Brokerage Firm** ☐ **Buyer** ☐ **Other** _____.

Brokerage Firm's Name: _____
Broker's Name: _____

_____
Broker's Signature   Date

Address: _____
_____

Phone No.: _____
Fax No.: _____
Electronic Address: _____

34. BROKER'S ACKNOWLEDGMENTS AND COMPENSATION DISCLOSURE.
(To be completed by Broker working with Seller)

Broker ☐ **Does** ☐ **Does Not** acknowledge receipt of Earnest Money deposit and, while not a party to the Contract, agrees to cooperate upon request with any mediation concluded under § 23. Broker agrees that if Brokerage Firm is the Earnest Money Holder and, except as provided in § 24, if the Earnest Money has not already been returned following receipt of a Notice to Terminate or other written notice of termination, Earnest Money Holder shall release the Earnest Money as directed by the written mutual instructions. Such release of Earnest Money shall be made within five days of Earnest Money Holder's receipt of the executed written mutual instructions, provided the Earnest Money check has cleared. Broker agrees that if Earnest Money Holder is other than the Brokerage Firm identified in § 33 or § 34, Closing Instructions signed by Buyer, Seller, and Earnest Money Holder must be obtained on or before delivery of Earnest Money to Earnest Money Holder.

Broker is working with Seller as a ☐ **Seller's Agent** ☐ **Buyer's Agent** ☐ **Transaction-Broker** in this transaction.
☐ This is a **Change of Status**.

Brokerage Firm's compensation or commission is to be paid by ☐ **Seller** ☐ **Buyer** ☐ **Other** _____.

Brokerage Firm's Name: _____
Broker's Name: _____

_____
Broker's Signature   Date

Address: _____
_____

Phone No.: _____
Fax No.: _____
Electronic Address: _____

679

CBS1-10-11. CONTRACT TO BUY AND SELL REAL ESTATE (RESIDENTIAL)   Page 15 of 15

7. Seller's Property Disclosure (All Types of Properties)

The printed portions of this form, except differentiated additions, have been approved by the Colorado Real Estate Commission. (SPD19-10-11) (Mandatory 1-12)

THIS FORM HAS IMPORTANT LEGAL CONSEQUENCES AND THE PARTIES SHOULD CONSULT LEGAL AND TAX OR OTHER COUNSEL BEFORE SIGNING.

SELLER'S PROPERTY DISCLOSURE
(ALL TYPES OF PROPERTIES)

THIS DISCLOSURE SHOULD BE COMPLETED BY SELLER, NOT BY BROKER.

Seller states that the information contained in this Disclosure is correct to Seller's CURRENT ACTUAL KNOWLEDGE as of this Date. **Any changes will be disclosed by Seller to Buyer promptly after discovery.** Seller hereby receipts for a copy of this Disclosure. **If the Property is part of a Common Interest Community, this Disclosure is limited to the Property or Unit itself, except as stated in Section L.** Broker may deliver a copy of this Disclosure to prospective buyers.

Note: If an item is not present at the Property or if an item is not to be included in the sale, mark the "N/A" column. The Contract to Buy and Sell Real Estate, not this Disclosure form, determines whether an item is included or excluded; if there is an inconsistency between this form and the Contract, the Contract controls.

Date: _____

Property Address: _____

Seller: _____

I. IMPROVEMENTS					
☐ If this box is checked, there are no structures or improvements on the Property; do not complete Sections A-G.					

A.	STRUCTURAL CONDITIONS Do any of the following conditions **now exist or have they ever existed**:	Yes	No	Do Not Know	N/A	Comments
1	Structural problems					
2	Moisture and/or water problems					
3	Damage due to termites, other insects, birds, animals or rodents					
4	Damage due to hail, wind, fire or flood					
5	Cracks, heaving or settling problems					
6	Exterior wall or window problems					
7	Exterior Artificial Stucco (EIFS)					
8	Any additions or alterations made					
9	Building code, city or county violations					

B.	ROOF Do any of the following conditions **now exist**:	Yes	No	Do Not Know	N/A	Comments
1	Roof problems					
2	Roof material: _____ Age _____ Roof material: _____ Age _____					
3	Roof leak: Past					
4	Roof leak: Present					
5	Damage to roof: Past					
6	Damage to roof: Present					
7	Roof under warranty until _____. Transferable _____					
8	Roof work done while under current roof warranty					
9	Skylight problems					
10	Gutter or downspout problems					

NOTES ON USE:

For a discussion of home inspections and the use of this disclosure form, see § 5.8.1.

Appendix 1: Forms

	IN WORKING CONDITION					
C. APPLIANCES Are the following **now** in working condition:	Yes	No	Do Not Know	Age If Known	N/A	Comments
1 Built-in vacuum system & accessories						
2 Clothes dryer						
3 Clothes washer						
4 Dishwasher						
5 Disposal						
6 Freezer						
7 Gas grill						
8 Hood						
9 Microwave oven						
10 Oven						
11 Range						
12 Refrigerator						
13 T.V. antenna: ☐ Owned ☐ Leased						
14 Satellite system or DSS dish: ☐ Owned ☐ Leased						
15 Trash compactor						

	IN WORKING CONDITION					
D. ELECTRICAL & TELECOMMUNICATIONS Are the following **now** in working condition:	Yes	No	Do Not Know	Age If Known	N/A	Comments
1 Security system: ☐ Owned ☐ Leased						
2 Smoke/fire detectors: ☐ Battery ☐ Hardwire						
3 Carbon Monoxide Alarm: ☐ Battery ☐ Hardwire						
4 Light fixtures						
5 Switches & outlets						
6 Aluminum wiring (110)						
7 Electrical: Phase _____ Voltage _____ Amps _____						
8 Telecommunications (T1, fiber, cable, satellite)						
9 Inside telephone wiring & blocks/jacks						
10 Abandoned communication cables: ☐ Yes ☐ No						
11 Ceiling fans						
12 Garage door opener						
13 Garage door control(s) #_____						
14 Intercom/doorbell						
15 In-wall speakers						
16 220 volt service						
17 Landscape lighting						

	IN WORKING CONDITION					
E. MECHANICAL Are the following **now** in working condition:	Yes	No	Do Not Know	Age If Known	N/A	Comments
1 Air conditioning:						
Evaporative cooler						
Window units						
Central						
Computer room						
2 Attic/whole house fan						
3 Vent fans						
4 Humidifier						

5	Air purifier						
6	Sauna						
7	Hot tub or spa						
8	Steam room/shower						
9	Pool						
10	Heating system: Type _____ Fuel _____ Type _____ Fuel _____						
11	Water heater: Number of _____ Fuel type _____ Capacity _____						
12	Fireplace: Type _____ Fuel _____						
13	Fireplace insert						
14	Stove: Type _____ Fuel _____						
15	When was fireplace/wood stove, chimney/flue last cleaned: Date: _____ ☐ Do not know						
16	Fuel tanks: ☐ Owned ☐ Leased						
17	Radiant heating system: ☐ Interior ☐ Exterior Hose Type _____						
18	Overhead door						
19	Entry gate system						
20	Elevator/escalators						
21	Lift/hoist/crane						

		IN WORKING CONDITION					
F.	**WATER, SEWER & OTHER UTILITIES** Are the following **now** in working condition:	**Yes**	**No**	**Do Not Know**	**Age If Known**	**N/A**	**Comments**
1	Water filter system: ☐ Owned ☐ Leased						
2	Water softener: ☐ Owned ☐ Leased						
3	Sewage problems: ☐ Yes ☐ No ☐ Do not know						
4	Lift station (sewage ejector pump)						
5	Drainage, storm sewers, retention ponds						
6	Grey water storage/use						
7	Plumbing problems: ☐ Yes ☐ No ☐ Do not know						
8	Sump pump						
9	Underground sprinkler system						
10	Fire sprinkler system						
11	Polybutylene pipe: ☐ Yes ☐ No ☐ Do not know						
12	Galvanized pipe: ☐ Yes ☐ No ☐ Do not know						
13	Backflow prevention device: ☐ Domestic ☐ Irrigation ☐ Fire ☐ Sewage						
14	Irrigation pump						
15	Well pump						

		IN WORKING CONDITION					
G.	**OTHER DISCLOSURES – IMPROVEMENTS**	**Yes**	**No**	**Do Not Know**	**Age If Known**	**N/A**	**Comments**
1	Included fixtures and equipment **now** in working condition						

Appendix 1: Forms

	II. GENERAL					
H.	**USE, ZONING & LEGAL ISSUES** Do any of the following conditions **now exist**:	**Yes**	**No**	**Do Not Know**	**N/A**	**Comments**
1	Current use of the Property					
2	Zoning violation, variance, conditional use, violation of an enforceable PUD or non-conforming use					
3	Notice or threat of condemnation proceedings					
4	Notice of any adverse conditions from any governmental or quasi-governmental agency that have not been resolved					
5	Violation of restrictive covenants or owners' association rules or regulations					
6	Any building or improvements constructed within the past one year from this Date without approval by the Association or the designated approving body					
7	Notice of zoning action related to the Property					
8	Notice of ADA complaint or report					
9	Other legal action					

I.	**ACCESS, PARKING, DRAINAGE & SIGNAGE** Do any of the following conditions **now exist**:	**Yes**	**No**	**Do Not Know**	**N/A**	**Comments**
1	Any access problems					
2	Roads, driveways, trails or paths through the Property used by others					
3	Public highway or county road bordering the Property					
4	Any proposed or existing transportation project that affects or is expected to affect the Property					
5	Encroachments, boundary disputes or unrecorded easements					
6	Shared or common areas with adjoining properties					
7	Cross-parking agreement, covenants, easements					
8	Requirements for curb, gravel/paving, landscaping					
9	Flooding or drainage problems: Past					
10	Flooding or drainage problems: Present					
11	Signs: ☐ Owned ☐ Leased					
12	Signs: Government or private restriction problems					

J.	**WATER & SEWER SUPPLY** Do any of the following conditions **now exist**:	**Yes**	**No**	**Do Not Know**	**N/A**	**Comments**
1	Water Rights: Type _____					
2	Water tap fees paid in full					
3	Sewer tap fees paid in full					
4	Subject to augmentation plan					
5	Well required to be metered					
6	Type of water supply: ☐ Public ☐ Community ☐ Well ☐ Shared Well ☐ Cistern ☐ None If the Property is served by a Well, a copy of the Well Permit ☐ **Is** ☐ **Is Not attached**. Well Permit #: _____ ☐ Drilling Records ☐ Are ☐ Are not attached. Shared Well Agreement ☐ **Yes** ☐ **No**. The **Water Provider** for the Property can be contacted at: Name: _____ Address: _____ Web Site: _____ Phone No.: _____ ☐ There is neither a Well nor a Water Provider for the Property. The source of potable water for the Property is [describe source]: **SOME WATER PROVIDERS RELY, TO VARYING DEGREES, ON NONRENEWABLE GROUND WATER. YOU MAY WISH TO CONTACT YOUR PROVIDER (OR INVESTIGATE THE DESCRIBED SOURCE) TO DETERMINE THE LONG-TERM SUFFICIENCY OF THE PROVIDER'S WATER SUPPLIES.**					
7	Type of sanitary sewer service: ☐ Public ☐ Community ☐ Septic System ☐ None ☐ Other _____ If the Property is served by an on-site septic system, supply to buyer a copy of the permit. Type of septic system: ☐ Tank ☐ Leach ☐ Lagoon					

SPD19-10-11. SELLER'S PROPERTY DISCLOSURE (ALL TYPES OF PROPERTIES)   Page 4 of 7

K.	**ENVIRONMENTAL CONDITIONS** Do any of the following conditions **now exist or have they ever existed**:	Yes	No	Do Not Know	N/A	Comments
1	Hazardous materials on the Property, such as radioactive, toxic, or biohazardous materials, asbestos, pesticides, herbicides, wastewater sludge, radon, methane, mill tailings, solvents or petroleum products					
2	Underground storage tanks					
3	Aboveground storage tanks					
4	Underground transmission lines					
5	Animals kept in the residence					
6	Property used as, situated on, or adjoining a dump, land fill or municipal solid waste land fill					
7	Monitoring wells or test equipment					
8	Sliding, settling, upheaval, movement or instability of earth or expansive soils on the Property					
9	Mine shafts, tunnels or abandoned wells on the Property					
10	Within governmentally designated geological hazard or sensitive area					
11	Within governmentally designated flood plain or wetland area					
12	Governmentally designated noxious weeds (within last 3 years only) If yes, see Section O.					
13	Dead, diseased or infested trees or shrubs					
14	Environmental assessments, studies or reports done involving the physical condition of the Property					
15	Property used for any mining, graveling, or other natural resource extraction operations such as oil and gas wells					
16	Endangered species on the Property					
17	Archeological features, fossils, or artifacts on the Property					
18	Interior of improvements of Property tobacco smoke-free					
19	Other environmental problems					

L.	**COMMON INTEREST COMMUNITY – ASSOCIATION PROPERTY** Do any of the following conditions **now exist**:	Yes	No	Do Not Know	N/A	Comments
1	Property is part of an owners' association					
2	Special assessments or increases in regular assessments approved by owners' association but not yet implemented					
3	Has the Association made demand or commenced a lawsuit against a builder or contractor alleging defective construction of improvements of the Association Property (common area or property owned or controlled by the Association but outside the Seller's Property or Unit).					

M.	**OTHER DISCLOSURES – GENERAL** Do any of the following conditions **now exist**:	Yes	No	Do Not Know	N/A	Comments
1	Any part of the Property leased to others (written or oral)					
2	Written reports of any building, site, roofing, soils or engineering investigations or studies of the Property					
3	Any property insurance claim submitted (whether paid or not)					
4	Structural, architectural and engineering plans and/or specifications for any existing improvements					
5	Property was previously used as a methamphetamine laboratory and not remediated to state standards					
6	Government special improvements approved, but not yet installed, that may become a lien against the Property					

	III. LAND					

N.	**CROPS, LIVESTOCK & LEASES** Do any of the following conditions **now exist**:	**Yes**	**No**	**Do Not Know**	**N/A**	**Comments**
1	Crops being grown on the Property					
2	Seller owns all crops					
3	Livestock on the Property					
4	Any land leased from others: ☐ State ☐ BLM ☐ Federal ☐ Private ☐ Other _____					

O.	**NOXIOUS WEEDS** Do any of the following conditions **now exist**:					
	The Colorado Noxious Weed Management Act (35-5.5-101-119 C.R.S) enables County and City governments to implement noxious weeds management programs to reclaim infested acres and protect weed-free land. For a directory of county weed supervisors call 303-239-4173 or see: www.colorado.gov/ag/weeds.					
	Have any of the following occurred to the Property:	**Yes**	**No**	**Do Not Know**	**N/A**	**Comments**
1	Have any noxious weeds on the Property been identified?					
2	Have there been any weed enforcement actions on the Property?					
3	Has a noxious weed management plan for the Property been entered into?					
4	Have noxious weed management actions been implemented?					
5	Have herbicides been applied?					

P.	**OTHER DISCLOSURES – LAND** Do any of the following conditions **now exist**:	**Yes**	**No**	**Do Not Know**	**N/A**	**Comments**
1	Any part of the Property enrolled in any governmental programs such as Conservation Reserve Program (CRP), Wetlands Reserve Program (WRP), etc.					
2	Conservation easement					

Seller and Buyer understand that the real estate brokers do not warrant or guarantee the above information on the Property. Property inspection services may be purchased and are advisable. This form is **not** intended as a substitute for an inspection of the Property.

ADVISORY TO SELLER:

Failure to disclose a known material defect may result in legal liability.

The information contained in this Disclosure has been furnished by Seller, who certifies to the truth thereof based on Seller's CURRENT ACTUAL KNOWLEDGE.

_____ _____   _____ _____
Seller   Date   Seller   Date

ADVISORY TO BUYER:

1.   Even though Seller has answered the above questions to Seller's current actual knowledge, Buyer should thoroughly inspect the Property and obtain expert assistance to accurately and fully evaluate the Property to confirm the status of the following matters:
      a.   the physical condition of the Property;
      b.   the presence of mold or other biological hazards;
      c.   the presence of rodents, insects and vermin including termites;
      d.   the legal use of the Property and legal access to the Property;
      e.   the availability and source of water, sewer, and utilities;

f.   the environmental and geological condition of the Property;

g.   the presence of noxious weeds; and

h.   any other matters that may affect Buyer's use and ownership of the Property that are important to Buyer as Buyer decides whether to purchase the Property.

2.   Seller states that the information is correct to "Seller's current actual knowledge" as of the date of this form. The term "current actual knowledge" is intended to limit Seller's disclosure only to facts actually known by the Seller and does not include "constructive knowledge" or "common knowledge" or what Seller "should have known" about the Property. The Seller has no duty to inspect the Property when this Disclosure is filled in and signed.

3.   Valuable information may be obtained from various local/state/federal agencies, and other experts may assist Buyer by performing more specific evaluations and inspections of the Property.

4.   Boundaries, location and ownership of fences, driveways, hedges, and similar features of the Property may become the subjects of a dispute between a property owner and a neighbor. A survey may be used to determine the likelihood of such problems.

5.   Whether any item is included or excluded is determined by the contract between Buyer and Seller and not this Seller's Property Disclosure.

6.   Buyer acknowledges that Seller does not warrant that the Property is fit for Buyer's intended purposes or use of the Property. Buyer acknowledges that Seller's indication that an item is "working" is not to be construed as a warranty of its continued operability or as a representation or warranty that such item is fit for Buyer's intended purposes.

7.   Buyer hereby receipts for a copy of this Disclosure.

_____   _____
Buyer   Date   Buyer   Date

Appendix 1: Forms

8. Lead-Based Paint Disclosure (Sales)

The printed portions of this form except differentiated additions, have been approved by the Colorado Real Estate Commission. (LP45-5-04

Lead-Based Paint Disclosure (Sales)

Attachment to Contract to Buy and Sell Real Estate for the Property known as:

Street Address	City	State	Zip

WARNING! LEAD FROM PAINT, DUST, AND SOIL CAN BE DANGEROUS IF NOT MANAGED PROPERLY

Penalties for failure to comply with Federal Lead-Based Paint Disclosure Laws include treble (3 times) damages, attorney fees, costs, and a penalty up to $10,000 (plus adjustment for inflation) for each violation.

Disclosure of Information on Lead-Based Paint and/or Lead-Based Paint Hazards

Lead Warning Statement

Every purchaser of any interest in residential real property on which a residential dwelling was built prior to 1978 is notified that such property may present exposure to lead from lead-based paint that may place young children at risk of developing lead poisoning. Lead poisoning in young children may produce permanent neurological damage, including learning disabilities, reduced intelligence quotient, behavioral problems, and impaired memory. Lead poisoning also poses a particular risk to pregnant women. The Seller of any interest in residential real property is required to provide the buyer with any information on lead-based paint hazards from risk assessments or inspections in the Seller's possession and notify the buyer of any known lead-based paint hazards. A risk assessment or inspection for possible lead-based paint hazards is recommended prior to purchase.

Seller's Disclosure to Buyer and Real Estate Licensee(s) and Acknowledgment

(a) Seller acknowledges that Seller has been informed of Seller's obligations. Seller is aware that Seller must retain a copy of this disclosure for not less than three years from the completion date of the sale.

(b) Presence of lead-based paint and/or lead-based paint hazards (check one box below):

❑ Seller has no knowledge of any lead-based paint and/or lead-based paint hazards present in the housing.

❑ Seller has knowledge of lead-based paint and/or lead-based paint hazards present in the housing (explain):

_____

(c) Records and reports available to Seller (check one box below):

❑ Seller has no reports or records pertaining to lead-based paint and/or lead-based paint hazards in the housing.

❑ Seller has provided Buyer with all available records and reports pertaining to lead-based paint and/or lead-based paint hazards in the housing (list documents below):

_____

_____

Buyer's Acknowledgment

(d) Buyer has read the Lead Warning Statement above and understands its contents.

(e) Buyer has received copies of all information, including any records and reports listed by Seller above.

(f) Buyer has received the pamphlet "Protect Your Family From Lead in Your Home".

(g) Buyer acknowledges federal law requires that before a buyer is obligated under any contract to buy and sell real estate, Seller shall permit Buyer a 10-day period (unless the parties mutually agree, in writing, upon a different period of time) to conduct a risk assessment or inspection for the presence of lead-based paint and/or lead-based paint hazards.

(h) Buyer, after having reviewed the contents of this form, and any records and reports listed by Seller, has elected to (check one box below):

❑ Obtain a risk assessment or an inspection of the Property for the presence of lead-based paint and/or lead-based paint hazards, within the time limit and under the terms of Section 10 of the Contract to Buy and Sell Real Estate; or

❑ Waive the opportunity to conduct a risk assessment or inspection for the presence of lead-based paint and/or lead-based paint hazards.

LP 45-5-04   LEAD-BASED PAINT DISCLOSURE (SALES)   Page 1 of 2

NOTES ON USE:

For a discussion on the use of this form and the law regarding lead-based paint, see §§ 5.8.5 and 5.9.

Real Estate Licensee's Acknowledgment

Each real estate licensee signing below acknowledges receipt of the above Seller's Disclosure, has informed Seller of Seller's obligations and is aware of licensee's responsibility to ensure compliance.

Certification of Accuracy

I certify that the statements I have made are accurate to the best of my knowledge.

Date: _____   Date: _____

_____   _____
Seller   Seller

Date: _____   Date: _____

_____   _____
Buyer   Buyer

Date: _____   Date: _____

_____   _____
Real Estate Licensee (Listing)   Real Estate Licensee (Selling)

LP 45-5-04   **LEAD-BASED PAINT DISCLOSURE (SALES)**   **Page 2 of 2**

9. Inspection Objection

3

4 **THIS FORM HAS IMPORTANT LEGAL CONSEQUENCES AND THE PARTIES SHOULD CONSULT LEGAL AND**
5 **TAX OR OTHER COUNSEL BEFORE SIGNING.**

6

7 ## INSPECTION OBJECTION

8
9 Date: _____

10
11 This document affects the contract dated _____, between _____

12 _____, (Seller) and _____ (Buyer)

13 relating to the sale and purchase of the Property known as: _____

14 _____ (Contract). Terms used herein shall have the same meaning as in the Contract.

15 **1.   BUYER'S NOTIFICATION OF UNSATISFACTORY PHYSICAL CONDITION.**
16 **1.1.**   Pursuant to § 10.2.2 of the Contract, Buyer notifies Seller that Buyer requires Seller, on or before _____,
17 to correct or resolve the following unsatisfactory physical conditions of the Property or Inclusions:

18 _____

19 _____

20 _____

21 If more space is required, attached are _____ additional pages.

22 **1.2.**   A copy of the inspection report ☐ **Is** ☐ **Is Not** provided in conjunction with this Notice.

23 Pursuant to § 10.4 of the Contract, items set forth in § 1.1, or otherwise in this document, shall be paid by Seller.

24 Pursuant to § 10.3 of the Contract, if Buyer and Seller have not agreed in writing to a settlement of the above matters on or before
25 the Inspection Resolution Deadline, the Contract will terminate unless Seller receives written notice from Buyer withdrawing this
26 Inspection Objection no later than before expiration of the Inspection Resolution Deadline.
27

_____   _____   _____   _____
Buyer   Date   Buyer   Date

_____   _____   _____   _____
Seller   Date   Seller   Date

28
29
30 Seller: ☐ **Seller's Alternative Resolution in Part 2 of this document.**

31   ☐ **Rejects** to correct all items in § 1.1 _____
32   Initials of Seller
33

_____

NOTES ON USE:
For a discussion of home inspections and the use of this form, see § 5.8.1.

34
35 **2.** **SELLER'S ALTERNATIVE RESOLUTION:**
36 _____
37 _____
38 _____
39

_____   _____
Seller   Date   Seller   Date

_____   _____
Buyer   Date   Buyer   Date
40

41
42 Buyer: ☐ **Rejects** Seller's Alternative Resolution _____
43   Initials of Buyer

44
45
46 **3.** **SURVIVAL.** If any agreed upon correction requires action after Closing, the obligations agreed upon shall survive Closing.

47
48
49
50
51
52
53
54
55
56 **4.** **BUYER'S WITHDRAWAL OF INSPECTION OBJECTION.**

57
58 Buyer withdraws the Inspection Objection and elects to proceed with the Contract.
59

_____   _____
Buyer   Date   Buyer   Date
60

10. Counterproposal

<table>
<tr><td>1</td><td colspan="2">The printed portions of this form, except differentiated additions, have been approved by the Colorado Real Estate Commission.</td></tr>
<tr><td>2</td><td colspan="2">(CP40-10-11) (Mandatory 1-12)</td></tr>
</table>

3
4 **THIS FORM HAS IMPORTANT LEGAL CONSEQUENCES AND THE PARTIES SHOULD CONSULT LEGAL AND TAX OR**
5 **OTHER COUNSEL BEFORE SIGNING.**
6
7 ## COUNTERPROPOSAL
8
9 Date: _____
10
11 **1.** This Counterproposal shall supersede and replace any previous counterproposal. This Counterproposal amends the proposed
12 contract dated _____ (Contract), between _____
13 (Seller), and _____ (Buyer), relating to the sale and purchase
14 of the following legally described real estate in the County of _____, Colorado:
15
16
17
18 known as No. _____ (Property).
19   Street Address   City   State   Zip
20
21 **NOTE: If the table is omitted, or if any item is left blank or is marked in the "No Change" column, it means no change to**
22 **the corresponding provision of the Contract. If any item is marked in the "Deleted" column, it means that the**
23 **corresponding provision of the Contract to which reference is made is deleted.**
24
25 **2.   § 3. DATES AND DEADLINES.** [Note: This table may be omitted if inapplicable.]

Item No.	Reference	Event	Date or Deadline	No Change	Deleted
1	§ 4.2	Alternative Earnest Money Deadline			
		Title and Association			
2	§ 7.1	Record Title Deadline			
3	§ 7.2	Exceptions Request Deadline			
4	§ 8.1	Record Title Objection Deadline			
5	§ 8.2	Off-Record Title Deadline			
6	§ 8.2	Off-Record Title Objection Deadline			
7	§ 8.3	Title Resolution Deadline			
8	§ 7.3	Association Documents Deadline			
9	§ 7.3	Association Documents Objection Deadline			
10	§ 8.5	Right of First Refusal Deadline			
		Seller's Property Disclosure			
11	§ 10.1	Seller's Property Disclosure Deadline			
		Loan and Credit			
12	§ 5.1	Loan Application Deadline			
13	§ 5.2	Loan Conditions Deadline			
14	§ 5.3	Buyer's Credit Information Deadline			
15	§ 5.3	Disapproval of Buyer's Credit Information Deadline			
16	§ 5.4	Existing Loan Documents Deadline			
17	§ 5.4	Existing Loan Documents Objection Deadline			
18	§ 5.4	Loan Transfer Approval Deadline			
		Appraisal			
19	§ 6.2	Appraisal Deadline			
20	§ 6.2	Appraisal Objection Deadline			
		Survey			
21	§ 9.1	Current Survey Deadline			
22	§ 9.2	Current Survey Objection Deadline			

NOTES ON USE:

For a discussion of counterproposals (also called counteroffers), see § 5.10.

		Inspection and Due Diligence			
23	§ 10.2	Inspection Objection Deadline			
24	§ 10.3	Inspection Resolution Deadline			
25	§ 10.5	Property Insurance Objection Deadline			
26	§ 10.6	Due Diligence Documents Delivery Deadline			
27	§ 10.7	Due Diligence Documents Objection Deadline			
28	§ 10.8	Environmental Inspection Objection Deadline CBS2, 3, 4			
29	§ 10.8	ADA Evaluation Objection Deadline CBS2, 3, 4			
30	§ 11.2	Tenant Estoppel Statements Deadline CBS2, 3, 4			
31	§ 11.2	Tenant Estoppel Statements Objection Deadline CBS2, 3, 4			
		Closing and Possession			
32	§ 12.3	Closing Date			
33	§ 17	Possession Date			
34	§ 17	Possession Time			

26 **3.   § 4. PURCHASE PRICE AND TERMS.** [Note: This table may be omitted if inapplicable.]

27 The Purchase Price set forth below shall be payable in U. S. Dollars by Buyer as follows:

Item No.	Reference	Item	Amount	Amount
1	§ 4.1	Purchase Price	$	
2	§ 4.2	Earnest Money		$
3	§ 4.5	New Loan		
4	§ 4.6	Assumption Balance		
5	§ 4.7	Seller or Private Financing		
6				
7				
8	§ 4.3	Cash at Closing		
9		**TOTAL**	$	$

28
29 **4.   ATTACHMENTS.** The following are a part of this Counterproposal:
30
31
32
33 Note: The following disclosure forms **are attached** but are **not** a part of this Counterproposal:
34
35
36
37 **5.   OTHER CHANGES.**
38
39
40
41 **6.   ACCEPTANCE DEADLINE.** This Counterproposal shall expire unless accepted in writing by Seller and Buyer as
42 evidenced by their signatures below and the offering party to this document receives notice of such acceptance on or before
43 _____.
44 Date   Time
45
46 If accepted, the Contract, as amended by this Counterproposal, shall become a contract between Seller and Buyer. All other terms
47 and conditions of the Contract shall remain the same.
48

Buyer's Name: _____   Buyer's Name: _____

Buyer's Signature   Date   Buyer's Signature   Date

CP40-10-11. COUNTERPROPOSAL   Page 2 of 3

Address: _____	Address: _____
Phone No.: _____	Phone No.: _____
Fax No.:	Fax No.:
Electronic Address: _____	Electronic Address: _____
Seller's Name: _____	Seller's Name: _____
_____	_____
Seller's Signature Date	Seller's Signature Date
Address: _____	Address: _____
Phone No.: _____	Phone No.: _____
Fax No.:	Fax No.:
Electronic Address: _____	Electronic Address: _____

49   **Note:** When this Counterproposal form is used, the Contract is **not** to be signed by the party initiating this Counterproposal.
50   Brokers must complete and sign the Broker's Acknowledgments and Compensation Disclosure portion of the Contract.
51

11. Agreement to Amend/Extend Contract

1	The printed portions of this form, except differentiated additions, have been approved by the Colorado Real Estate Commission.
2	(AE41-10-11) (Mandatory 1-12)

3

4 **THIS FORM HAS IMPORTANT LEGAL CONSEQUENCES AND THE PARTIES SHOULD CONSULT LEGAL AND TAX OR**
5 **OTHER COUNSEL BEFORE SIGNING.**

6

7 ## AGREEMENT TO AMEND/EXTEND CONTRACT

8

9 Date: _____

10

11 **1.** This agreement amends the contract dated _____ (Contract), between _____
12 _____ (Seller), and _____
13 (Buyer), relating to the sale and purchase of the following legally described real estate in the County of _____,
14 Colorado:

15

16

17

18 known as No. _____ (Property).
19   Street Address   City   State   Zip

20

21 **NOTE: If the table is omitted, or if any item is left blank or is marked in the "No Change" column, it means no change to**
22 **the corresponding provision of the Contract. If any item is marked in the "Deleted" column, it means that the**
23 **corresponding provision of the Contract to which reference is made is deleted.**

24

25 **2. § 3. DATES AND DEADLINES.** [Note: This table may be omitted if inapplicable.]

Item No.	Reference	Event	Date or Deadline	No Change	Deleted
1	§ 4.2	Alternative Earnest Money Deadline			
		Title and Association			
2	§ 7.1	Record Title Deadline			
3	§ 7.2	Exceptions Request Deadline			
4	§ 8.1	Record Title Objection Deadline			
5	§ 8.2	Off-Record Title Deadline			
6	§ 8.2	Off-Record Title Objection Deadline			
7	§ 8.3	Title Resolution Deadline			
8	§ 7.3	Association Documents Deadline			
9	§ 7.3	Association Documents Objection Deadline			
10	§ 8.5	Right of First Refusal Deadline			
		Seller's Property Disclosure			
11	§ 10.1	Seller's Property Disclosure Deadline			
		Loan and Credit			
12	§ 5.1	Loan Application Deadline			
13	§ 5.2	Loan Conditions Deadline			
14	§ 5.3	Buyer's Credit Information Deadline			
15	§ 5.3	Disapproval of Buyer's Credit Information Deadline			
16	§ 5.4	Existing Loan Documents Deadline			
17	§ 5.4	Existing Loan Documents Objection Deadline			
18	§ 5.4	Loan Transfer Approval Deadline			
		Appraisal			
19	§ 6.2	Appraisal Deadline			
20	§ 6.2	Appraisal Objection Deadline			
		Survey			
21	§ 9.1	Current Survey Deadline			
22	§ 9.2	Current Survey Objection Deadline			

AE41-10-11. AGREEMENT TO AMEND/EXTEND CONTRACT   Page 1 of 2

NOTES ON USE:

For a discussion of amendments to the contract to purchase property, see § 5.11.

		Inspection and Due Diligence			
23	§ 10.2	Inspection Objection Deadline			
24	§ 10.3	Inspection Resolution Deadline			
25	§ 10.5	Property Insurance Objection Deadline			
26	§ 10.6	Due Diligence Documents Delivery Deadline			
27	§ 10.7	Due Diligence Documents Objection Deadline			
28	§ 10.8	Environmental Inspection Objection Deadline CBS2, 3, 4			
29	§ 10.8	ADA Evaluation Objection Deadline CBS2, 3, 4			
30	§ 11.1	Tenant Estoppel Statements Deadline CBS2, 3, 4			
31	§ 11.2	Tenant Estoppel Statements Objection Deadline CBS2, 3, 4			
		Closing and Possession			
32	§ 12.3	**Closing Date**			
33	§ 17	Possession Date			
34	§ 17	Possession Time			

26
27   **3.**   Other dates or deadlines set forth in the Contract shall be changed as follows:
28
29
30
31   **4.**   Additional amendments:
32
33
34
35   All other terms and conditions of the Contract shall remain the same.
36
37
38   This proposal shall expire unless accepted in writing by Seller and Buyer as evidenced by their signatures below and the offering
39   party to this document receives notice of such acceptance on or before _____.
40   Date   Time
41
42

Buyer's Name: _____   Buyer's Name: _____

_____   _____
Buyer's Signature   Date   Buyer's Signature   Date

Seller's Name: _____   Seller's Name: _____

_____   _____
Seller's Signature   Date   Seller's Signature   Date
43

12A. General Warranty Deed (to Joint Tenants)

WARRANTY DEED

THIS DEED, is dated _____ , 20 ____ , and is made between

_____ , (whether one, or more than one), the "Grantor," of the

* _____ County of _____ and State of _____ , and

_____ , the "Grantees,"

whose legal address is _____

of the _____ County of _____ and State of _____ .

WITNESS, that the Grantor, for and in consideration of the sum of

_____ DOLLARS,

($ _____), the receipt and sufficiency of which is hereby acknowledged, hereby grants, bargains, sells, conveys and confirms unto the Grantees and the Grantees' heirs and assigns forever, not in tenancy in common but in joint tenancy, all the real property, together with any improvements thereon, located in the _____ County of _____ and State of Colorado, described as follows:

also known by street address as: _____
and assessor's schedule or parcel number: _____

TOGETHER with all and singular the hereditaments and appurtenances thereunto belonging, or in anywise appertaining, the reversions, remainders, rents, issues and profits thereof, and all the estate, right, title, interest, claim and demand whatsoever of the Grantor, either in law or equity, of, in and to the above bargained premises, with the hereditaments and appurtenances;

TO HAVE AND TO HOLD the said premises above bargained and described, with the appurtenances, unto the Grantees and the Grantees' heirs and assigns forever.

The Grantor, for the Grantor and the Grantor's heirs and assigns, does covenant, grant, bargain, and agree to and with the Grantees, and the Grantees' heirs and assigns: that at the time of the ensealing and delivery of these presents, the Grantor is well seized of the premises above described; has good, sure, perfect, absolute and indefeasible estate of inheritance, in law and in fee simple; and has good right, full power and lawful authority to grant, bargain, sell and convey the same in manner and form as aforesaid; and that the same are free and clear from all former and other grants, bargains, sales, liens, taxes, assessments, encumbrances and restrictions of whatever kind or nature soever, except and subject to: ☐ none; or ☐ the following matters:

And the Grantor shall and will WARRANT THE TITLE AND DEFEND the above described premises, *but not any adjoining vacated street or alley,* if any, in the quiet and peaceable possession of the Grantees and the heirs and assigns of the Grantees, against all and every person or persons claiming the whole or any part thereof.

IN WITNESS WHEREOF, the Grantor has executed this deed on the date set forth above.

_____   _____

_____   _____

_____   _____

STATE OF COLORADO

County of _____   } ss.

The foregoing instrument was acknowledged before me this ____ day of _____ , 20 ____ ,
by _____

Witness my hand and official seal.
My commission expires: _____

*Insert "City and" if applicable.   _____ Notary Public

Name and Address of Person Creating Newly Created Legal Description (§38-35-106.5, C.R.S.)

No. 921A. Rev. 10-09. WARRANTY DEED (To Joint Tenants))
Bradford Publishing, 1743 Wazee St., Denver, CO 80202 — 303-292-2590 — www.bradfordpublishing.com

---

NOTES ON USE:
For a discussion of the different kinds of deeds, see § 6.3.1.

12B. General Warranty Deed

WARRANTY DEED

THIS DEED, is dated _____ , 20 ____ , and is made between

_____

(whether one, or more than one), the "Grantor,"

of the *_____ County of _____ and State of _____ ,

and

_____

(whether one, or more than one), the "Grantee,"

whose legal address is _____

of the _____ County of _____ and State of _____ .

 WITNESS, that the Grantor, for and in consideration of the sum of _____ DOLLARS,

($_____), the receipt and sufficiency of which is hereby acknowledged, hereby grants, bargains, sells, conveys and confirms unto the Grantee and the Grantee's heirs and assigns forever, all the real property, together with any improvements thereon, located in the _____ County of _____ and State of Colorado, described as follows:

also known by street address as:

and assessor's schedule or parcel number:

 TOGETHER with all and singular the hereditaments and appurtenances thereunto belonging, or in anywise appertaining, the reversions, remainders, rents, issues and profits thereof, and all the estate, right, title, interest, claim and demand whatsoever of the Grantor, either in law or equity, of, in and to the above bargained premises, with the hereditaments and appurtenances;

 TO HAVE AND TO HOLD the said premises above bargained and described, with the appurtenances, unto the Grantee and the Grantee's heirs and assigns forever.

 The Grantor, for the Grantor and the Grantor's heirs and assigns, does covenant, grant, bargain, and agree to and with the Grantee, and the Grantee's heirs and assigns: that at the time of the ensealing and delivery of these presents, the Grantor is well seized of the premises above described; has good, sure, perfect, absolute and indefeasible estate of inheritance, in law and in fee simple; and has good right, full power and lawful authority to grant, bargain, sell and convey the same in manner and form as aforesaid; and that the same are free and clear from all former and other grants, bargains, sales, liens, taxes, assessments, encumbrances and restrictions of whatever kind or nature soever, except and subject to: ☐ none; or ☐ the following matters:

 And the Grantor shall and will WARRANT THE TITLE AND DEFEND the above described premises, *but not any adjoining vacated street or alley*, if any, in the quiet and peaceable possession of the Grantee and the heirs and assigns of the Grantee, against all and every person or persons claiming the whole or any part thereof.

 IN WITNESS WHEREOF, the Grantor has executed this deed on the date set forth above.

_____ _____

_____ _____

_____ _____

STATE OF COLORADO   } ss.

County of _____

The foregoing instrument was acknowledged before me this _____ day of _____ , 20 ____ ,

by _____

   Witness my hand and official seal.

   My commission expires:

   _____

*Insert "City and" if applicable.   Notary Public

_____

Name and Address of Person Creating Newly Created Legal Description (§38-35-106.5, C.R.S.)

No. 932A. Rev. 10-09. WARRANTY DEED

Bradford Publishing, 1743 Wazee St., Denver, CO 80202 — 303-292-2590 — www.bradfordpublishing.com

_____

NOTES ON USE:

For a discussion of the different kinds of deeds, see § 6.3.1.

12C. Special Warranty Deed (to Joint Tenants)

SPECIAL WARRANTY DEED

THIS DEED, is dated _____ , 20 ____ , and is made between

_____ '

(whether one, or more than one), the "Grantor," of the *   County of _____
and State of _____ , and

the "Grantees," whose legal address is _____ '

of the _____ County of _____ and State of _____ .

    WITNESS, that the Grantor, for and in consideration of the sum of _____
_____ DOLLARS,
($_____), the receipt and sufficiency of which is hereby acknowledged, hereby grants, bargains,
sells, conveys and confirms unto the Grantees and the Grantees' heirs and assigns forever, not in tenancy in common but
in joint tenancy, all the real property, together with any improvements thereon, located in the   County
of _____ and State of Colorado, described as follows:

also known by street address as:
and assessor's schedule or parcel number:
    TOGETHER with all and singular the hereditaments and appurtenances thereunto belonging, or in anywise
appertaining, the reversions, remainders, rents, issues and profits thereof, and all the estate, right, title, interest, claim
and demand whatsoever of the Grantor, either in law or equity, of, in and to the above bargained premises, with the
hereditaments and appurtenances;
    TO HAVE AND TO HOLD the said premises above bargained and described, with the appurtenances, unto the
Grantees and the Grantees' heirs and assigns forever. The Grantor, for the Grantor and the Grantor's heirs and assigns,
does covenant and agree that the Grantor shall and will WARRANT THE TITLE AND DEFEND the above described
premises, *but not any adjoining vacated street or alley*, if any, in the quiet and peaceable possession of the Grantees and
the heirs and assigns of the Grantees, against all and every person or persons claiming the whole or any part thereof, by,
through or under the Grantor except and subject to: ☐ none; or ☐ the following matters:

    IN WITNESS WHEREOF, the Grantor has executed this deed on the date set forth above.

_____   _____

_____   _____

_____   _____

STATE OF COLORADO   ⎫
                               ⎬ ss.
County of _____   ⎭

    The foregoing instrument was acknowledged before me this _____ day of _____ , 20 ____ ,
by _____ .

Witness my hand and official seal.
My commission expires: _____

*Insert "City and" if applicable.   _____
                                      Notary Public

_____
Name and Address of Person Creating Newly Created Legal Description (§38-35-106.5, C.R.S.)

No. 515. Rev. 10-09. SPECIAL WARRANTY DEED (to Joint Tenants)
Bradford Publishing, 1743 Wazee St., Denver, CO 80202 — 303-292-2590 — www.bradfordpublishing.com

---

NOTES ON USE:

For a discussion of the different kinds of deeds, see § 6.3.1.

12D. Special Warranty Deed

SPECIAL WARRANTY DEED

THIS DEED, is dated   , 20   , and is made between

(whether one, or more than one), the "Grantor," of the *   County of
and State of   , and

(whether one, or more than one), the "Grantee," whose legal address is

of the   County of   and State of   .

WITNESS, that the Grantor, for and in consideration of the sum of

DOLLARS,

($_____), the receipt and sufficiency of which is hereby acknowledged, hereby grants, bargains, sells, conveys and confirms unto the Grantee and the Grantee's heirs and assigns forever, all the real property, together with any improvements thereon, located in the   County of   and State of Colorado, described as follows:

also known by street address as:
and assessor's schedule or parcel number:

TOGETHER with all and singular the hereditaments and appurtenances thereunto belonging, or in anywise appertaining, the reversions, remainders, rents, issues and profits thereof, and all the estate, right, title, interest, claim and demand whatsoever of the Grantor, either in law or equity, of, in and to the above bargained premises, with the hereditaments and appurtenances;

TO HAVE AND TO HOLD the said premises above bargained and described, with the appurtenances, unto the Grantee and the Grantee's heirs and assigns forever. The Grantor, for the Grantor and the Grantor's heirs and assigns, does covenant and agree that the Grantor shall and will WARRANT THE TITLE AND DEFEND the above described premises, *but not any adjoining vacated street or alley*, if any, in the quiet and peaceable possession of the Grantee and the heirs and assigns of the Grantee, against all and every person or persons claiming the whole or any part thereof, by, through or under the Grantor except and subject to: ☐ none; or ☐ the following matters:

IN WITNESS WHEREOF, the Grantor has executed this deed on the date set forth above.

_____   _____

_____   _____

_____   _____

STATE OF COLORADO
                                        } ss.
County of

The foregoing instrument was acknowledged before me this   day of   , 20   ,
by   .

Witness my hand and official seal.

_____
Notary Public

*Insert "City and" when applicable.   My commission expires: _____

Name and Address of Person Creating Newly Created Legal Description (§38-35-106.5, C.R.S.)

No. 16. Rev. 12-09. SPECIAL WARRANTY DEED

Bradford Publishing, 1743 Wazee St., Denver, CO 80202 — 303-292-2500 — www.bradfordpublishing.com

NOTES ON USE:

For a discussion of the different kinds of deeds, see § 6.3.1.

12E. Personal Representative's Deed (Sale)

PERSONAL REPRESENTATIVE'S DEED
(Sale)

THIS DEED is dated   , 20   , and is made between

the "Grantor," as Personal Representative of the estate of

                                                                    , deceased, and

(whether one, or more than one), the "Grantee," whose legal address is

of the   * County of   and State of   .

WHEREAS, the decedent died on the date of   and Grantor was duly appointed
Personal Representative of said estate by the   Court in and for the
County of   , State of Colorado, Probate No.   , on the date of
                    , and is now qualified and acting in said capacity;

NOW THEREFORE, pursuant to the powers conferred upon Grantor by the Colorado Probate Code, Grantor does
hereby sell and convey unto Grantee (in joint tenancy),** for and in consideration of
                                        Dollars, ($),
the following described real property situate in the   County of   ,
State of Colorado:

also known by street address as:
and assessor's schedule or parcel number:

With all appurtenances.

IN WITNESS WHEREOF, the Grantor has executed this deed on the date set forth above.

_____

_____
Personal Representative of the estate of
_____, Deceased

STATE OF COLORADO

COUNTY OF   } ss.

The foregoing instrument was acknowledged before me this   day of   , 20   ,
by   as Personal Representative of
the estate of   , Deceased.

Witness my hand and official seal.

_____

*Insert "City and" where applicable.   Notary Public
**Strike as required.   My commission expires: _____

Name and Address of Person Creating Newly Created Legal Description (§ 38-35-106.5, C.R.S.)

No. 46. Rev. 1-06. PERSONAL REPRESENTATIVE'S DEED (Sale) ©
Bradford Publishing, 1743 Wazee St., Denver, CO 80202 — 303-292-2590 — www.bradfordpublishing.com

---

NOTES ON USE:

For a discussion of the different kinds of deeds, see § 6.3.1.

12F. Personal Representative's Deed of Distribution

**PERSONAL REPRESENTATIVE'S
DEED OF DISTRIBUTION**

THIS DEED is dated   , 20   , and is made between

,

the "Grantor," as Personal Representative of the estate of

, deceased, and

(whether one, or more than one), the "Grantee," whose legal address is

,

of the   * County of   and State of   .

WHEREAS, the decedent died on the date of   and Grantor was duly appointed
Personal Representative of said estate by the   Court in and for the
County of   , State of Colorado, Probate No.   , on the date of
                    , and is now qualified and acting in said capacity;

NOW THEREFORE, pursuant to the powers conferred upon Grantor by the Colorado Probate Code, Grantor does
hereby convey, assign, transfer and release unto Grantee (in joint tenancy),** as the person entitled to distribution, the
following described real property situate in the   County of   ,
State of Colorado:

also known by street address as:
and assessor's schedule or parcel number:

With all appurtenances.

IN WITNESS WHEREOF, the Grantor has executed this deed on the date set forth above.

_____

_____
Personal Representative of the estate of

_____, Deceased

STATE OF COLORADO   }
                                                          } ss.
COUNTY OF   }

The foregoing instrument was acknowledged before me this   day of   , 20   ,
by   as Personal Representative of
the estate of   , Deceased.

Witness my hand and official seal.

_____

*Insert "City and" where applicable.   Notary Public
**Strike as required.   My commission expires: _____

Name and Address of Person Creating Newly Created Legal Description (§ 38-35-106.5, C.R.S.)

No. 47. Rev. 1-06. PERSONAL REPRESENTATIVE'S DEED OF DISTRIBUTION ©
Bradford Publishing, 1743 Wazee St., Denver, CO 80202 — 303-292-2590 — www.bradfordpublishing.com

---

NOTES ON USE:

For a discussion of the different kinds of deeds, see § 6.3.1.

12G. Bargain and Sale Deed

BARGAIN AND SALE DEED

KNOW ALL BY THESE PRESENTS, That

(whether one, or more than one), the "Grantor,"
whose legal address is

of the   *County of   and State of   ,
for the consideration of

DOLLARS, ($),
in hand paid, hereby sells and conveys to

(whether one, or more than one), the "Grantee",
whose legal address is

of the   *County of   and State of   ,
the following real property in the   *County of   and State of Colorado,
to wit:

also known by street address as:
and assessor's schedule or parcel number:

with all its appurtenances.

Signed this   day of   , 20   .

_____   _____

_____   _____

_____   _____

STATE OF COLORADO
                                        } ss.
County of

The foregoing instrument was acknowledged before me this   day of   , 20   ,
by

Witness my hand and official seal.
My commission expires:

*Insert "City and" where applicable.   Notary Public

Name and Address of Person Creating Newly Created Legal Description (§ 38-35-106.5, C.R.S.)

No. 901. Rev. 1-06. BARGAIN AND SALE DEED (Statutory Form) Copyright 1988
Bradford Publishing, 1743 Wazee St., Denver, CO 80202 — (303) 292-2590 — www.bradfordpublishing.com

NOTES ON USE:
For a discussion of the different kinds of deeds, see § 6.3.1.

12H. Quitclaim Deed

QUITCLAIM DEED

THIS DEED is dated   , 20   , and is made between

                                                                                    , (whether one, or more than one), the "Grantor,"

of the *   County of   and State of

and

                                                                                    , the "Grantees,"

whose legal address is

of the   * County of   and State of   .

WITNESS, that the Grantor, for and in consideration of the sum of

                                                            DOLLARS, ($),

the receipt and sufficiency of which is hereby acknowledged, does hereby remise, release, sell and QUITCLAIM unto the Grantees and the Grantees' heirs and assigns, forever, not in tenancy in common but in joint tenancy, all the right, title, interest, claim and demand which the Grantor has in and to the real property, together with any improvements thereon, located in the   County of   and State of Colorado, described as follows:

also known by street address as:
and assessor's schedule or parcel number:

TO HAVE AND TO HOLD the same, together with all and singular the appurtenances and privileges thereunto belonging, or in anywise thereunto appertaining, and all the estate, right, title, interest and claim whatsoever of the Grantor, either in law or equity, to the only proper use, benefit and behoof of the Grantee, and the Grantees' heirs and assigns, forever.

IN WITNESS WHEREOF, the Grantor has executed this deed on the date set forth above.

_____   _____

_____   _____

_____   _____

STATE OF COLORADO   }
                                            } ss.
County of   }

The foregoing instrument was acknowledged before me this   day of   , 20   ,
by   .

Witness my hand and official seal.
My commission expires:

*Insert "City and" where applicable.   _____
                                                                        Notary Public

Name and Address of Person Creating Newly Created Legal Description (§ 38-35-106.5, C.R.S.)

No. 962. Rev. 1-06. QUITCLAIM DEED (To Joint Tenants)
Bradford Publishing, 1743 Wazee St., Denver, CO 80202 — (303) 292-2590 — www.bradfordpublishing.com

---

NOTES ON USE:

For a discussion of the different kinds of deeds, see § 6.3.1.

12I. Quitclaim Deed

QUITCLAIM DEED

THIS DEED is dated   , 20   , and is made between

                                                                          ,

                                                        (whether one, or more than one), the "Grantor,"

of the *   County of   and State of   ,
and

                                                        (whether one, or more than one), the "Grantee,"

whose legal address is

of the   County of   and State of   .

WITNESS, that the Grantor, for and in consideration of the sum of

                                                        DOLLARS, ($),
the receipt and sufficiency of which is hereby acknowledged, does hereby remise, release, sell and QUITCLAIM unto the Grantee and the Grantee's heirs and assigns, forever, all the right, title, interest, claim and demand which the Grantor has in and to the real property, together with any improvements thereon, located in the   County of and State of Colorado, described as follows:

also known by street address as:
and assessor's schedule or parcel number:

TO HAVE AND TO HOLD the same, together with all and singular the appurtenances and privileges thereunto belonging, or in anywise thereunto appertaining, and all the estate, right, title, interest and claim whatsoever of the Grantor, either in law or equity, to the only proper use, benefit and behoof of the Grantee, and the Grantee's heirs and assigns, forever.

IN WITNESS WHEREOF, the Grantor has executed this deed on the date set forth above.

_____   _____

_____   _____

_____   _____

STATE OF COLORADO   }
                            } ss.
County of   }

The foregoing instrument was acknowledged before me this   day of   , 20   ,
by   .

Witness my hand and official seal.
My commission expires:

*Insert "City and" where applicable.   _____
                                               Notary Public

Name and Address of Person Creating Newly Created Legal Description (§ 38-35-106.5, C.R.S.)

No. 933. Rev. 1-06. QUITCLAIM DEED
Bradford Publishing, 1743 Wazee St., Denver, CO 80202 — (303) 292-2590 — www.bradfordpublishing.com

NOTES ON USE:

For a discussion of the different kinds of deeds, see § 6.3.1.

Appendix 1: Forms

13. Promissory Note

1 The printed portions of this form, except differentiated additions, have been approved by the Colorado Real Estate Commission.
2 (NTD81-10-06) (Mandatory 1-07)

3 **IF THIS FORM IS USED IN A CONSUMER CREDIT TRANSACTION, CONSULT LEGAL COUNSEL.**

4 **THIS IS A LEGAL INSTRUMENT. IF NOT UNDERSTOOD, LEGAL, TAX OR OTHER COUNSEL SHOULD BE CONSULTED BEFORE SIGNING.**

5 **PROMISSORY NOTE**

6 U.S. $_____   _____, Colorado

7   Date: _____

8 1.   FOR VALUE RECEIVED, the undersigned (Borrower) promise(s) to pay
9
10
11 (Note Holder) or order, the principal sum of
12   Dollars,
13 with interest on the unpaid principal balance from   , until paid, at the rate
14 of _____ percent per annum. Principal and interest shall be payable at
15   ,
16 or such other place as Note Holder may designate, in _____ payments of
17   Dollars (U.S. $_____),
18 due on the _____ day of each _____, beginning _____.
19 Such payments shall continue until the entire indebtedness evidenced by this Note is fully paid; provided, however, if
20 not sooner paid, the entire principal amount outstanding and accrued interest thereon, shall be due and payable on
21 _____.

22 2.   Borrower shall pay to Note Holder a late charge of _____% of any payment not received by Note Holder within
23 _____ days after the payment is due.

24 3.   Payments received for application to this Note shall be applied first to the payment of late charges, if any, second to
25 the payment of accrued interest at the default rate specified below, if any, third to accrued interest first specified above,
26 and the balance applied in reduction of the principal amount hereof.

27 4.   If any payment required by this Note is not paid when due, or if any default under any Deed of Trust securing this
28 Note occurs, the entire principal amount outstanding and accrued interest thereon shall at once become due and payable
29 at the option of Note Holder (Acceleration); and the indebtedness shall bear interest at the rate of _____ percent per
30 annum from the date of default. Note Holder shall be entitled to collect all reasonable costs and expense of collection
31 and/or suit, including, but not limited to reasonable attorneys' fees.

32 5.   Borrower may prepay the principal amount outstanding under this Note, in whole or in part, at any time without
33 penalty except
34
35
36
37
38 Any partial prepayment shall be applied against the principal amount outstanding and shall not postpone the due date of
39 any subsequent payments or change the amount of such payments.

40 6.   Borrower and all other makers, sureties, guarantors, and endorsers hereby waive presentment, notice of dishonor
41 and protest, and they hereby agree to any extensions of time of payment and partial payments before, at, or after maturity.
42 This Note shall be the joint and several obligation of Borrower and all other makers, sureties, guarantors and endorsers,
43 and their successors and assigns.

No. NTD81-10-06. PROMISSORY NOTE   Page 1 of 2 _____
                                                                            Initial
Bradford Publishing, 1743 Wazee St., Denver, CO 80202 — (303) 292-2590 — www.bradfordpublishing.com

NOTES ON USE:
For a discussion of promissory notes, see § 6.3.2.

44   7. Any notice to Borrower provided for in this Note shall be in writing and shall be given and be effective upon (a)
45   delivery to Borrower or (b) by mailing such notice by first class U.S. mail, addressed to Borrower at Borrower's address
46   stated below, or to such other address as Borrower may designate by notice to Note Holder. Any notice to Note Holder
47   shall be in writing and shall be given and be effective upon (a) delivery to Note Holder or (b) by mailing such notice by
48   first class U.S. mail, to Note Holder at the address stated in the first paragraph of this Note, or to such other address as
49   Note Holder may designate by notice to Borrower.

50   8. The indebtedness evidenced by this Note is secured by a Deed of Trust dated _____,
51   and until released said Deed of Trust contains additional rights of Note Holder. Such rights may cause Acceleration of
52   the indebtedness evidenced by this Note. Reference is made to said Deed of Trust for such additional terms. Said Deed
53   of Trust grants rights in the following legally described property located in the _____ County of
54   _____, State of Colorado:

55
56
57
58
59
60
61
62
63
64   known as No. _____ (Property Address).
65   Street Address   City   State   Zip

66   (CAUTION: SIGN ORIGINAL NOTE ONLY/RETAIN COPY)

67   IF BORROWER IS NATURAL PERSON(S):

68   _____   _____

69   _____   doing business as _____

70   IF BORROWER IS CORPORATION:

71   ATTEST: _____
72   Name of Corporation

73   _____   By _____
74   Secretary   President

75   (SEAL)

76   IF BORROWER IS PARTNERSHIP: _____
77   Name of Partnership

78   _____   By _____
79   General Partner

80   Borrower's address: _____

81   _____

82   KEEP THIS NOTE IN A SAFE PLACE. THE ORIGINAL OF THIS NOTE MUST BE EXHIBITED TO THE PUBLIC TRUSTEE IN ORDER
83   TO RELEASE A DEED OF TRUST SECURING THIS NOTE.

14. Deed of Trust (Due on Transfer - Strict)

1	The printed portions of this form, except differentiated additions, have been approved by the Colorado Real Estate Commission.
2	(TD72-8-10) (Mandatory 1-11)

4 **IF THIS FORM IS USED IN A CONSUMER CREDIT TRANSACTION, CONSULT LEGAL COUNSEL.**

5 **THIS IS A LEGAL INSTRUMENT. IF NOT UNDERSTOOD, LEGAL, TAX OR OTHER COUNSEL SHOULD BE**
6 **CONSULTED BEFORE SIGNING.**

DEED OF TRUST
(Due on Transfer – Strict)

11 THIS DEED OF TRUST is made this _____ day of _____, 20____, between _____
12 _____ (Borrower), whose
13 address is _____ ; and the
14 Public Trustee of the County in which the Property (see § 1) is situated (Trustee); for the benefit of _____
15 _____ (Lender), whose address is _____
16 _____ .

18 Borrower and Lender covenant and agree as follows:
19   **1.**   **Property in Trust.** Borrower, in consideration of the indebtedness herein recited and the trust herein created,
20 hereby grants and conveys to Trustee in trust, with power of sale, the following legally described property located in the
21 _____ County of _____, State of Colorado:

25 known as No. _____ (Property Address),
26   Street Address   City   State   Zip
27 together with all its appurtenances (Property).
28   **2.**   **Note: Other Obligations Secured.** This Deed of Trust is given to secure to Lender:
29   **2.1.**   the repayment of the indebtedness evidenced by Borrower's note (Note) dated _____
30 in the principal sum of _____ Dollars
31 (U.S. $_____), with interest on the unpaid principal balance from _____ until
32 paid, at the rate of _____ percent per annum, with principal and interest payable at _____
33 _____ or such other place as Lender may designate,
34 in _____ payments of _____ Dollars
35 (U.S. $_____), due on the _____ day of each _____ beginning _____ ;
36 such payments to continue until the entire indebtedness evidenced by said Note is fully paid; however, if not sooner paid,
37 the entire principal amount outstanding and accrued interest thereon shall be due and payable on _____ ;
38 and Borrower is to pay to Lender a late charge of _____% of any payment not received by Lender within _____ days
39 after payment is due; and Borrower has the right to prepay the principal amount outstanding under said Note, in whole or in
40 part, at any time without penalty except _____ ;
41   **2.2.**   the payment of all other sums, with interest thereon at _____% per annum, disbursed by Lender in
42 accordance with this Deed of Trust to protect the security of this Deed of Trust; and
43   **2.3.**   the performance of the covenants and agreements of Borrower herein contained.
44   **3.**   **Title.** Borrower covenants that Borrower owns and has the right to grant and convey the Property, and warrants
45 title to the same, subject to general real estate taxes for the current year, easements of record or in existence, and recorded
46 declarations, restrictions, reservations and covenants, if any, as of this date; and subject to _____ .
47   **4.**   **Payment of Principal and Interest.** Borrower shall promptly pay when due the principal of and interest on the
48 indebtedness evidenced by the Note, and late charges as provided in the Note and shall perform all of Borrower's other
49 covenants contained in the Note.
50   **5.**   **Application of Payments.** All payments received by Lender under the terms hereof shall be applied by Lender
51 first in payment of amounts due pursuant to § 23 (Escrow Funds for Taxes and Insurance), then to amounts disbursed by

NOTES ON USE:

For a discussion of deeds of trust, see § 6.3.2.

52 Lender pursuant to § 9 (Protection of Lender's Security), and the balance in accordance with the terms and conditions of the
53 Note.
54   **6.   Prior Mortgages and Deeds of Trust; Charges; Liens.** Borrower shall perform all of Borrower's obligations
55 under any prior deed of trust and any other prior liens. Borrower shall pay all taxes, assessments and other charges, fines
56 and impositions attributable to the Property which may have or attain a priority over this Deed of Trust, and leasehold
57 payments or ground rents, if any, in the manner set out in § 23 (Escrow Funds for Taxes and Insurance) or, if not required
58 to be paid in such manner, by Borrower making payment when due, directly to the payee thereof. Despite the foregoing,
59 Borrower shall not be required to make payments otherwise required by this section if Borrower, after notice to Lender,
60 shall in good faith contest such obligation by, or defend enforcement of such obligation in, legal proceedings which operate
61 to prevent the enforcement of the obligation or forfeiture of the Property or any part thereof, only upon Borrower making
62 all such contested payments and other payments as ordered by the court to the registry of the court in which such
63 proceedings are filed.
64   **7.   Property Insurance.** Borrower shall keep the improvements now existing or hereafter erected on the Property
65 insured against loss by fire or hazards included within the term "extended coverage" in an amount at least equal to the
66 lesser of (a) the insurable value of the Property or (b) an amount sufficient to pay the sums secured by this Deed of Trust as
67 well as any prior encumbrances on the Property. All of the foregoing shall be known as "Property Insurance."
68   The insurance carrier providing the insurance shall be qualified to write Property Insurance in Colorado and shall be
69 chosen by Borrower subject to Lender's right to reject the chosen carrier for reasonable cause. All insurance policies and
70 renewals thereof shall include a standard mortgage clause in favor of Lender, and shall provide that the insurance carrier
71 shall notify Lender at least ten (10) days before cancellation, termination or any material change of coverage. Insurance
72 policies shall be furnished to Lender at or before closing. Lender shall have the right to hold the policies and renewals
73 thereof.
74   In the event of loss, Borrower shall give prompt notice to the insurance carrier and Lender. Lender may make proof of
75 loss if not made promptly by Borrower.
76   Insurance proceeds shall be applied to restoration or repair of the Property damaged, provided said restoration or repair
77 is economically feasible and the security of this Deed of Trust is not thereby impaired. If such restoration or repair is not
78 economically feasible or if the security of this Deed of Trust would be impaired, the insurance proceeds shall be applied to
79 the sums secured by this Deed of Trust, with the excess, if any, paid to Borrower. If the Property is abandoned by
80 Borrower, or if Borrower fails to respond to Lender within 30 days from the date notice is given in accordance with § 16
81 (Notice) by Lender to Borrower that the insurance carrier offers to settle a claim for insurance benefits, Lender is
82 authorized to collect and apply the insurance proceeds, at Lender's option, either to restoration or repair of the Property or
83 to the sums secured by this Deed of Trust.
84   Any such application of proceeds to principal shall not extend or postpone the due date of the installments referred to
85 in §§ 4 (Payment of Principal and Interest) and 23 (Escrow Funds for Taxes and Insurance) or change the amount of such
86 installments. Notwithstanding anything herein to the contrary, if under § 18 (Acceleration; Foreclosure; Other Remedies)
87 the Property is acquired by Lender, all right, title and interest of Borrower in and to any insurance policies and in and to the
88 proceeds thereof resulting from damage to the Property prior to the sale or acquisition shall pass to Lender to the extent of
89 the sums secured by this Deed of Trust immediately prior to such sale or acquisition.
90   All of the rights of Borrower and Lender hereunder with respect to insurance carriers, insurance policies and insurance
91 proceeds are subject to the rights of any holder of a prior deed of trust with respect to said insurance carriers, policies and
92 proceeds.
93   **8.   Preservation and Maintenance of Property.** Borrower shall keep the Property in good repair and shall not
94 commit waste or permit impairment or deterioration of the Property and shall comply with the provisions of any lease if this
95 Deed of Trust is on a leasehold. Borrower shall perform all of Borrower's obligations under any declarations, covenants,
96 by-laws, rules, or other documents governing the use, ownership or occupancy of the Property.
97   **9.   Protection of Lender's Security.** Except when Borrower has exercised Borrower's rights under § 6 above, if
98 Borrower fails to perform the covenants and agreements contained in this Deed of Trust, or if a default occurs in a prior
99 lien, or if any action or proceeding is commenced which materially affects Lender's interest in the Property, then Lender, at
100 Lender's option, with notice to Borrower if required by law, may make such appearances, disburse such sums and take such
101 action as is necessary to protect Lender's interest, including, but not limited to:
102   **9.1.**   any general or special taxes or ditch or water assessments levied or accruing against the Property;
103   **9.2.**   the premiums on any insurance necessary to protect any improvements comprising a part of the Property;
104   **9.3.**   sums due on any prior lien or encumbrance on the Property;

No. TD72-8-10.   DEED OF TRUST (Due on Transfer – Strict)   Page 2 of 6

105   **9.4.**   if the Property is a leasehold or is subject to a lease, all sums due under such lease;

106   **9.5.**   the reasonable costs and expenses of defending, protecting, and maintaining the Property and Lender's
107 interest in the Property, including repair and maintenance costs and expenses, costs and expenses of protecting and securing
108 the Property, receiver's fees and expenses, inspection fees, appraisal fees, court costs, attorney fees and costs, and fees and
109 costs of an attorney in the employment of Lender or holder of the certificate of purchase;

110   **9.6.**   all other costs and expenses allowable by the evidence of debt or this Deed of Trust; and

111   **9.7.**   such other costs and expenses which may be authorized by a court of competent jurisdiction.

112   Borrower hereby assigns to Lender any right Borrower may have by reason of any prior encumbrance on the Property
113 or by law or otherwise to cure any default under said prior encumbrance.

114   Any amounts disbursed by Lender pursuant to this § 9, with interest thereon, shall become additional indebtedness of
115 Borrower secured by this Deed of Trust. Such amounts shall be payable upon notice from Lender to Borrower requesting
116 payment thereof, and Lender may bring suit to collect any amounts so disbursed plus interest specified in § 2.2 (Note: Other
117 Obligations Secured). Nothing contained in this § 9 shall require Lender to incur any expense or take any action hereunder.

118   **10.**   **Inspection.** Lender may make or cause to be made reasonable entries upon and inspection of the Property,
119 provided that Lender shall give Borrower notice prior to any such inspection specifying reasonable cause therefore related
120 to Lender's interest in the Property.

121   **11.**   **Condemnation.** The proceeds of any award or claim for damages, direct or consequential, in connection with
122 any condemnation or other taking of the Property, or part thereof, or for conveyance in lieu of condemnation, are hereby
123 assigned and shall be paid to Lender as herein provided. However, all of the rights of Borrower and Lender hereunder with
124 respect to such proceeds are subject to the rights of any holder of a prior deed of trust.

125   In the event of a total taking of the Property, the proceeds shall be applied to the sums secured by this Deed of Trust,
126 with the excess, if any, paid to Borrower. In the event of a partial taking of the Property, the proceeds remaining after
127 taking out any part of the award due any prior lien holder (net award) shall be divided between Lender and Borrower, in the
128 same ratio as the amount of the sums secured by this Deed of Trust immediately prior to the date of taking bears to
129 Borrower's equity in the Property immediately prior to the date of taking. Borrower's equity in the Property means the fair
130 market value of the Property less the amount of sums secured by both this Deed of Trust and all prior liens (except taxes)
131 that are to receive any of the award, all at the value immediately prior to the date of taking.

132   If the Property is abandoned by Borrower or if, after notice by Lender to Borrower that the condemnor offers to make
133 an award or settle a claim for damages, Borrower fails to respond to Lender within 30 days after the date such notice is
134 given, Lender is authorized to collect and apply the proceeds, at Lender's option, either to restoration or repair of the
135 Property or to the sums secured by this Deed of Trust.

136   Any such application of proceeds to principal shall not extend or postpone the due date of the installments referred to
137 in §§ 4 (Payment of Principal and Interest) and 23 (Escrow Funds for Taxes and Insurance) nor change the amount of such
138 installments.

139   **12.**   **Borrower not Released.** Extension of the time for payment or modification of amortization of the sums secured
140 by this Deed of Trust granted by Lender to any successor in interest of Borrower shall not operate to release, in any manner,
141 the liability of the original Borrower, nor Borrower's successors in interest, from the original terms of this Deed of Trust.
142 Lender shall not be required to commence proceedings against such successor or refuse to extend time for payment or
143 otherwise modify amortization of the sums secured by this Deed of Trust by reason of any demand made by the original
144 Borrower nor Borrower's successors in interest.

145   **13.**   **Forbearance by Lender Not a Waiver.** Any forbearance by Lender in exercising any right or remedy
146 hereunder, or otherwise afforded by law, shall not be a waiver or preclude the exercise of any such right or remedy.

147   **14.**   **Remedies Cumulative.** Each remedy provided in the Note and this Deed of Trust is distinct from and
148 cumulative to all other rights or remedies under the Note and this Deed of Trust or afforded by law or equity, and may be
149 exercised concurrently, independently or successively.

150   **15.**   **Successors and Assigns Bound; Joint and Several Liability; Captions.** The covenants and agreements herein
151 contained shall bind, and the rights hereunder shall inure to, the respective successors and assigns of Lender and Borrower,
152 subject to the provisions of § 24 (Transfer of the Property; Assumption). All covenants and agreements of Borrower shall
153 be joint and several. The captions and headings of the sections in this Deed of Trust are for convenience only and are not to
154 be used to interpret or define the provisions hereof.

155   **16.**   **Notice.** Except for any notice required by law to be given in another manner, (a) any notice to Borrower
156 provided for in this Deed of Trust shall be in writing and shall be given and be effective upon (1) delivery to Borrower or
157 (2) mailing such notice by first class U.S. mail, addressed to Borrower at Borrower's address stated herein or at such other

158   address as Borrower may designate by notice to Lender as provided herein, and (b) any notice to Lender shall be in writing
159   and shall be given and be effective upon (1) delivery to Lender or (2) mailing such notice by first class U.S. mail, to
160   Lender's address stated herein or to such other address as Lender may designate by notice to Borrower as provided herein.
161   Any notice provided for in this Deed of Trust shall be deemed to have been given to Borrower or Lender when given in any
162   manner designated herein.

163   **17.   Governing Law; Severability.** The Note and this Deed of Trust shall be governed by the law of Colorado. In
164   the event that any provision or clause of this Deed of Trust or the Note conflicts with the law, such conflict shall not affect
165   other provisions of this Deed of Trust or the Note which can be given effect without the conflicting provision, and to this
166   end the provisions of the Deed of Trust and Note are declared to be severable.

167   **18.   Acceleration; Foreclosure; Other Remedies.** Except as provided in § 24 (Transfer of the Property;
168   Assumption), upon Borrower's breach of any covenant or agreement of Borrower in this Deed of Trust, or upon any default
169   in a prior lien upon the Property, (unless Borrower has exercised Borrower's rights under § 6 above), at Lender's option, all
170   of the sums secured by this Deed of Trust shall be immediately due and payable (Acceleration). To exercise this option,
171   Lender may invoke the power of sale and any other remedies permitted by law. Lender shall be entitled to collect all
172   reasonable costs and expenses incurred in pursuing the remedies provided in this Deed of Trust, including, but not limited
173   to, reasonable attorney's fees.

174   If Lender invokes the power of sale, Lender shall give written notice to Trustee of such election. Trustee shall give
175   such notice to Borrower of Borrower's rights as is provided by law. Trustee shall record a copy of such notice and shall
176   cause publication of the legal notice as required by law in a legal newspaper of general circulation in each county in which
177   the Property is situated, and shall mail copies of such notice of sale to Borrower and other persons as prescribed by law.
178   After the lapse of such time as may be required by law, Trustee, without demand on Borrower, shall sell the Property at
179   public auction to the highest bidder for cash at the time and place (which may be on the Property or any part thereof as
180   permitted by law) in one or more parcels as Trustee may think best and in such order as Trustee may determine. Lender or
181   Lender's designee may purchase the Property at any sale. It shall not be obligatory upon the purchaser at any such sale to
182   see to the application of the purchase money.

183   Trustee shall apply the proceeds of the sale in the following order: (a) to all reasonable costs and expenses of the sale,
184   including, but not limited to, reasonable Trustee's and attorney's fees and costs of title evidence; (b) to all sums secured by
185   this Deed of Trust; and (c) the excess, if any, to the person or persons legally entitled thereto.

186   **19.   Borrower's Right to Cure Default.** Whenever foreclosure is commenced for nonpayment of any sums due
187   hereunder, the owners of the Property or parties liable hereon shall be entitled to cure said defaults by paying all delinquent
188   principal and interest payments due as of the date of cure, costs, expenses, late charges, attorney's fees and other fees all in
189   the manner provided by law. Upon such payment, this Deed of Trust and the obligations secured hereby shall remain in full
190   force and effect as though no Acceleration had occurred, and the foreclosure proceedings shall be discontinued.

191   **20.   Assignment of Rents; Appointment of Receiver; Lender in Possession.** As additional security hereunder,
192   Borrower hereby assigns to Lender the rents of the Property; however, Borrower shall, prior to Acceleration under § 18
193   (Acceleration; Foreclosure; Other Remedies) or abandonment of the Property, have the right to collect and retain such rents
194   as they become due and payable.

195   Lender or the holder of the Trustee's certificate of purchase shall be entitled to a receiver for the Property after
196   Acceleration under § 18 (Acceleration; Foreclosure; Other Remedies), and shall also be so entitled during the time covered by
197   foreclosure proceedings and the period of redemption, if any; and shall be entitled thereto as a matter of right without regard to
198   the solvency or insolvency of Borrower or of the then owner of the Property, and without regard to the value thereof. Such
199   receiver may be appointed by any Court of competent jurisdiction upon ex parte application and without notice; notice being
200   hereby expressly waived.

201   Upon Acceleration under § 18 (Acceleration; Foreclosure; Other Remedies) or abandonment of the Property, Lender,
202   in person, by agent or by judicially-appointed receiver, shall be entitled to enter upon, take possession of and manage the
203   Property and to collect the rents of the Property including those past due. All rents collected by Lender or the receiver shall
204   be applied, first to payment of the costs of preservation and management of the Property, second to payments due upon
205   prior liens, and then to the sums secured by this Deed of Trust. Lender and the receiver shall be liable to account only for
206   those rents actually received.

207   **21.   Release.** Upon payment of all sums secured by this Deed of Trust, Lender shall cause Trustee to release this
208   Deed of Trust and shall produce for Trustee the Note. Borrower shall pay all costs of recordation and shall pay the statutory
209   Trustee's fees. If Lender shall not produce the Note as aforesaid, then Lender, upon notice in accordance with § 16 (Notice)

No. TD72-8-10.   DEED OF TRUST (Due on Transfer – Strict)   Page 4 of 6

210 from Borrower to Lender, shall obtain, at Lender's expense, and file any lost instrument bond required by Trustee or pay
211 the cost thereof to effect the release of this Deed of Trust.
212   **22.**   **Waiver of Exemptions.** Borrower hereby waives all right of homestead and any other exemption in the
213 Property under state or federal law presently existing or hereafter enacted.
214   **23.**   **Escrow Funds for Taxes and Insurance.** This § 23 is not applicable if Funds, as defined below, are being paid
215 pursuant to a prior encumbrance. Subject to applicable law, Borrower shall pay to Lender, on each day installments of
216 principal and interest are payable under the Note, until the Note is paid in full, a sum (herein referred to as "Funds") equal
217 to _____ of the yearly taxes and assessments which may attain priority over this Deed of Trust, plus
218 _____ of yearly premium installments for Property Insurance, all as reasonably estimated initially and from
219 time to time by Lender on the basis of assessments and bills and reasonable estimates thereof, taking into account any
220 excess Funds not used or shortages.
221   The principal of the Funds shall be held in a separate account by Lender in trust for the benefit of Borrower and
222 deposited in an institution, the deposits or accounts of which are insured or guaranteed by a federal or state agency. Lender
223 shall apply the Funds to pay said taxes, assessments and insurance premiums. Lender may not charge for so holding and
224 applying the Funds, analyzing said account or verifying and compiling said assessments and bills. Lender shall not be
225 required to pay Borrower any interest or earnings on the Funds. Lender shall give to Borrower, without charge, an annual
226 accounting of the Funds showing credits and debits to the Funds and the purpose for which each debit to the Funds was
227 made. The Funds are pledged as additional security for the sums secured by this Deed of Trust.
228   If the amount of the Funds held by Lender shall not be sufficient to pay taxes, assessments and insurance premiums as
229 they fall due, Borrower shall pay to Lender any amount necessary to make up the deficiency within 30 days from the date
230 notice is given in accordance with § 16 (Notice) by Lender to Borrower requesting payment thereof. Provided however, if
231 the loan secured by this Deed of Trust is subject to RESPA or other laws regulating Escrow Accounts, such deficiency,
232 surplus or any other required adjustment shall be paid, credited or adjusted in compliance with such applicable laws.
233   Upon payment in full of all sums secured by this Deed of Trust, Lender shall simultaneously refund to Borrower any
234 Funds held by Lender. If under § 18 (Acceleration; Foreclosure; Other Remedies) the Property is sold or the Property is
235 otherwise acquired by Lender, Lender shall apply, no later than immediately prior to the sale of the Property or its acquisition
236 by Lender, whichever occurs first, any Funds held by Lender at the time of application as a credit against the sums secured by
237 this Deed of Trust.
238   **24.**   **Transfer of the Property; Assumption.** The following events shall be referred to herein as a "Transfer": (i) a
239 transfer or conveyance of title (or any portion thereof, legal or equitable) of the Property (or any part thereof or interest
240 therein); (ii) the execution of a contract or agreement creating a right to title (or any portion thereof, legal or equitable) in
241 the Property (or any part thereof or interest therein); (iii) or an agreement granting a possessory right in the Property (or any
242 portion thereof), in excess of 3 years; (iv) a sale or transfer of, or the execution of a contract or agreement creating a right to
243 acquire or receive, more than fifty percent (50%) of the controlling interest or more than fifty percent (50%) of the
244 beneficial interest in Borrower and (v) the reorganization, liquidation or dissolution of Borrower. Not to be included as a
245 Transfer are (x) the creation of a lien or encumbrance subordinate to this Deed of Trust; (y) the creation of a purchase
246 money security interest for household appliances; or (z) a transfer by devise, descent or by operation of the law upon the
247 death of a joint tenant. At the election of Lender, in the event of each and every Transfer:
248   **24.1.**   All sums secured by this Deed of Trust shall become immediately due and payable (Acceleration).
249   **24.2.**   If a Transfer occurs and should Lender not exercise Lender's option pursuant to this § 24 to Accelerate,
250 Transferee shall be deemed to have assumed all of the obligations of Borrower under this Deed of Trust including all sums
251 secured hereby whether or not the instrument evidencing such conveyance, contract or grant expressly so provides. This
252 covenant shall run with the Property and remain in full force and effect until said sums are paid in full. Lender may without
253 notice to Borrower deal with Transferee in the same manner as with Borrower with reference to said sums including the
254 payment or credit to Transferee of undisbursed reserve Funds on payment in full of said sums, without in any way altering
255 or discharging Borrower's liability hereunder for the obligations hereby secured.
256   **24.3.**   Should Lender not elect to Accelerate upon the occurrence of such Transfer then, subject to § 24.2 above,
257 the mere fact of a lapse of time or the acceptance of payment subsequent to any of such events, whether or not Lender had
258 actual or constructive notice of such Transfer, shall not be deemed a waiver of Lender's right to make such election nor
259 shall Lender be estopped therefrom by virtue thereof. The issuance on behalf of Lender of a routine statement showing the
260 status of the loan, whether or not Lender had actual or constructive notice of such Transfer, shall not be a waiver or
261 estoppel of Lender's said rights.

No. TD72-8-10.   **DEED OF TRUST (Due on Transfer – Strict)**   Page 5 of 6

262   **25.   Borrower's Copy.** Borrower acknowledges receipt of a copy of the Note and this Deed of Trust.
263
264   EXECUTED BY BORROWER.

IF BORROWER IS NATURAL PERSON(s):

_____   _____

                                              doing business as _____

IF BORROWER IS CORPORATION:
ATTEST: _____
                                              Name of Corporation

                                              By _____
_____
Secretary   President

        (SEAL)

IF BORROWER IS PARTNERSHIP: _____
                                              Name of Partnership

                                              By _____
                                                 A General Partner

IF BORROWER IS LIMITED LIABILITY COMPANY: _____
                                              Name of Limited Liability Company

                                              By _____
                                                 Its Authorized Representative

                                              _____
                                              Title of Authorized Representative

            STATE OF COLORADO
_____ COUNTY OF _____

    The foregoing instrument was acknowledged before me this _____ day of _____, 20_____,
by *_____.

                                              Witness my hand and official seal.
                                              My commission expires: _____

                                              _____
                                              Notary Public

265   *If a natural person or persons, insert the name(s) of such person(s). If a corporation, insert, for example, "John Doe as President and
266   Jane Doe as Secretary of Doe & Co., a Colorado corporation." If a partnership, insert, for example, "Sam Smith as general partner in and
267   for Smith & Smith, a general partnership." A Statement of Authority may be required if borrower is a limited liability company or other
268   entity (§ 38-30-172, C.R.S.)

No. TD72-8-10.   **DEED OF TRUST (Due on Transfer – Strict)**   Page 6 of 6

15. Bill of Sale

BILL OF SALE

KNOW ALL BY THESE PRESENTS, That

of the _____ *County of _____ , State of Colorado, (Seller), for and in consideration of

_____ Dollars,

to him in hand paid, at or before the ensealing or delivery of these presents by

of the _____ County of _____ , in the State of Colorado, (Buyer), the receipt of which is hereby acknowledged, has bargained and sold, and by these presents does grant and convey unto the said Buyer, his personal representatives, successors and assigns, the following property, goods and chattels, to wit:

located at

TO HAVE AND TO HOLD the same unto the said Buyer, his personal representatives, successors and assigns, forever. The said Seller covenants and agrees to and with the Buyer, his personal representatives, successors and assigns, to WARRANT AND DEFEND the sale of said property, goods and chattels, against all and every person or persons whomever. When used herein, the singular shall include the plural, the plural the singular, and the use of any gender shall be applicable to all genders.

IN WITNESS WHEREOF, the Seller has executed this Bill of Sale on _____ .

Date

_____

_____

STATE OF COLORADO,
} ss.
_____ County of _____

The foregoing instrument was acknowledged before me this _____ day of _____ , _____ ,

by _____

Witness my hand and official seal.

My Commission expires _____ .

_____

* Insert "City and" where applicable. | Notary Public

No. 35A. Rev. 9-83. BILL OF SALE

Bradford Publishing, 1743 Wazee St., Denver, CO 80202 — (303) 292-2590 — www.bradfordpublishing.com

---

NOTES ON USE:

For a discussion of the Bill of Sale, see § 6.3.3.

16. Real Property Transfer Declaration

REAL PROPERTY TRANSFER DECLARATION — (TD-1000)

GENERAL INFORMATION

Purpose: The Real Property Transfer Declaration provides essential information to the county assessor to help ensure fair and uniform assessments for all property for property tax purposes. Refer to 39-14-102(4), Colorado Revised Statutes (C.R.S.).

Requirements: All conveyance documents (deeds) subject to the documentary fee submitted to the county clerk and recorder for recordation must be accompanied by a Real Property Transfer Declaration. This declaration must be completed and signed by the grantor (seller) or grantee (buyer). Refer to 39-14-102(1)(a), C.R.S.

Penalty for Noncompliance: Whenever a Real Property Transfer Declaration does not accompany the deed, the clerk and recorder notifies the county assessor who will send a notice to the buyer requesting that the declaration be returned within thirty days after the notice is mailed.

If the completed Real Property Transfer Declaration is not returned to the county assessor within the 30 days of notice, the assessor may impose a penalty of $25.00 or .025% (.00025) of the sale price, whichever is greater. This penalty may be imposed for any subsequent year that the buyer fails to submit the declaration until the property is sold. Refer to 39-14-102(1)(b), C.R.S.

Confidentiality: The assessor is required to make the Real Property Transfer Declaration available for inspection to the buyer. However, it is only available to the seller if the seller filed the declaration. Information derived from the Real Property Transfer Declaration is available to any taxpayer or any agent of such taxpayer subject to confidentiality requirements as provided by law. Refer to 39-5-121.5, C.R.S and 39-13-102(5)(c), C.R.S.

---

1. Address and/or legal description of the real property sold: Please do not use P.O. box numbers.

    _____

    _____

2. Type of property purchased: ☐ Single Family Residential ☐ Townhome ☐ Condominium ☐ Multi-Unit Res
    ☐ Commercial ☐ Industrial ☐ Agricultural ☐ Mixed Use ☐ Vacant Land ☐ Other _____

3. Date of closing:

    _____
    Month   Day   Year

    Date of contract if different than date of closing:

    _____
    Month   Day   Year

4. Total sale price: Including all real and personal property.
    $ _____

5. Was any personal property included in the transaction? Personal property would include, but is not limited to, carpeting, draperies, free standing appliances, equipment, inventory, furniture. If the personal property is not listed, the entire purchase price will be assumed to be for the real property as per 39-13-102, C.R.S.
    ☐ Yes ☐ No   If yes, approximate value $_____ Describe _____

6. Did the total sale price include a trade or exchange of additional real or personal property? If yes, give the approximate value of the goods or services as of the date of closing.
    ☐ Yes ☐ No   If yes, approximate value $_____
    If yes, does this transaction involve a trade under IRS Code Section 1031? ☐ Yes ☐ No

7. Was 100% interest in the real property purchased? Mark "no" if only a partial interest is being purchased.
    ☐ Yes ☐ No   If no, interest purchased _____%

8. Is this a transaction among related parties? Indicate whether the buyer or seller are related. Related parties include persons within the same family, business affiliates, or affiliated corporations. ☐ Yes ☐ No

---

NOTES ON USE:

For a discussion of the Real Property Transfer Declaration, see § 6.3.4 and § 7.5.

Appendix 1: Forms

9. Check any of the following that apply to the condition of the improvements at the time of purchase.
   ☐ New   ☐ Excellent   ☐ Good   ☐ Average   ☐ Fair   ☐ Poor   ☐ Salvage.

If the property is financed, please complete the following.

10. Total amount financed. $_____

11. Type of financing: (Check all that apply)
    ☐ New
    ☐ Assumed
    ☐ Seller
    ☐ Third Party
    ☐ Combination; Explain _____

12. Terms:
    ☐ Variable; Starting interest rate _____%
    ☐ Fixed; Interest rate _____%
    ☐ Length of time _____ years
    ☐ Balloon payment ☐ Yes ☐ No   If yes, amount _____ Due date _____

13. Please explain any special terms, seller concessions, or financing and any other information that would help the assessor understand the terms of sale.
    _____
    _____
    _____

For properties other than residential (Residential is defined as: single family detached, townhomes, apartments and condominiums) please complete questions 14-16 if applicable. Otherwise, skip to #17 to complete.

14. Did the purchase price include a franchise or license fee? ☐ Yes ☐ No
    If yes, franchise or license fee value $

15. Did the purchase price involve an installment land contract? ☐ Yes ☐ No
    If yes, date of contract

16. If this was a vacant land sale, was an on-site inspection of the property conducted by the buyer prior to the closing?
    ☐ Yes ☐ No

Remarks: Please include any additional information concerning the sale you may feel is important.
_____
_____
_____

17. Signed this _____ day of _____, 20_____.
    Enter the day, month, and year, have at least one of the parties to the transaction sign the document, and include an address and a daytime phone number. Please designate buyer or seller.

_____
Signature of Grantee (Buyer) ☐ or Grantor (Seller) ☐

18. All future correspondence (tax bills, property valuations, etc.) regarding this property should be mailed to:

_____   (____) _____
Address (mailing)   Daytime Phone

_____
City, State and Zip Code

No. TD-1000. REAL PROPERTY TRANSFER DECLARATION (Page 2 of 2)

161

Appendix 2:
Colorado Counties Providing Property Information

Adams County   http://www.co.adams.co.us/
Alamosa County   http://www.alamosacounty.org/
Arapahoe County   http://www.co.arapahoe.co.us/
Archuleta County   http://www.archuletacounty.org/
Boulder County   http://www.co.boulder.co.us/
Broomfield County   http://www.ci.broomfield.co.us/
Chaffee County   http://www.chaffeecounty.org/
Clear Creek County   http://www.co.clear-creek.co.us/
Costilla County   http://www.colorado.gov/cs/Satellite/ CNTY-Costilla/CBON/1251592888581

Custer County   http://www.custercountygov.com/
Delta County   http://www.deltacounty.com/
Denver County   http://www.denvergov.org/
Dolores County   http://www.qpublic.net/co/dolores/
Douglas County   http://www.douglas.co.us/
Eagle County   http://www.eaglecounty.us/
El Paso County   http://www.elpasoco.com/
Elbert County   http://www.elbertcounty-co.gov/
Fremont County   http://www.fremontco.com/
Garfield County   http://www.garfield-county.com/
Gilpin County   http://co.gilpin.co.us/
Grand County   http://co.grand.co.us/
Gunnison County   http://www.gunnisoncounty.org/
Hinsdale County   http://www.hinsdalecountycolorado.us/
Jefferson County   http://co.jefferson.co.us/
Kit Carson County   http://www.kitcarsoncounty.org/
Lake County   http://www.lakecountyco.com/
La Plata County   http://co.laplata.co.us/
Larimer County   http://www.larimer.org/
Las Animas County   http://www.tlac.net/
Logan County   http://www.loganco.gov/
Mesa County   http://www.mesacounty.us/
Moffat County   http://www.co.moffat.co.us/
Montezuma County   http://www.co.montezuma.co.us/
Montrose County   http://www.co.montrose.co.us/
Ouray County   http://ouraycountyco.gov/
Park County   http://www.parkco.us/
Pitkin County   http://www.aspenpitkin.com/
Prowers County   http://www.prowerscounty.net/

Pueblo County	http://www.co.pueblo.co.us/
Rio Blanco County	http://www.co.rio-blanco.co.us/
Rio Grande County	http://www.riograndecounty.org/
Routt County	http://www.co.routt.co.us/
Saguache County	http://www.saguachecounty.net/
San Miguel County	http://www.sanmiguelcounty.org/
Summit County	http://www.co.summit.co.us/
Teller County	http://www.co.teller.co.us/
Weld County	http://www.co.weld.co.us/
Yuma County	http://www.yumacounty.net/

NOTE: Some Colorado counties have not yet developed an official website. Other counties have websites but do not provide property information on them.

Index